The Country Life Companion to

Architecture in Britain and Europe

Bruce Allsopp

COUNTRY LIFE
BOOKS

Contents

Published by
Country Life Books
an imprint of Newnes Books
a division of the
Hamlyn Publishing Group Limited
84-88 The Centre, Feltham, Middlesex, TW13 4BH
and distributed for them by
Hamlyn Distribution Services Limited
Rushden, Northants, England

First published 1985

ISBN 0 600 34259 X Hardback
ISBN 0 600 34265 4 Softback

Printed in Italy by Poligrafici Calderara S.p.a., Bologna

How to use this book

This is a guide to architecture as it is now, as tourists and students see it. Some is very old and has changed through time. Some is young and almost as it was when the building was finished. This is not a history book, but we have to be aware of how time and change constantly affect architecture. Architecture is born by building. The building has a life-span and a death by decay or demolition. It is necessary to recognise buildings as living creations rather than static objects.

Part One is about the nature of architecture, what it is, the different kinds of architecture, how it was built, how it was designed and for what purpose. You need to read *Part One.*

Part Two is about the styles and periods of architecture in Europe, how and why they came into being through the people who built them. There is much that is common to all the countries of Europe so this part is constantly referred to in *Part Three* which consists of a regional breakdown.

Parts Three and *Four* are specific to countries or regions, indicating regional characteristics and the reasons for them; *Part Three* covering roughly that area included in the Roman Empire, and *Four* the regions beyond it.

To cover the whole range of European architecture in a single handbook it has been essential to avoid repetition and to be concise but without being merely factual. The text is meant to be read, mainly as explanation of how and why. The illustrations convey visually many of the facts of architecture and the captions do not duplicate the text. Text, pictures and captions on each pair of pages are a package, like one house in a street. The cross references are important to avoid repetition and by using them you may increase your capacity to appreciate architecture and probably your desire to extend your travels.

This book is about architecture and the people who built. It aims to help you to enjoy architecture quite apart from all the associations with people who have acted out their lives on the stage the buildings provided. You can learn of these as well as some details about the buildings from the local guides, but we think that nowhere else in such concise form can you learn to see individual buildings, from cathedrals to cottages, in the context of European architecture.

The quantity of building done in the present century may exceed everything built before it. We have chosen to use time as a scale, not quantity, so the Modernist period gets less space than the Middle Ages or even the Renaissance.

From the beginning, architecture has had a basic standard. The great sculptor Auguste Rodin called it *Taste*. He wrote, 'Taste is the adaptation of human will and human forces to the will and forces of nature.'

About the middle of the present century man began to believe that the will and forces of nature could and should be subject to man's technology. Where this will lead we do not know. Architecture has changed: man is fearful but the heritage remains – though precariously.

Finally, in this book the word *architecture* is 'meaningful' or 'significant' building and *architect* means any person or people who have designed buildings which are architecture.

Part One

The Nature of Architecture

If a bunch of flowers is gathered and put in a vase it is almost impossible for a sensitive person not to adjust them so that they look better. This may be the studied artistic act of a trained florist or it may be an instinctive manifestation of a sense of design which most people have and apply in many activities, one of which is building.

We may arrange flowers so that they themselves look their best, or we may make a wreath which gives a recognisable meaning to our arrangement. Similarly in architecture we may design so as to express the nature of the materials, the structure of the building and its place in its setting; or alternatively we may design it to excite reverence, fear, friendliness or familiarity. Architecture can be sublime or snobbish, materialistic, repressive, joyous or sombre, licentious or puritanical, academic or vulgar; but it is never without meaning.

Architecture is the sort of building to which the people who made it have given meaning. The way of giving meaning to building is the art of architectural design. It is born in most of us. Every person who takes care about the appearance of the home is, in a simple way, an architect; likewise every craftsman who insists on 'making a proper job'. Architecture, like all the other arts, can be practised at many different levels and the creative care of ordinary people for the appearance and significance of things may produce admirable results. Indeed the quality of our environment depends very much upon people, and their representatives in government, trade unions and management, caring about architecture, its seemliness and its beauty. But, above the level of folk architecture and the common practice of decent and seemly building, there is the work of people who have studied deeply in the traditions and principles of the art and have so educated an inborn genius that they

The little hut (aedicule), seen by the 18th-century Frenchman Abbé Laugier as the basis of architecture, for both the home and the temple (p. 36). Constructed in various ways of local materials, it consists of a cell, a porch and a precinct (or defensible space).

St Quirin, eastern France, on the river Sarre; a blend of Western and Eastern styles on a frontier.

can produce masterpieces in architecture equal to those in painting, sculpture and music which have enriched civilisations and set enduring standards of attainment.

St Aidan, Fourstones, Northumberland, England. An ordinary timber building differentiated by its belfry, cross and Gothic windows, which make it recognisably a church.

Architecture is so emotionally significant and symbolically important that it has sometimes given rise to violent acts: as when early Christians toppled the columns of the pagan temples of Mercury on Montmartre in Paris and the Puy de Dôme; or English puritans in the seventeenth century turned their destructive wrath upon Gothic decoration in churches and French Huguenots burned Orléans cathedral; or revolutionaries burned the Bastille prison in 1789 as the symbolic act of liberation that is still celebrated as a public holiday in France.

But these things are on the negative side. In France the late seventeenth-century Second Church of the Invalides is a national shrine and throughout the world there are buildings which similarly are focal points and symbols.

The English Victorian architect Sir George Gilbert Scott said that architecture was the decoration of structure. There is truth in this because the principal way in which building has been given the meanings which qualify it to be architecture is by decoration in the widest sense, including perfection of proportion and the meaningfully decorative exposure of the beauty of structure and materials.

Just dumping your bluebells in an empty jam-jar and letting them die of thirst has its counterpart in the kind of building which is not architecture.

If we learn to read it, architecture can tell us about how people felt towards each other; that is the social side of architectural history. Wealth and poverty, the rule of law or the prevalence of disorder, security, civic or national pride, personal vanity, trade and the state of the economy are also reflected in architecture. But even more importantly architecture tells how people felt about their relationship to the world, and how they could share with nature in the creation of beauty.

The cottage, a development of the hut, becomes a social symbol and a simple ideal.

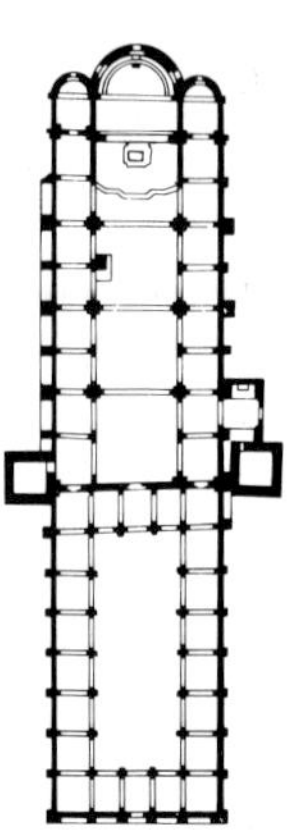

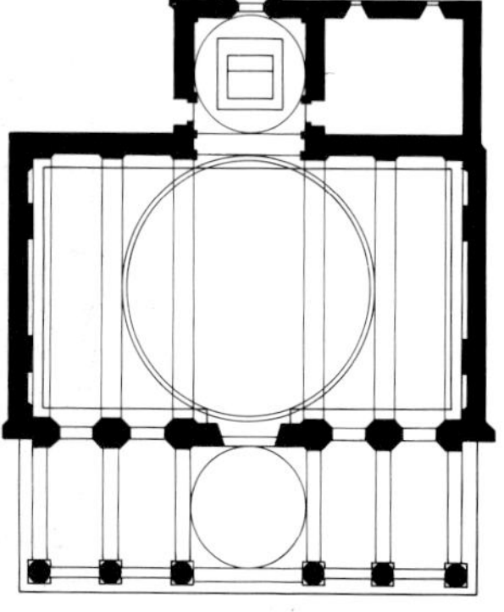

Right Neuschwanstein Castle, southern Germany; a mid-19th century fantasy.

Far left and plan left S. Ambrogio, Milan; a Romanesque church with an atrium (see also p. 177).

Left and plan far left The Second Church of Les Invalides, Paris; a 17th-century hospital church which became a national shrine when Napoleon was buried there.

Right The Beaubourg, or Pompidou Centre, Paris; 1976. A very sophisticated modernist building for an essentially popular purpose. As a technological fantasy it is an alternative to the eclecticism of Neuschwanstein, but for 'ordinary people' rather than a monarch.

Far left and plan left The Pazzi Chapel, Florence; 1429–46 by Brunelleschi. Like many of the trendsetting buildings in history, it is small.

Arcane, Folk and Common Architecture

We often make a distinction between 'music' and 'folk music', 'art' and 'folk art', 'science' and 'folk lore', 'architecture' and 'folk architecture'. The boundaries are not always easy to define but we are aware of the difference. It is tempting to think that architecture evolved from folk architecture but this is not so, indeed the contrary is often the case.

From early times the houses of the chief and the priest or medicine man have been given arcane significance. This word 'arcane' is not commonly used nowadays but (as *arcanus*) it was important to the Romans and meant mysterious, secret and even holy: 'the arcane part of divine wisdom' as George Berkeley wrote. In many ancient civilisations medicine was a priestly craft, a fact demonstrated by the still acknowledged relevance if not actual sanctity of the Hippocratic Oath. Architecture has never developed a comparable ethic or set of rules for its practitioners but it has been closely associated with religion, and the main streams of architectural development were in religious architecture from seventh-century BC Greece until the Industrial Revolution. The

Proportions

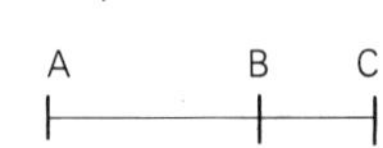

Golden Section
BC:AB::AB:AC

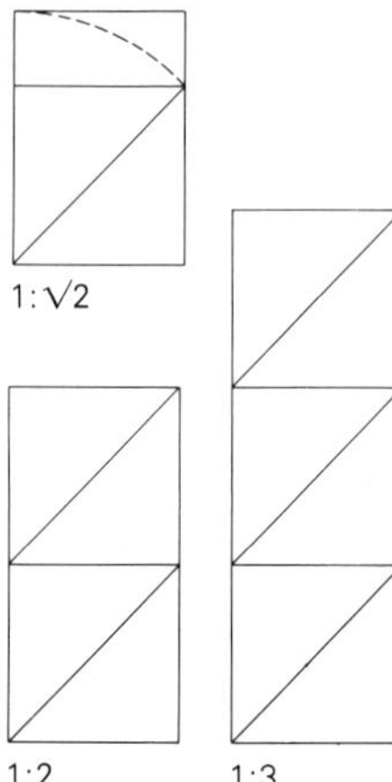

Below Arcane architecture: Palazzo Chiericati, Vicenza; 1550–80. Designed by Palladio on a strict proportional system.

Right A house in Amsterdam: common architecture derived from Renaissance rules though without the architect actually knowing them.

Below Maulbronn, West Germany: Two stages in the development of folk architecture: expressed structure in the timber frames, and an added façade on the building on the left.

architecture of power and pomp – palaces – has tended to adapt designs worked out for temples and churches. It would have been almost unthinkable to adopt styles for these palaces from folk architecture, except very rarely as a quaint conceit, such as *Le Hameau* at Versailles (p. 235).

Military architecture, whether defensive or oppressive, has been essentially functional in inspiration but after the invention of explosives and artillery, some military buildings were adapted for domestic use and sometimes included features from folk architecture.

Greek architecture did not originate in folk architecture. Instead it maintained a distinction between what was proper for religious or public buildings and what was right for houses. The Romans blurred this distinction, as was perhaps appropriate considering that they gave divine status to Caesar. Provincial governors who wielded the authority of Caesar built ostentatious residences in imitation of imperial palaces. Since Roman times we find many examples of arcane architecture influencing folk architecture, but only a few the other way round. In what are generally regarded as the great periods, the arcane qualities of architecture have been prominent. Architects have worked within a cult, following principles which were mysterious and in some periods (as in Italy in the fifteenth century) thought to be of divine origin. This is still true in modern architectural practice, where the nature of the mystery is probably more obscure than ever: pursue any architect with relentless reasoning and he will retreat into the mystery of design! Architecture is, in fact, an art and operates beyond the limits of human reasoning. This is one reason why some buildings which long ago became totally useless remain beautiful and fascinating. Beauty in a building does not depend upon its utility.

Blaise Hamlet, near Bristol, England; an early 19th-century prototype of suburbia. Its architect John Nash, who also designed Regent's Park terraces and Brighton Pavilion, has often been censured for his versatility. It might be better to admire his realism and recognition of the fact that one architecture cannot meet all needs and situations.

Between arcane and folk architecture there is a great deal of unpretentious building which can properly be called 'common' architecture (cf. 'common' white butterfly, or *sternus vulgaris* – the starling). Most buildings have been designed, by architects or builders, without pretensions to greatness. They may adopt arcane motifs for decoration, but avoid the loftiest aims of arcane architecture. We may liken this common architecture to good workaday prose, folk architecture to genuine dialect and arcane to literature. In all of these poetry is possible, though rare.

The Royal Pavilion, Brighton, England; 1815–21, by John Nash and built for the Prince Regent. It is a 'pleasure dome' which almost miraculously has survived the prejudices and idealisms of later times. Now as functionally irrelevant as the Parthenon, it is enjoyed for its exotic beauty. It is also a creditable example of English restoration and conservation (compare with the French policy, as at Carcassonne, p. 251).

Fantasy Architecture

Architecture, in the widest sense including man-managed landscape, is the scenery for our lives and there are few places on Earth which remain entirely free of it. This scenery may be grand, squalid, pastoral or of many other kinds but mankind, which has the imagination to tell fairy tales, dance round maypoles, create ballet and opera and write science fiction, also uses architecture as a vehicle for fantasy. Great painters have pictured fantasy architecture in the fresco decoration of buildings (such as those by Giotto in Assisi). Book illustrators in many lands have visualised fantasy architecture and their art has been extended into cartoon films. Indeed, medieval decoration and stained glass extended real architecture towards fantasy by depicting buildings beyond the limitations of physical construction on Earth.

At many periods in Europe, and even more in the Far East, people have wanted to build for sheer enjoyment and realise the imagined architecture of the illustrators. To take such architecture seriously is to miss the point. It is meant to be enjoyed though there have always been people who think this hedonistic approach is naughty if not actually evil.

There is an element of fantasy in almost all great buildings. Fantasy holds up the picture of the imaginable to what we actually do.

Ways of Building

You can experience almost all the stresses in a building with your own body – in actuality or in your imagination

Stresses In and On Buildings

The forces in buildings have never changed, they are the same for us as for the megalith builders. The rules don't change but some things we build are vulnerable; high-rise buildings, for instance, are specially susceptible to the problem of wind.

A tall building is not only a column resting on the ground but also a cantilever sticking up against the force of the wind.

A slab is stronger from the ends than the sides. A spire is strong where the stress is greatest, and is equally strong in all directions.

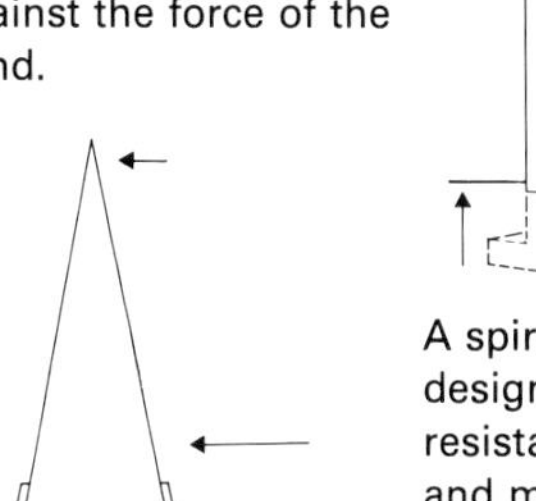

A spire is a sensible design, offering least resistance at the top and most at the bottom where the greatest leverage is.

Rigidity

No building is completely rigid. There is always movement caused by internal and external stresses and changes of temperature. Most buildings are made as rigid as possible.

The most stable shape is a pyramid. Then a triangle. Three pieces of wood joined with one nail at each corner make a rigid triangle.

A rectangle is a more convenient shape but it has to be stabilised to be rigid. Roof trusses, girders and some domes are built of triangles.

Solid walls are not always rigid. Arches have to be supported laterally by an abutment – that is, something to push against.

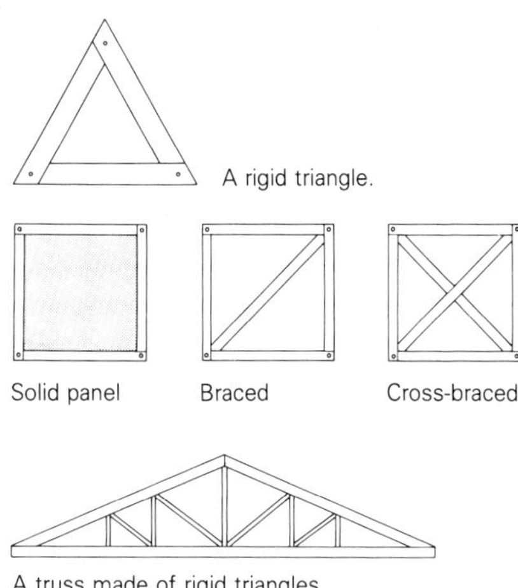

A rigid triangle.

Solid panel Braced Cross-braced

A truss made of rigid triangles.

Foundations and Forces

Isaac Newton's Third Law of Motion states that for every action there is an equal and opposite reaction. In other words, if you walk into a wall it hits you as hard as you hit it. That's why it hurts.

A building standing on the ground exerts a force downwards. The ground has to be strong enough to hit back.

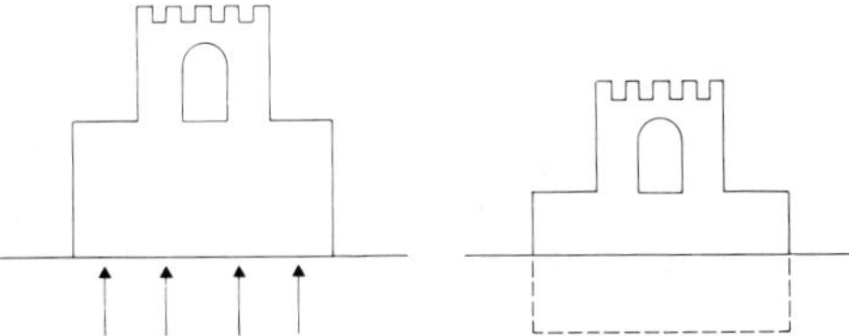

On soft foundations the load is spread by using footings or even rafts.

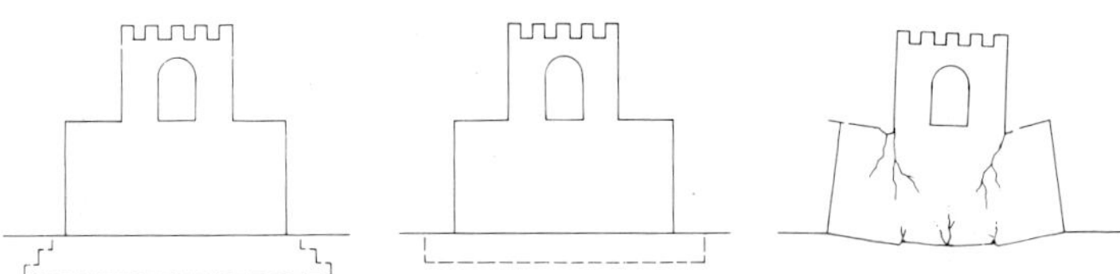

Or by using friction. On marshes, swamps or other very soft ground piles are used. A pile works by friction on the sides of the pile.

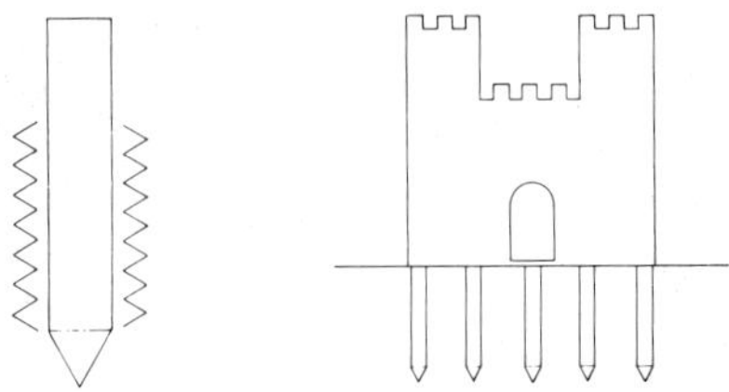

Venice was built on piles in a swamp. The piles do not go down to anything hard; they work by friction.

Forces in Competition

If you walk into a wall, the reaction is to you. The wall does not hit you until you hit it. But what happens if two forces are moving? If they meet head-on, the big force pushes the little force; the result is a function of their relative weights and speed. If two forces act in different directions, the objects will move in relation to the strength and direction of the forces. Tendency to movement in this different direction is called the *resultant* force.

The best example in architecture is the structure of a Gothic cathedral; the arrows show the directions in which forces are acting. We tend to think of the forces as though they were in movement. This would be true if the building failed, but we build so that it will not fail. If the forces are in pure equilibrium there is no safety factor and a puff of wind might make it fall down. There has to be a safety factor. This is now usually calculated at four times the original force but until recently forces could not be calculated accurately. What was safe was learned by intuition, imagination and experience. We still have to imagine the structure – design it – before we can calculate its forces, not the other way round. We do not calculate structures; we design and then test by calculation.

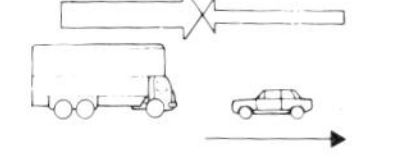

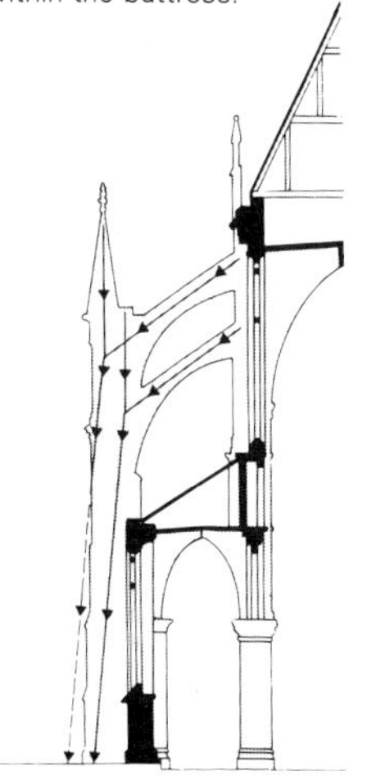

Forces in a Gothic cathedral; the weight of the pinnacles deflects the thrust of roof and vault downwards within the structure: the resultant forces are contained within the buttress.

Below Salginatobel Bridge, Switzerland; 1929–30, by Robert Maillart. Like most original works of architecture and engineering, it was imagined first and calculated afterwards. Computations are an aid to, not a substitute for, imagination.

Structural Materials

Timber

Timber is of two kinds; hard and soft. Softwood timber (which is known as deal) comes from coniferous trees which generally grow straight, can be cut into convenient lengths and rip-sawn into long scantlings. Soft woods are universal in modern carpentry. Larch has been favoured since Roman times for posts in the ground, for its durability and some fire resistance (Vitruvius).

Timber structural walls are historically found in coniferous forest areas and took two forms. In the first horizontal logs, half-notched at the corners, provide stable walls (a horizontal frame) which will carry a roof.

Alternatively, logs or thick planks (staves) are used vertically as walls, diagonally braced on the inside for stability. When the staves are sunk in the ground they have tended to rot, and the more durable method has been to have them resting on ground-sills. Bracing is subsidiary to the structural idea of timber walls. Until about AD 1100, the idea was that walls themselves were the main structure supporting the roof, and columns were thought of as 'interrupted walls'. This 'stressed-skin' principle (now very modern and used in aircraft) also persisted in shipbuilding until about 1100 when skeletal (framed) designs were introduced.

Framing is now the commonest principle in constructing buildings of timber (also in steel and concrete). The frame is constructed first and then covered or infilled to provide enclosure. The typical half-timbered building was made of hardwood. Big timbers were cut from trunks of trees but the basis of timber-framed construction was provided by coppicing oak on a 25–30 year cycle. Coppiced oak provided timber of convenient size without rip-sawing; this could be adzed square. In a sense, carpentry began in the forests, since curved timbers were actually grown to the required shapes.

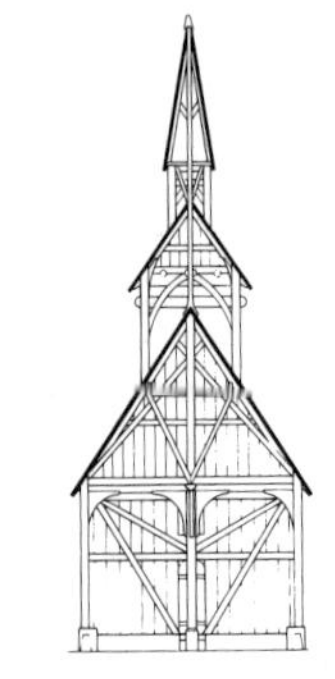

Section of a Norwegian timber 'stave' church.

A Russian log cabin, with the timbers halved onto each other at the corners.

English medieval cruck construction, precursor of the portal frame.

Timber-framed house, usually in oak.

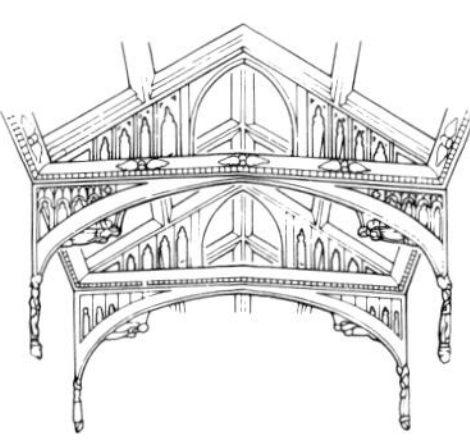

Medieval tie-beam roof: carpenters lagged behind masons in their structural thinking.

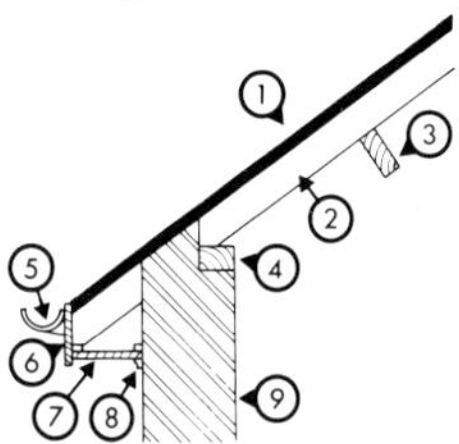

The normal eave of a building – the origin of the Classical cornice.
1 Roof coverings
2 Rafter
3 Purlin
4 Wall plate (timber)
5 Gutter
6 Fascia
7 Soffit
8 Bed mould
9 Wall (in section)

Structurally a rectangle is a less stable shape than a triangle. Rectangles can be made rigid by the strength of the corner joints, by battening, or by infilling with panels of wood, brick, wattle and daub, plaster or laths, stone or by bracing.

Wide pieces of timber are hard to get and split with shrinkage. Traditional methods of building with timber therefore use small units and allow for shrinkage and expansion with variations of humidity. Timber is never still, in spite of seasoning, and traditional craft techniques of design take this into account. Modern plywoods, chipboards and so on reduce this problem and allow the designer to use larger surfaces.

Timber is also the main material for the structure of pitched roofs. Battens carry tiles, slates or thatch. Rafters carry battens and rest upon purlins which span between trusses or walls. A truss is a framed structure built up of triangles and because it is a composite beam its bottom member is kept in tension. With roofs that are open from below, the tension member may seem ugly, so that arched or hammer-beam roofs are designed to have minimal lateral thrust. They consist of superimposed brackets.

From about 1700 weather boarding of softwood, followed by tongue-and-grooved boarding, became common as an outside covering for timber-framed and sometimes for brick buildings. Clinker built boats became usual about the same date. In some modern buildings glues are used but nobody knows how long the glues will stand the fatigue of the constant movement common to all timber structures.

Lamination, the principle used in plywood, is now employed for beams.

The main hazards to timber are fire, insects, lack of ventilation (which causes dry-rot) and alternation of dry and damp conditions.

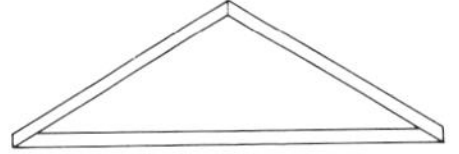

Trussed rafter, with the lower member of the roof in tension.

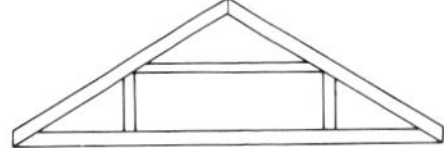

Queen post truss; it works but it contains a rectangle – an 'indeterminate' structure.

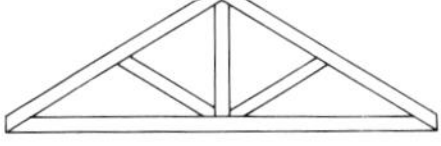

King post truss, made of triangles.

Stone and Brick

Nearly all the world's greatest buildings are made of stone, but even though the Earth's crust consists entirely of rock and its derivatives such as sand and clay, good building stone is not easy to come by. Granite and other igneous rocks are hard and difficult to work, so that simple and austere architectural forms are appropriate to these materials. Polished granite ranks with marble as a superb material for wall-linings and columns.

Hard, even and undisturbed beds of sedimentary rocks yield the best building stones. Sandstones, being granular, are best for plain walling and simple mouldings. They must be laid in the plane in which they were formed – on their bed as masons say. Hard limestones, which were formed under water by the fossilisation of organisms, make the finest building stone. These are particularly suitable for carving but, like marbles, they are very vulnerable to atmospheric pollution.

The term marble is loosely applied to many kinds of stone that can be polished and used decoratively. Most are limestones which have been subjected to volcanic heat and pressure. Though occasionally used structurally, as in Athens (p. 101) and Pisa (p. 52), they are generally turned as columns or sawn into sheets for lining walls. The traditional and still-used method of sawing marble is by means of a rope passing over two pulleys, dipping into wet sand and then cutting the marble by friction. Since the first century AD Italy has been the home of marble craftsmanship.

European bricks are made of clay, sometimes mixed with sand, broken tiles or clinker and burnt in a kiln. Bricks have been extensively used in areas where good building stone was not available and in forest areas as infilling for timber-framed buildings. The Romans used bricks on an enormous scale, often as shells for walls which were filled-in with rubble and rough concrete by unskilled labour. Gradually bricks became standardised

Random rubble. Large stones are often wedged with pebbles.

Snecked or coursed rubble. Snecks are small stones used to adjust the course line.

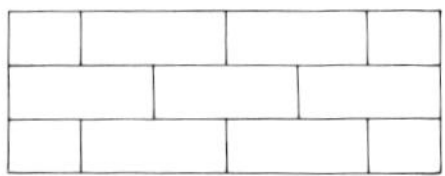

Ashlar, dressed stone masonry; normally laid in courses.

to dimensions which could be made without undue distortion in the kiln and could be easily handled by the bricklayer: approximately 23cm × 11.5cm × 50–75cm (9″ × 4.5″ × 2–3″) became the accepted form throughout Europe.

Until about 1860 bricklayers exploited the natural unevenness of shape and colour and used thick joints of lime mortar to accommodate variations. Bricks were hand-made and each one was a work of craftsmanship. Bricklayers *chose* their bricks, mingling or grouping them to produce beautiful surfaces.

The late nineteenth-century passion for machinery led to a new type of brickwork, composed of precision-made, smooth, sharp-edged bricks laid with very fine joints of mortar, often blackened with soot. The Arts and Crafts Movement reversed this trend and established, especially in Britain, Scandinavia and Benelux, a new idiom of beautiful brickwork though this was lost again under the influence of Modernism.

Stone and brick are weak in tension and cannot span wide openings as beams (except by subterfuge) but since Roman times they have been used for arches.

Some sandstones and shales (slates) can be split to be used for roofing or hung on walls as weather-proofing. Tiles made of baked clay are used for the same purposes. A crucial factor in the durability of slate and tiling is the method of fixing them to the supporting battens. This varies from the old, bone peg or bronze nail, to the modern nib, moulded onto the tile and lasting about 25 years.

The ceramic techniques used in pottery have been exploited from Etruscan times to make building components – often highly decorative – with the generalised name of *terra-cotta*. Glazed tiles are a major element in Islamic decoration, as in the Blue Mosque at Istanbul. The 19th-century fashion for polychromy is exemplified in the use of glazed tiles and mouldings in the entrance hall of Liverpool University by Alfred Waterhouse.

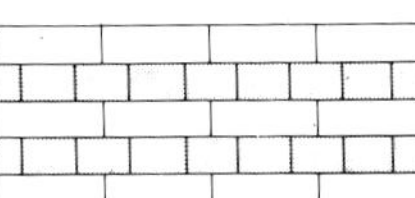

English bond brickwork: alternate courses of headers and stretchers.

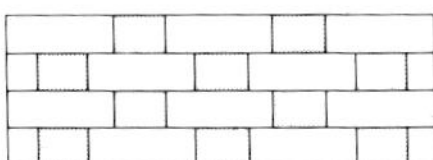

Flemish bond brickwork: alternate headers and stretchers in each course.

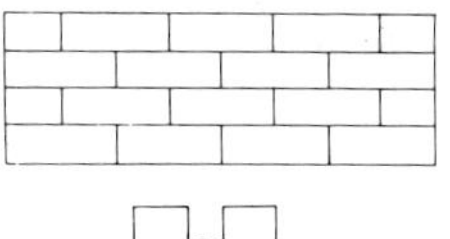

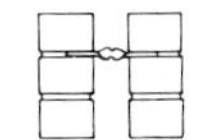

Cavity wall, usually built in stretcher bond.
Wall tie (galvanised iron).

Mud, Mortar and Concrete

As a building material mud is older than man; swallows still use it for their nests. It is used in two forms: prefabricated pieces called bricks, which are usually joined with mortar, and as a plastic which generally needs support (shuttering) until it has set or dried. The best muds contain clay and can be made waterproof (puddled clay) as in the dew ponds constructed by Neolithic people. Mud lends itself to the construction of corbelled domes. These are made in a series of rings, each allowed to harden before the next is made.

Muds made with clay are vulnerable to rain, but clays which have been burnt by volcanic heat produce a mud which sets hard, even under water. Such muds occur naturally and were used by the Romans under the name *pozzolana*. They came from the volcanic system of Vesuvius and were mined at Pozzuoli near Naples.

Another way of making hard mud is by mixing sand and lime but this is not fully waterproof. Modern cements (Portland cement) are made by applying heat to lime and clay and grinding the product. High alumina cements set quickly but whatever the sophistication of manufacture and composition, all cements are mud and all require support until set. When set they are hard and can carry heavy loads, under compression, but they are weak in tension. Concrete is thus no better than stone for beams, so the technique of reinforcing it with steel on the underside of beams and on the outside of columns has been developed. In simple terms the twentieth century has discovered how to give tensile strength to mud.

To build in concrete you need a temporary supporting structure and it has been fashionable to commemorate the original structure in the 'board-marking' of the concrete, but the aesthetics of concrete building remain unsettled. The material starts semi-fluid and becomes hard, but to withstand tension it has to have an invisible reinforcement of steel.

The mud hut is the origin of one of the noblest architectural forms, the dome. It is made of rings of mud, each being allowed to harden in the sun before the next is placed upon it. The result is an egg-shaped structure.

The Einstein Tower, Potsdam; 1920–21 by Erich Mendelsohn. The Romans developed concrete as a hard material; modernists saw it as a plastic medium, like clay, but the size of the buildings for which it was used meant that it had to be held in place by rigid shuttering until it became rigid itself.

Visually, reinforced concrete is the biggest con-trick in architectural history. The stability of a building is no longer apparent but depends upon built-in reinforcements which may or may not have been correctly calculated. The aesthetic implications of this have hardly begun to be appreciated but if structure can no longer be assessed by appearance the aesthetic qualities of buildings must rely instead upon non-structural aspects of design – 'commodity' and 'delight' (would that 'firmness' could be taken for granted).

As mortar (which comprises sand and lime), and as plaster (calcined gypsum with or without sand), mud is still the most common interior surfacing material for walls and the main means of sticking bricks together.

Cement mortar (instead of lime) is commonly tolerated by modern architects but is disastrous for stone buildings and hazardous, as well as ugly, for brickwork because it is too hard except for the hardest bricks. It should rarely be used in restoration work.

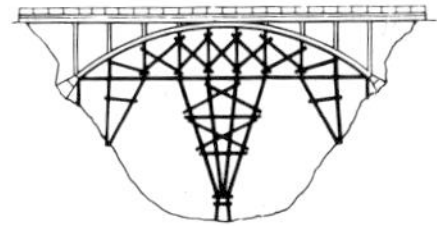

A re-inforced concrete bridge with the timber temporary structure used to support it during construction.

The National Theatre, London; 1976.The incoherent exterior is mainly the enclosure of temporary structures which, when removed, leave a fascinating collection of related 'caves' in the concrete.

Metals and Glass

A sheet lead roof on Lincoln chapter house (13th century).

Apart from nails and screws, locks, bolts, hinges and other fittings, metal has been used structurally since Roman times, when bronze was used for casing wooden beams, for cramping stones together and cramping marble wall-linings back to brick, stone or concrete walls. (Brass is now used for this purpose). Lead was the ideal material for church roofs, whether pitched or flat, and for gutters and down-comers. Frequently it was melted and moulded, or made into sheets, on sand beds, on-site and could be restored by melting and remaking in the same way.

Stained glass is mounted in lead cames, before being inserted in stone or iron frames or tracery. Until recently lead has been the main material for water pipes and commonly used for fixing iron cramps or fittings, such as lamp brackets, into masonry. Lead was, and still is, the best material for flashings (covering joints in roofs). Zinc and copper are less malleable than lead but copper roofs which weather to a beautiful blue-green patina (especially near the sea) are conspicuous in Scandinavia and from there southwards to Austria and Savoy. Zinc is the metal which gives the silvery greys of the Paris rooftops.

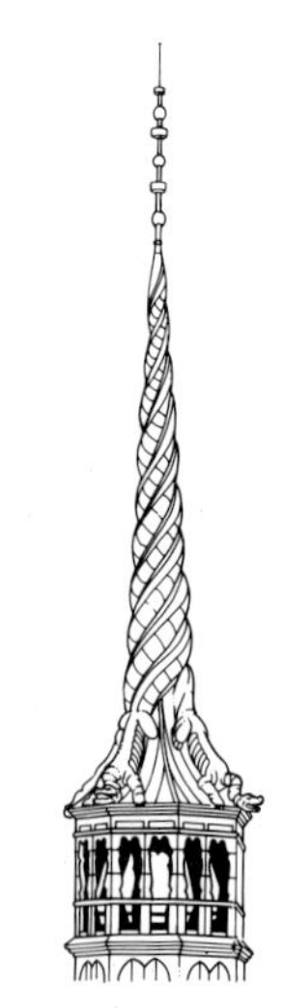

The copper-covered spire of Copenhagen Exchange; 1619–30.

Iron was used sparingly because it rusts, but wrought iron became a popular decorative material in the sixteenth and seventeenth centuries; and with improvements in manufacture, possibly derived from sword-smiths, and the development of lead paints in a linseed oil medium (first used by Dutch artists) and above all the discovery of how to use coal for melting iron ore, cast and wrought iron became important structural materials. The techniques developed to make railway lines in the nineteenth century were quickly adapted for building purposes, not least in railway stations. Steel and the RSJ (rolled steel joist) became standard building materials and by means of compound beams, such as lattice girders, larger spans than ever before could be constructed. There was no concealment of the construction in station roofs and bridges, or the pioneer metal-framed buildings made for exotic plants.

The Romans made beautiful decorative glassware – especially in the Rhineland (as at Trier) and Hellenesque mosaic artists used glass *tesserae* along with cubes of marble, tile and even semi-precious stones. Window glass became important in the eleventh and twelfth centuries. Design in glass is always related to the frames which support it and this is true of an English Georgian sash window, a Tudor lattice or a medieval church window. Crown glass, which was blown and spun and flashed with mineral colours, was not obtainable in large sheets. The centre bulls-eye was a cheap remainder and used for cottage windows. To make larger panes of window glass before the nineteenth century broad glass was blown into a long cylinder, the ends of which were cut off with a diamond. The cylinder was cut lengthwise, then heated and opened out to form a sheet. This retained the slightly uneven reflective qualities of blown glass and is a particularly beautiful feature of eighteenth-century buildings, especially with white-painted glazing bars and sashes set in hand-made brickwork. Techniques of rolling glass developed in the Industrial Revolution alongside the processes for rolling other metals, and the availability of large sheets of window glass led to the change from the small Georgian panes to the big undivided sashes of the mid-nineteenth century. Polished plate glass was developed in France from 1665 but was expensive in labour and breakages in manufacture.

Spanish wrought-iron work.

The Palm House of the Royal Botanic Gardens, Kew; 1845–47, by Decimus Burton and Richard Turner. A very clean structural design with reticent Greek decoration of the ironwork. A more elegant structure than the Eiffel Tower or the Beaubourg. Decimus Burton had assisted the gardener Joseph Paxton in the design of the Great Stove at Chatsworth House, Derbyshire, a prototype of the Crystal Palace (1850–51 by Paxton).

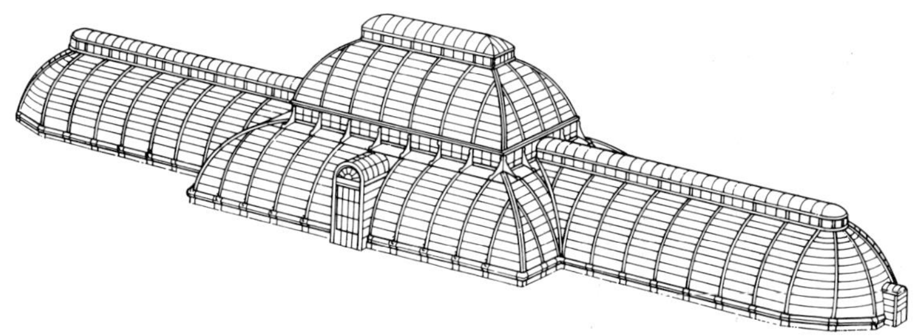

Elements of Architectural Design
The Architect's Palette

Common sense has prevailed through most of architectural history, though in some periods architects have designed in perverse and fantastic fashions which may be thought to reflect social tensions and insecurities. To recognise the abnormalities one needs to understand the sensible norms of architecture; it then becomes apparent that, even in the most extravagant phases of design, some elements persist and it is possible to distinguish between the froth and the beer, so to speak.

Below Palazzo Farnese, Caprarola; 1547–49 by Vignola, one of the most influential Classicists of the 16th century.

1 Pilaster
2 Cornice
3 Quoins
4 Parapet
5 Pediments
6 Balustrade
7 Podium
8 Rustication

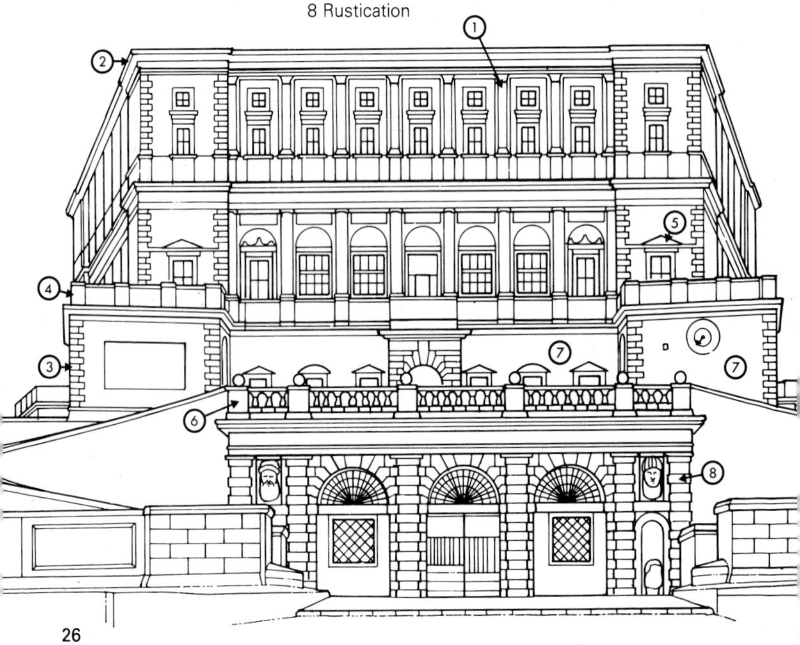

Above Detail of the Palazzo del Tè, Mantua; 1525–35. True Mannerism: breaking the rules 'for the hell of it'.

The Greek Temple of Poseidon, Paestum, southern Italy; c. 460 BC. The three steps (*stylobate*) on which the temple stands are footings, spreading the load of columns outwards.

Foundations, Podiums and Plinths
All buildings rest upon the ground and the load has to be spread evenly according to the bearing capacity of the ground. The place where the vertical walls meet the horizontal ground is vulnerable, no matter how the ground surface is treated. Below ground, walls are constantly damp; above it they vary with the weather but for comfort and durability they are kept as dry as possible. The bottom of walls and columns is also vulnerable to abrasion, impact, chemicals (e.g. urine), water running down the walls and frost, so it has seemed sensible to thicken the walls at the base. This is called a plinth. Visually a plinth makes a logical transition from vertical to horizontal and structurally it begins the process of spreading the load onto the ground. In Greek temples which were built upon surface rock the stepped *crepidoma* was both foundation and plinth.

Greek Doric columns were exceptional in not having base mouldings but earlier (e.g. Minoan) columns did, and all subsequent Classical columns have had bases which are part of the Order. This practice continued in Romanesque, Gothic and Renaissance styles.

Gothic column

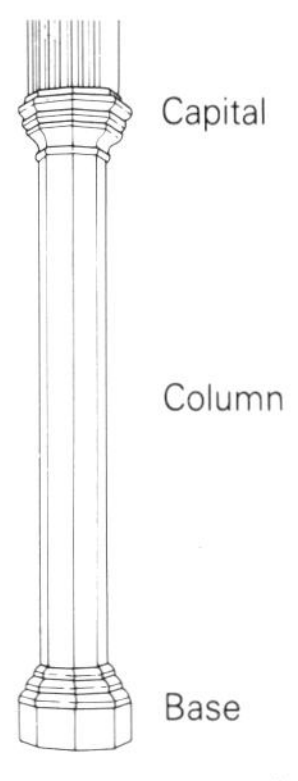

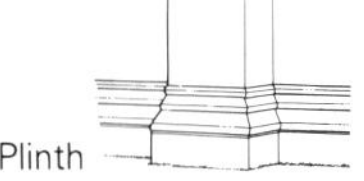

Walls and Columns

In European architecture walls are normally vertical. The thickness of a wall depends upon the method of construction, the load it has to carry and the insulation properties required. If the wall is to withstand battering rams or artillery, as in a fortress, the mass has to be more than proportionate to the impact. If the climate is extreme, thick walls provide better insulation than thin. Apart from such considerations the thickness of a wall is also determined by the method of construction and its height.

Where skilled labour is not available or costly, walls are constructed as two skins built by craftsmen and the core infilled with rubble, or concrete. This was done by the Romans, and in the Romanesque period. Walls built by craftsmen can be much thinner (as in ancient Greek or Anglo-Saxon building), since they are not only bonded on the surfaces but through the wall.

In buildings of more than one storey it is usual to diminish the thickness of the wall for each storey. This provides a seat for floor joists at each level, and it has been customary to mark the floor levels on the outside by string courses which indicate a stage in the building.

Rain is often driven by wind against walls and runs down them. Traditional building styles provide drip moulds to keep the water clear of the wall surface as far as possible. These occur sometimes under string courses and almost always under the mouldings which are placed above windows and doors.

Architectural theorists have differed in considering whether a column is a part of a discontinuous wall (the Classical view) or something different, such as a component of a frame. This is what it appears to be in Gothic, where verticality takes precedence over the horizontal component in design; possibly reflecting an upwards aspiration of the architects towards heaven rather than the presence of Classical gods here on Earth, among men and women.

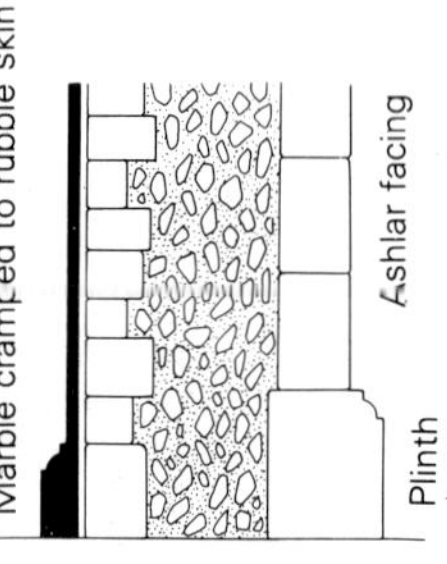

Rubble-filled wall – stones and mortar forming a poor concrete.

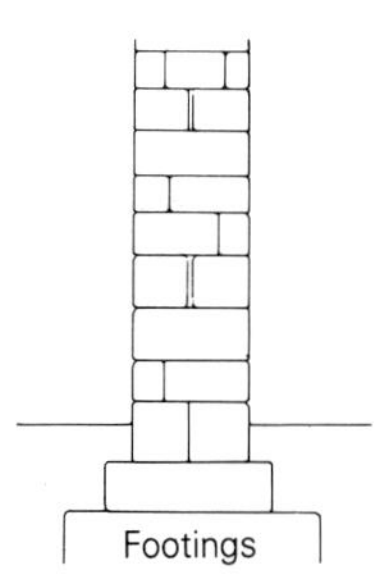

Masonry wall with through-stones. A better quality wall, as made, for instance, by the Anglo-Saxons.

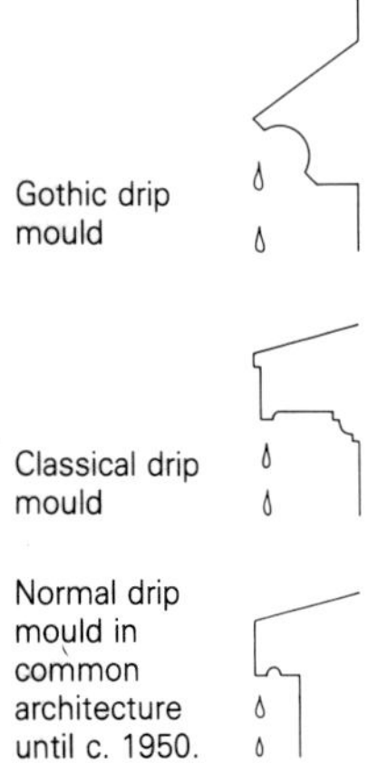

Gothic drip mould

Classical drip mould

Normal drip mould in common architecture until c. 1950.

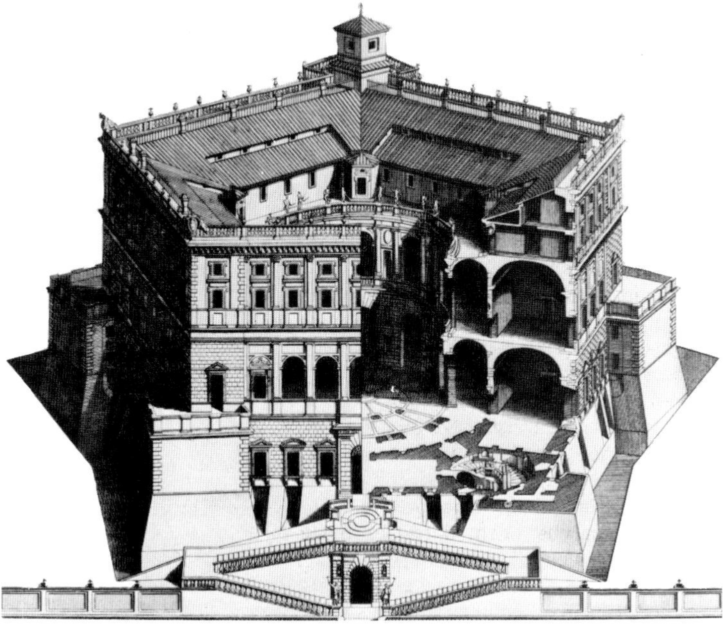

Above The structural form of the Palazzo Farnese (p. 26), revealed in section. In architectural design the section is the vital interface between plan and elevation.

Right Salisbury Cathedral chapter house; 1263–84. A central unifying column: beautiful but inconvenient in a committee room.

Roofs

In any climate where there is considerable rainfall, and especially where it may alternate with frost, the walls, which are the essential feature of any building, are protected, as far as possible, by the overhang of the roof, called the eaves. The roof is a hat with a brim to protect the walls – it is an astonishing phenomenon that the abandonment of cornices in architecture coincides with the unfashionableness of headgear!

Whatever the constructional logic the job of protecting the walls remains, and its effectiveness is in inverse proportion to the height of the wall. As a result the cornice of high-rise buildings has become vestigial.

The traditional eaves and cornice allow water from the roof to drip clear of the building. Gutters collect rain which falls on the roof and discharge it by spouts (gargoyles) or downcomers but the cornice still protects the walls and is retained in post-Renaissance buildings which have parapet gutters.

Visually a cornice expresses the change from walls to roof. The fully-elaborated Classical cornice originated from a pitched roof overhanging the walls – like a hat (p. 28).

The simplest and best way to cover a rectangular building is a double pitched roof, with gable ends which are triangular pieces of wall. The ridge of the roof is covered with ridge tiles, or a similar capping of stone or metal. In Classical temples, and later in Gothic churches, the gable end became the entrance front of the building. The axis of the building was naturally parallel to the ridge and the gable-end, a rectangle surmounted by a triangle, could be a satisfying geometrical composition. The low-pitched roofs of Mediterranean buildings were developed into the form known as a pediment in which the mouldings of the eaves were carried across the front of the building. The gutter mould (*cymatium*) was carried up the edge of the roof (verge) but never across the lower chord of the pediment, according to correct Classical theory (which has a common-sense basis,

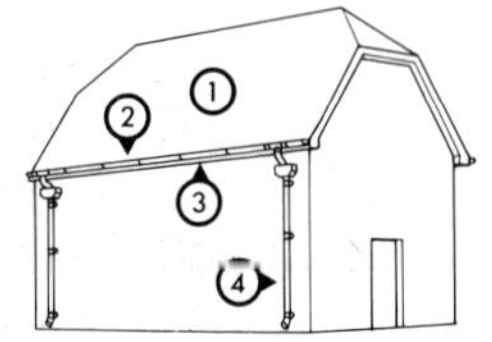

The roof is a hat on a building. It should throw water clear from the walls, or channel it down rainwater pipes (RWPs) to the ground
1 Roof
2 Gutter
3 Eaves
4 RWP

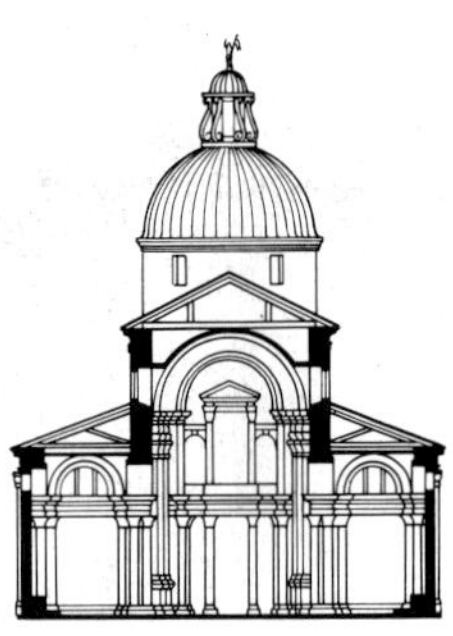

Section of a fully developed Classical building, but one also designed for the weather – S. Giorgio Maggiore, Venice; 1565 and later, by Palladio. One of the most famous 'picturesque' buildings.

Above Roman structural arches within a nonstructural frame of columns and cornices.

Left The Pantheon, Rome; 2nd century AD. A concrete dome on a circular plan.

Left The Palace of Labour, Turin; 1948–49, by P. L. Nervi. This may be compared with the chapter house of Salisbury (p. 29); but here cantilevers are used in a kind of mushroom construction but confused by beams.

Below The Dover Stage Hotel; 1950s.This is really an example of trilithon construction, but the columns here are V-shaped.

Floors and Stairs

Many of the greatest buildings are on a single floor and even if they are in ruins you can read the roof in the plan. But as early as 1500 BC in Crete architects were exploring changes of level as an architectonic experience. Some Gothic buildings (such as Mont St Michel and Rocamadour) are forced by their site to create vertical transitions but, in the late sixteenth century, movement from one level to another began to be a major obsession of architects. This can be experienced in buildings as widely different as the Scala Regia in Rome by Bernini (p. 194) and Hardwick Hall in England (p. 276). The most subtle as well as the most splendid example of this aspect of the art of architecture is the main staircase of the nineteenth-century Paris Opéra. The Royal Festival Hall and the National Theatre in London, and the Beaubourg in Paris are all modern examples of this phenomenon of being 'inside sculpture'. But changes of level (vertical circulation) in architecture do not have to be enclosed: they can be found wherever steps or ramps are related under the

Above The staircase in the Palazzo Farnese, Caprarola. One of the most subtle and difficult aspects in architectural design is 'vertical circulation', the easy change from one level to another. Ideally the plan, which is three-dimensional, indicates the way you should go.

The grand staircase of the Opéra, Paris; 1861–74. On a gala night (or any night) ascending the stairs is a memorable social experience, interpret it as you will!

Left Stairs in the Laurentian Library, Florence; 1559– , by Michelangelo and Vasari.

sky to buildings, as at the Acropolis at Athens (p. 158).

In castles, staircases were commonly spiral and eminently defensible because the defender was above the intruder. When stairs became part of a peaceful and ceremonial progression towards an experience – an audience, a judgement or a performance – architects designed the staircase as a way of extending a main axis to an upper level. Architecture showed the visitor the way to go, without resort to notices.

Doors and Windows

The French eighteenth-century theorist, Marc-Antoine Laugier, believed that the ideal building derived from the 'rustic hut', consisting only of columns, entablature and a roof, like the Parthenon; but even the Parthenon had walls to enclose the shrine and doors for access, though no windows. Walls, doors and windows were considered blemishes upon perfection but had to be accepted for practical reasons. Laugier called them *licences*.

The purpose of a doorway is to give access and of a door to control access. Windows are normally to admit light and provide a view out.

From the earliest times until Modernism, the main entrance to even the smallest building has received emphatic treatment. With Modernism it is assumed that everyone could read, and signs may be used to direct the visitor to an insignificant doorway. Castles and prisons have emphasised exclusion and constraint in their doorways, with such devices as barbicans (p. 45), towers, portcullises and drawbridges. Palaces have been more welcoming but still impressive – psychologically defensive.

Within buildings, the hierarchy of importance has been indicated by the size and design of doorways, the ultimate in privacy being the concealed doorway, and in discretion, the postern.

Windows have always been a problem demanding a variety of compromises. The disposition of windows in relation to each other and to the whole of the building (called the fenestration) has been one of the main preoccupations of architects from the Middle Ages to the present. In Classical theory (Palladio or Alberti) the proportions of the windows are prescribed and there is a calculable proportional relationship of all the voids and solids to the façade as a whole. It is this consistency of proportion which gives repose and dignity to many eighteenth-century buildings and the lack of it which gives a

The basic cottage, each unit having one door and two windows.

Rudimentary emphasis given to the entrance.

The stylised development of the 18th-century, Classically-derived, door.

The entrance subservient to the overall pattern of the building (by Gerrit Rietveld; 1924).

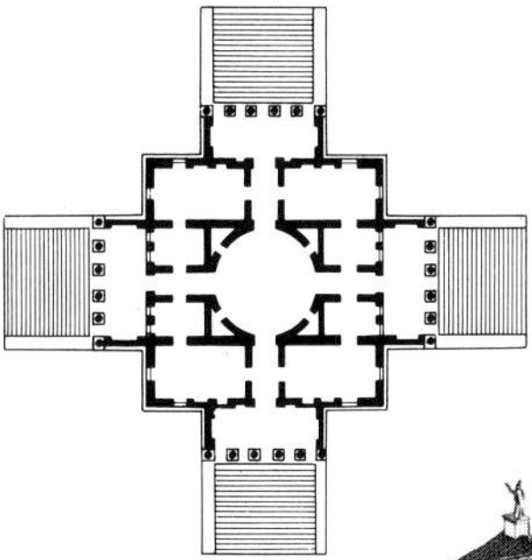

Below and plan left The Villa Capra, Vicenza; 1552– , by Palladio. Plan and sectioned view showing the relationship of interior and exterior.

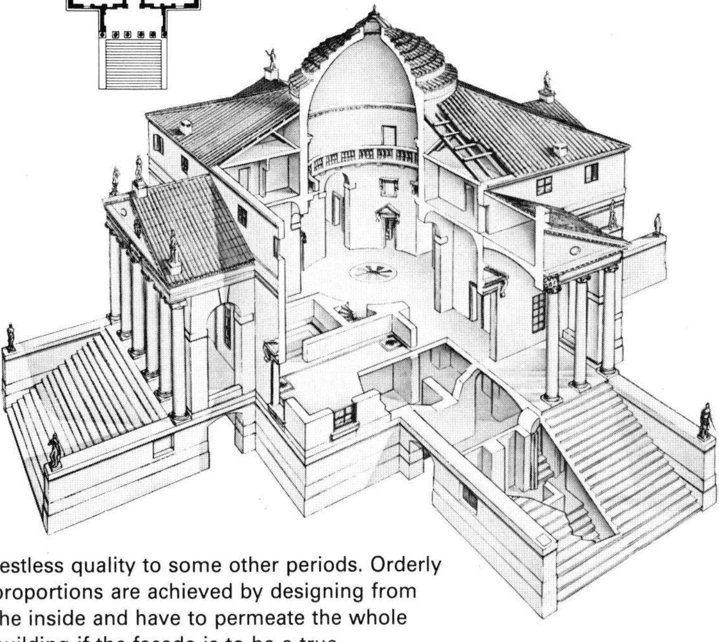

restless quality to some other periods. Orderly proportions are achieved by designing from the inside and have to permeate the whole building if the façade is to be a true expression of the interior. To achieve this is a severe discipline.

In folk and folk-based architecture there are established formulae of fenestration which are rooted in tradition and not to be varied without discordancy, except by an extremely sensitive master-designer. Modernism apart, successful fenestration depends upon regional tradition and/or arcane theory, but the state of law and order in any society also has a profound effect upon ground-floor windows. Climate and aspect also affect folk architecture but are commonly ignored in arcane architecture.

Below A handsome Classical palazzo window barred for security.

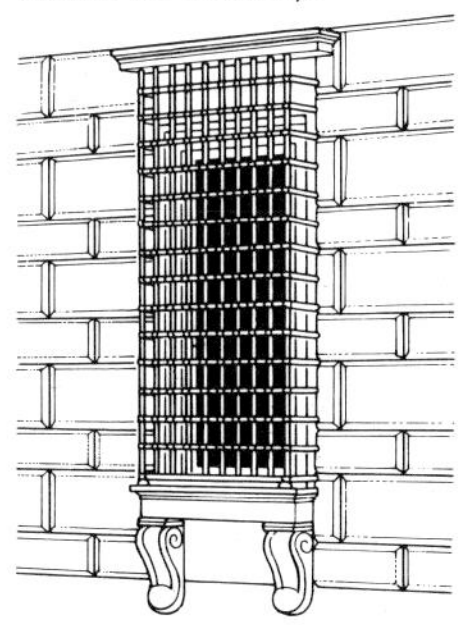

Types of Building Programme

What architects nowadays call the programme profoundly affects the way in which a building is designed. The programme indicates the purpose of the building, what accommodation will be required, how it will be used and probably the acceptable cost (even for a cathedral) but, in periods when labour resources were more important than money, attitudes to costing were different from what they are today. It remains true that many buildings eventually cost far more than the promoters have envisaged and some of the most wonderful buildings in the world would probably never have been started if the ultimate cost had been accurately assessed.

The programme states the function of the building but it is wrong to suppose that the architecture results only from the solution of the functional problem.

A building is hardly ever made without a purpose, but the function of a building may be purely decorative – to improve a view, for example. It may be a monument to commemorate a person, or an event, or it may be intended, as is much garden architecture, mainly to give pleasure.

The function of a building often indicates whether it should be arcane, folk or common in its architectural treatment.

The House

Domestic architecture is lived in by people. Its simplest form is the isolated hut but even this has a small territory round it, for growing vegetables, working, hanging out washing, storing wood, and as a playground for children. The basic human home is a hut plus a territory. This is something we have in common with animals and birds. The basic hut is a single room, occupied by the family and probably shared with animals.

The development of domestic architecture involves the grouping of huts for families and communities; the joining of huts to form

The basic croft-cottage, with a good standard of space, thermal insulation and heating, lacking internal sanitation but otherwise better than many modern accommodation units. Good external living space,and maintained with local materials and labour. Dry-stone walling resists rising damp and minimises condensation problems.

In towns and villages cottages are built in rows along streets. The single-storey cottage is the archetype for urban architecture.

The bay window improves outlook and is a step towards relating interior and exterior. Under bye-laws it could project beyond a building line – an economic advantage for developers.

The bay window is then added to the traditional country dwelling to give a touch of modernity and better outlook.

Evolution of a common architecture: case study – Scotland

The basic cottage is the nucleus of the small linear farm, extended at one or both ends. The use of a ceiling enables the loft to be used for storage or sleeping space, lit at first by sky-lights (a piece of glass placed in the roof instead of slates). The idea of the loft is adopted. The hipped roof, which is suitable for thatch, gives way to gables when squared slates are used.

Dormer windows (an idea from abroad) improve the attic but the single storey concept is maintained for the typical rural dwelling. A porch and a walled front garden complete the rural dwelling house, which now has electricity or bottled gas and internal sanitation.

The common architecture of the towns preserves the ground floor and roof line of the folk tradition, but inserting extra floors between these. Often, bay windows are stacked on each other.

rooms, the communalisation of living space to provide village greens, grazing lands, commons, allotments; communal defence by walls or by the grouping of houses; increasing specialisation and sub-division of the home, the relationship of living accommodation to work-space in farms and in cottage-industry factories, water-mills and the like. Living space was extended to the streets in many industrialised towns, and eliminated, with disastrous results, in high-rise housing developments of the Modernist period.

There are three classes of householder – owner, tenant and lessee. The owner-occupier has the greatest freedom to alter his home and modify its environment. This type of tenure has a marked effect upon the character of houses and districts; it allows for organic development within whatever communal regulations there may be (and these have existed even in the most primitive communities).

An 'open' village plan, centred on its green, which serves as a multi-purpose communal precinct.

Above A defended village, with controlled access.

Below Tourrette-sur-Loup, southern France; the houses are grouped to form a continuous wall, but are unfortified. There is a central castle.

Leaseholding usually involves some control by the freeholder and progressively diminishes the value of the house to the lessee. This can lead to progressive deterioration of maintenance and it has favoured eventual demolition for comprehensive redevelopment.

Legislation for the protection of tenants paradoxically has a bad effect upon the maintenance of architecture and necessitates the provision of publicly-owned housing for poorer people. The environmental character of areas of publicly owned and bureaucratically administered housing is recognisable throughout Europe.

The design of houses for the more prosperous has been affected by the availability and cost of servants and the standards of accommodation customarily provided for them. The accommodation for owners and for servants was separated in town houses from c.1750 to c.1930 in most European towns and cities. The apartment house was common in continental cities, and in Scotland, at all social levels, but rare in England except at the lowest levels until the end of the nineteenth century.

Flats in Paris by Auguste Perret; 1902. A communal expression of prosperity.

Council flats in Lewisham, London; 1960s. Enforced anonymity and bureaucratic domination.

Elaboration of the House

As more and more people 'go out to work' and even consider it a form of liberation to do so, we tend to forget that the architecture of the old Europe was made for people, from carpenters to kings, whose working life was centred upon or closely related to the home. Industrialisation and mechanical transport have exploded the old environmental patterns.

Before the Industrial Revolution many homes were also work-places. This is still true of almost all farmhouses, and even in industrial towns many shop-keepers still live 'over the shop'. To understand the character of many old towns and villages it is necessary to know that they were and, in many cases still are, hives of domestic industry. Even the precious artefacts of the Renaissance were mostly produced in studios or workshops where the artists lived. In times when everything was made by hand the distinction, if it existed, between the artist's studio and the craftsman's workshop was insignificant.

Until the invention of the steam engine the most impressive machinery was that used for grinding corn by wind or water power and the miller lived on the premises. Mines and quarries had cottages which were prototypes of nineteenth-century industrial housing. In seaports, although the main work of fishing and freighting was done away from the home, many ancillary activities were in or close to the home. In cloth-making communities weavers commonly worked on the top floors for a good light.

But the elaboration of the house did not stop with domestic industries. Fine town houses, which became common in the Renaissance, owed their existence in part to pride and in part to the cultivation of a gracious style of living. But in towns, the spacious rooms of merchants and bankers, as well as leading artists, lawyers, consuls, ambassadors and other officials, were part of a working apparatus in the social context of the time. Likewise, in the country, the great house or *château* was an administrative and

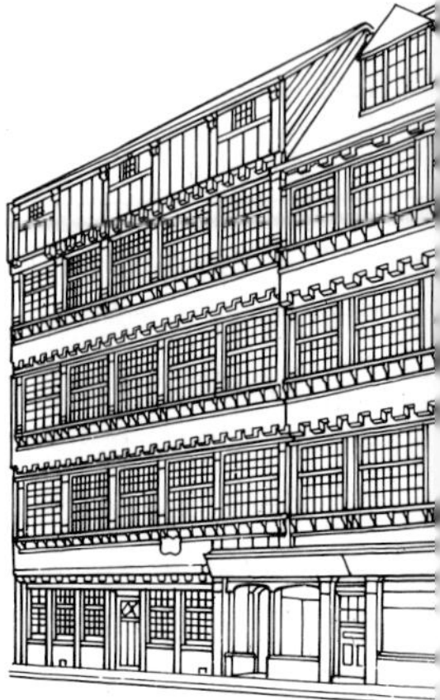

The merchant house; 17th-century, Newcastle-upon-Tyne. This is an unusually developed example of refined timber-framing.

The house as workplace – a water mill, Melin Bompren, Wales.

Right A French *château* famous for its wine – Clos-de-Vougeot, Burgundy.

social centre with accommodation far beyond the domestic needs of the resident family. The fact that the best wines are '*château-bottled*' indicates the working role of the great house in a country where wine-drinking is almost a religion.

If we see royal palaces simply as superlatively grand homes we misunderstand their nature. Louis XIV retired to a flat on the top floor of Versailles. A villa in the grounds served Louis XV, and Marie Antoinette delighted in the rustic simplicity of a romanticised farmhouse set in an 'English' garden (p. 235).

18th-century English houses with weaving rooms on the top floor.

Below An eastern European farmhouse, combining agricultural and domestic accommodation.

Defence

Military architecture is mainly defensive, though strong-points can form part of the tactics of aggression, and garrisons in occupied territory are defended as bases for domination.

After the Neolithic era (the date varied from place to place in Europe) people found it necessary to defend their homes and villages. Waves of aggressive penetration out of Asia into Europe coincided with the rising skills of the metal-workers, whose artefacts in gold, silver and bronze gave a new dimension to human covetousness and whose weapons, in bronze and later in iron, provided the means for defending the treasures which are commonly regarded as criteria of civilisation.

By about 1200 BC castles were being built in Greece. The architectural problem was solved from first principles and a pattern was established which persisted, with minor modifications, until explosives made castles obsolete. Nearly all the necessities of castle design, except enfilade (protection from the side) and machicolation (from above), are embodied in Mycenaean citadels, such as Tiryns.

The absolute priority is a well, a secure water source. Defences can be built round this and they will be better if the site itself is protected by gradients, cliffs, water or marsh. The designer of a castle has to imagine how it might be attacked. In the fifteenth and sixteenth centuries some of the greatest Italian artists, among them Leonardo and Michelangelo, were employed to design fortifications because they were imaginative and ingenious.

At the centre of the castle is that which is to be defended, the ruler, his family and his treasure, then his servants and personal guards; all this with due consideration for his dignity, social obligations, comfort and his role as a ruler, administrator and judge.

Next in order of necessity come secured stores of salted meat and fish, oil, cereals and dried fruit. A peculiarity of the Mycenaean

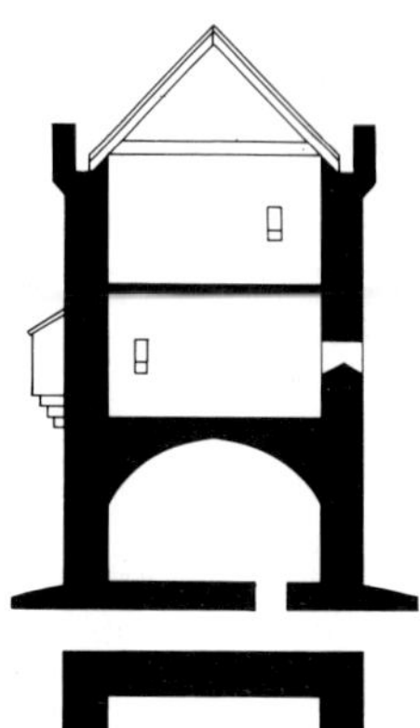

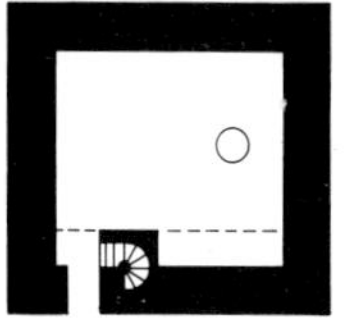

A tower house of the type common throughout Europe; the rudimentary castle and the origin of the keep. The entrance is on the first floor, and the house has its own water supply.

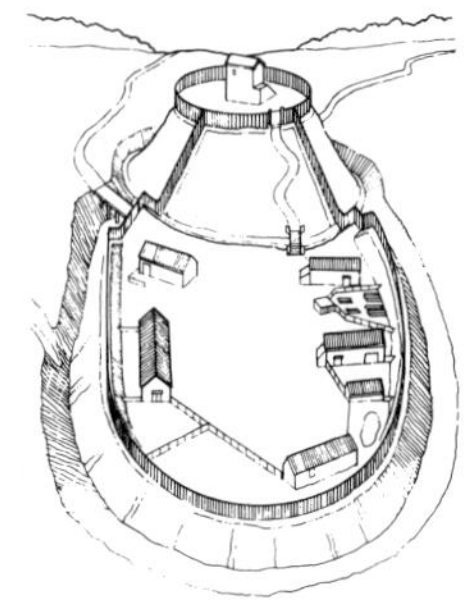

An 11th-century motte-and-bailey castle comprising mostly earthworks and timber stockades.

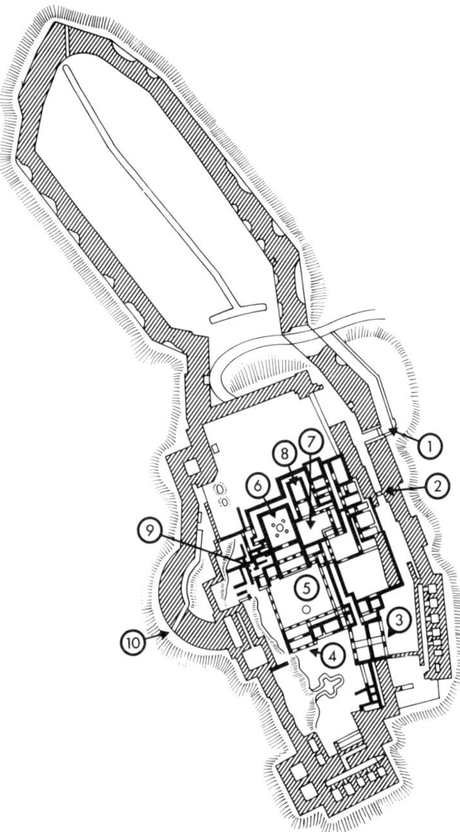

Left Tiryns; the best preserved Mycenaean citadel in Greece. It was one of many, including the Acropolis at Athens before it became a sacred site. Tiryns was more intelligently designed, both for accommodation and for defence, than such medieval castles as Caernarfon (p. 115) or Sirmione (p. 116).
1 Main gateway
2 Inner gateway
3 Greater propylaeum
4 Lesser propylaeum
5 Court to chief megaron
6 Chief megaron
7 Court to lesser megaron
8 Lesser megaron
9 Bathroom
10 Postern

castle is the provision of a bathroom adjoining reception and prior to audience.

The nucleus is defended by grouping the buildings as integral with the inner and outer walls. A postern may provide alternative ingress and egress, but the main approach is by a heavily defended barbican which, in turn, is approached outside the walls by a narrow inclined path, exposing the right or unshielded side of attacking soldiers to the defenders.

Attached to the citadel, and essential to it except in conditions of extreme danger, was a less heavily defended enclosure for the garrison, live-stock, and additional stores. This was a fortified cattle fold, which also served as parade ground and, if necessary, refuge for

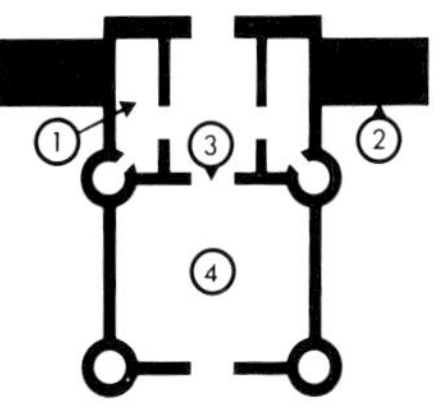

Below A medieval barbican at York: rather feeble compared to the long corridor that served the same purpose at Tiryns.
1 Gatehouse
2 Wall
3 Gate
4 Barbican

the local people. This part of a castle is called a bailey.

Roman conquest of most of Europe reduced the need for castles and substituted garrisons in rectangular 'camps' protected from local intrusion by ditches, embankments and walls or stockades. These camps were more like barracks than castles.

After the collapse of the Western Empire in AD 476 there was little castle building and though the ensuing period has a reputation for disorder, towns in much of Europe were mostly unwalled and villa estates continued to flourish without any fortifications. Battles were fought in the field, sometimes with devastating consequences for local communities, but military architecture seems to have been in abeyance.

The great age of castle building and fortified towns began in the eleventh century. There was no inheritance from the past and the problems were solved all over again, starting with a stockaded motte, then a bailey, then a keep and then a gatehouse. The main innovations in the thirteenth and fourteenth centuries were corbelled battlements (machicolation), round towers which were less vulnerable to sapping than square towers, and projecting towers with slits to enfilade the walls with archery and subsequently musketry. Though briars and other thorny plants were used to protect the approaches to

The medieval defended bridge over the river Lot at Cahors, France; as much an expression of pride as of military engineering.

Below Medina del Campo, Valladolid; one of the great, almost fabulous, Spanish strongholds; 1440–.

San Gimignano, central Italy; 12th-century and later towers of the nobility who were constrained to live in the towns. Ludicrous and uncomfortable, though picturesque. In most places they were superseded by *palazzi*.

castles, the picturesque trees which surround many of them today would not have been allowed in the Middle Ages. The ground around castles was kept clear and offered no cover to attackers.

In many places, such as the border between England and Scotland, where disorder prevailed for long periods, people built tower houses (peles) usually without outer defences. The ground floor had a well and also housed cattle. This room was vaulted for fire protection. The family quarters were above, approached by a retractable ladder. Tower houses were also built in cities where feuds and lawlessness made security a priority for wealthy people, but they also became status symbols like some modern high buildings.

Fortifications did not become obsolete with the invention of gunpowder and cannon but were modified to meet the new conditions. Battered walls presented an oblique target to artillery and were less easy to undermine. A 'low profile', if not actual concealment in the ground or in coastal cliffs, made the defences less identifiable as targets for guns. Garrisons became smaller and more specialised; the protection of ammunition became extremely important. Castles had been provocatively and proudly obvious in the fourteenth century; their twentieth-century counterparts were in concealed and camouflaged emplacements, with devious blast-resisting entrances.

Peles were simple tower houses often entered by retractable ladders at first-floor level. On the English-Scottish borders the clergy often lived in peles.

Religious

Most of the best architecture has been built in the service, propitiation or honour of God or the gods, of inscrutable spiritual power, and the ultimate mystery of existence. This is true for all countries and creeds. The programme for a religious building is not a mere statement of accommodation to be provided. The building is meaningful within the religious beliefs of the people. In the great majority of cases it is consecrated to the spiritual power which among believers is seen to be effective. If one can approach religious buildings in the belief that all religions are ways to the same destination, whatever one's own religion or lack of it may be, it becomes easier to understand and appreciate what was intended and achieved. The observance of certain customs and courtesies, such as removing one's shoes before entering a mosque, can be a helpful reminder. A merely secular and historical experience of a religious building leaves out the prime meaning of the architecture, like a swimming bath without water.

Religious architecture of Europe may be classified as follows:

Firstly, ordered arrangements of large stones (megaliths) which served to relate man to nature by observation of the skies and prediction of seasons and eclipses, by ceremonial, especially dancing and tuning-in to Earth rhythms which are less well understood now than they were 5000 years ago.

Secondly, the pagan Classical period of ancient Greece and Rome, when religious architecture was dedicated to particular gods. The gods were conceived as being like humans but immortal. Athens, for example, considered itself to be under the special protection of Athena, generally seen as the divine embodiment of the arts and crafts, of the olive oil industry, of commercial wisdom and the advantages of peace. In this period gods were essentially tribal and thus the deification of Caesar as head of the Roman

Above The *Alignement d'Erdiven* at Carnac, Brittany, one of the most complex arrangements of megaliths.

Left The Ionic temple of Wingless Victory (*Athena Niké*) at Athens; 427 BC.

Below A small Romanesque Christian church of S. Juan de Baños de Cerrato, Palencia, Spain; 661.

Empire was consistent, though vulgar.

Thirdly, medieval Christianity, divided from 1054 into the Greek Orthodox Church – which roughly coincided with the Eastern Roman Empire – and the Roman Catholic Church. Both forms involved congregational worship in large buildings which were themselves acts of worship, while including provision for individual prayer and shrines consecrated to particular saints.

The Orthodox Church suffered grievously from the Fourth Crusade of 1204 and the conquest of Constantinople by the Turks in 1453 but remained influential in architecture on the fringe between Islam and Western Christian Europe — from Russia and Scandinavia to Austria, Switzerland, Alpine France and Italy.

The Catholic Church was supreme in Western Europe (except Islamic Spain) throughout the Middle Ages and was the major patron of architecture.

Fourthly, the Renaissance Church emphasised humanism and the adaptation of Classical architecture to Christian use, upon a theoretical basis of Classical geometry which reflected the divine ordering of the world. From the 1520s, the Reformation introduced a diversity of sects, many of them puritanical and disposed to see church buildings simply as meeting places, and to find the Church in people rather than in structures. In parallel with this, the Counter-Reformation placed emphasis upon the *glory* of God in magnificent Baroque buildings and the life-style of bishops as princes of the Church.

Finally, in the nineteenth century a purification and revival of religion coincided with the revival of Gothic architecture. This led on to the ambivalence of the modern age, with its uncertainties reflected in mainly nondescript church buildings. Coventry Cathedral (1951–62) in England is a brave and successful attempt, by Sir Basil Spence, to re-create the medieval convergence of many arts in one building. Tapestry, glass, sculpture, paintings are all original works of art.

Right Coutances Cathedral, France; 1218–91. One of the greatest achievements of the Western tradition.

The opposite of the elaborate church – a Meeting House of the Society of Friends (Quakers), whose founder, George Fox, taught that the church is people not buildings.

Left The Cathedral of St Basil the Blessed in Moscow; 1554. Not a Disneyland frivolity but the culmination of the Hellenesque tradition, just as St Maclou, Rouen (p. 243) and King's College Chapel, Cambridge (p. 272) are the elaborate conclusion of the Romanesque-Gothic tradition in the Roman Catholic Church

Below St Lawrence, Wilten, Innsbruck; an 18th-century Rococo design which emphasises taste and beauty in the service of God. The design, like St Quirin (p. 7), is strongly influenced from eastern Europe (see also p. 335).

Temples, Churches and Mosques

The word temple (which derives from the Greek *temenos* and Latin *templum*) seems to have meant originally a defined or fenced piece of ground, a precinct such as a grove of trees, but came to mean a building set in a precinct with a shrine or statue inside and an altar outside, in front of the porch. We tend to apply the word to the building and forget that its setting, whether architectural or natural, was part of the scheme. Being the house of a god, a temple was arcane architecture.

A sacred precinct.

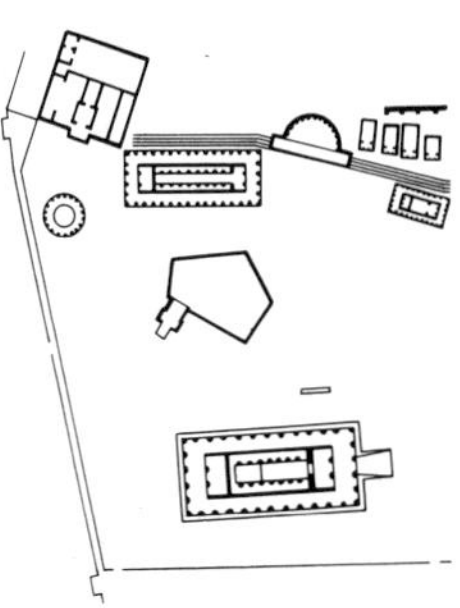

Plan of part of the *temenos* at Olympia, including temples of Hera and Zeus and other buildings; 2nd century AD.

Some pre-Christian cults brought the congregation inside a building to worship, and this continued in Christian churches, with the main altar generally at the east end inside the sanctuary. This place came to be enclosed by *cancelli* (lattices), hence the name chancel, but as with the Classical temple, the shrine was given a setting within columns (the *ciborium* or ambulatory or both) and approached by a columned nave, often leading to transepts which, by forming a crossing, gave the effect of a court in front of the sanctuary.

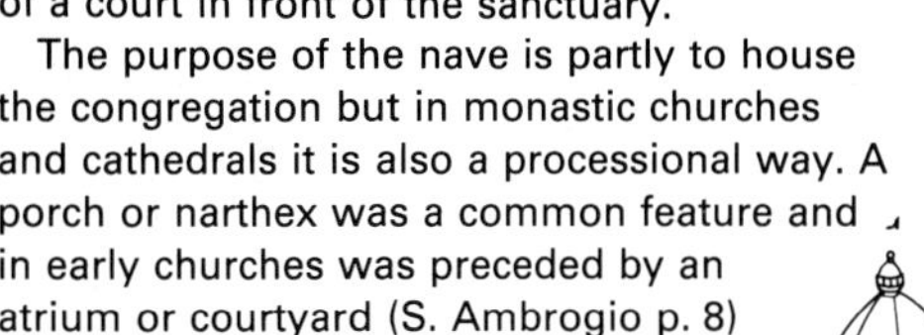

The purpose of the nave is partly to house the congregation but in monastic churches and cathedrals it is also a processional way. A porch or narthex was a common feature and in early churches was preceded by an atrium or courtyard (S. Ambrogio p. 8)

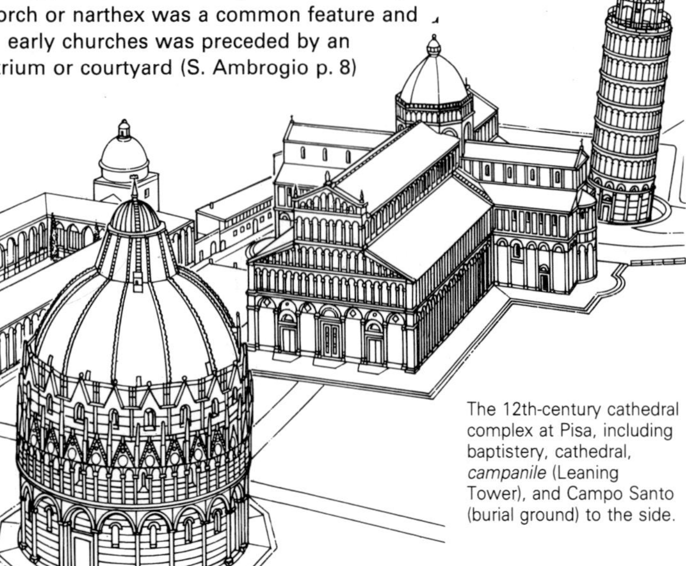

The 12th-century cathedral complex at Pisa, including baptistery, cathedral, *campanile* (Leaning Tower), and Campo Santo (burial ground) to the side.

In the Middle Ages the nave had many secular uses, as a parish hall for meetings, dancing and commerce, and there are records of people seeking sanctuary from the law who actually lived for months on end in the naves of cathedrals, unable to go out for fear of summary execution.

Small churches served by a single priest are really a different programme from cathedrals, approximating to the conditions of worship in homes during the Roman persecution. Their function as places of meeting for worship has been idealised by many non-conformist sects. Chapels and meeting houses generally place emphasis upon the coming together of people rather than upon the arcane significance of architecture.

Mosques, some of the finest of which are in Europe, inherited the form of Hellenesque churches but, in fact, they are stupendously beautiful meeting houses with no altar. The congregation worships 'out from' the mosque guided by a *mihrab* (prayer-niche) which indicates the direction of Mecca. There is also a *mimbar* which serves as pulpit and lectern. Since the ninth century figurative decoration has not been used. It is not prohibited by the Koran, but the Traditions (*Hadith*) warn that the artist will be required to breathe a soul into figures which attempt to rival the divine art of creation. Fortunately architecture does not come under this stricture.

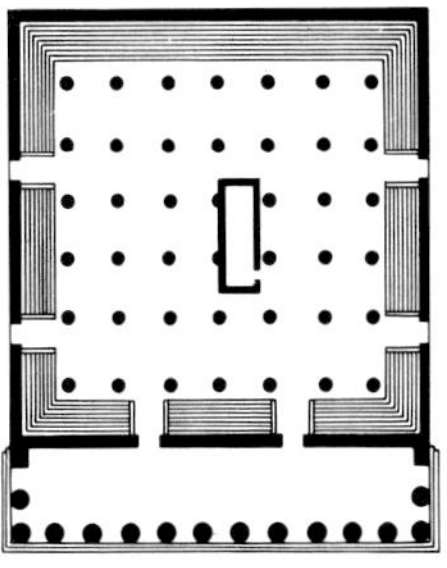

The Telesterion, Eleusis; a 5th-century BC meeting place, or Hall of the Mysteries.

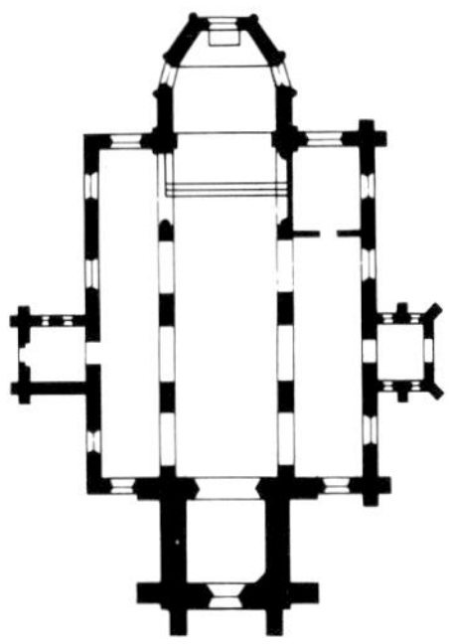

Plan of the small Anglo-Saxon church at Wing, Bucks., England, with chancel, aisled nave and porch.

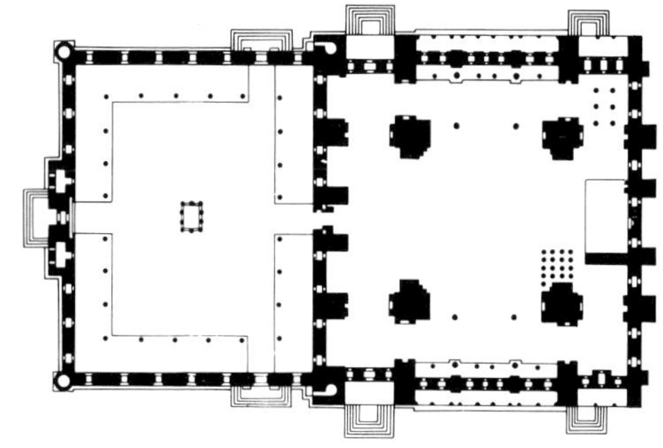

Left Plan of the Suleiman Mosque, Istanbul.
See p. 163.

Monastic

Monasteries played a vital role in the development of medieval architecture and its legacy to modern times. It should also be noted that many monasteries are active today, throughout western Europe, and one of the outstanding buildings of the Modernist period is the Cistercian monastery of La Tourette by Le Corbusier.

When the Frankish king Clovis I accepted Christianity (the official Roman religion) and was baptised by St Rémy at Rheims in 506, a relationship was established between the illiterate barbarian aristocracy and the educated Gallo-Roman people, and Roman culture was to some extent preserved. Romans of good family found their vocation in the Church and, having both clerical skills and spiritual authority, they became a powerful element in early medieval society. The clergy formed fraternities under the rule of abbots and in some cases bishops. Monasticism probably originated in Egypt, spread rapidly in Europe in the fourth and fifth centuries and was consolidated in the sixth century by St Benedict who established a short and workable code for the conduct of monasteries as self-contained religious families, living on

Below left St Martin du Canigou, France; a remote monastery in the eastern Pyrenees, centring upon the church and the cloister.

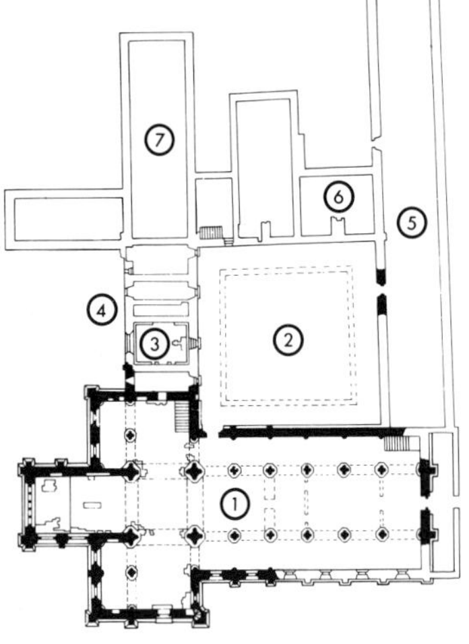

1 Church
2 Cloister
3 Chapter house
4 Treasury
5 Lay brothers' range
6 Kitchen
7 Novices' room

Sweetheart Abbey, Scotland (plan above) demonstrates the principle of hierarchy in the buildings themselves: the church for the worship of God, the cloister for the fraternity, the administrative rooms and the living accommodation. The same order can be seen in the monastery of La Tourette; 1955–59, by Le Corbusier (above right).

An idyllic monastic setting on Corfu, Greece. A Christian tribute to Apollo.

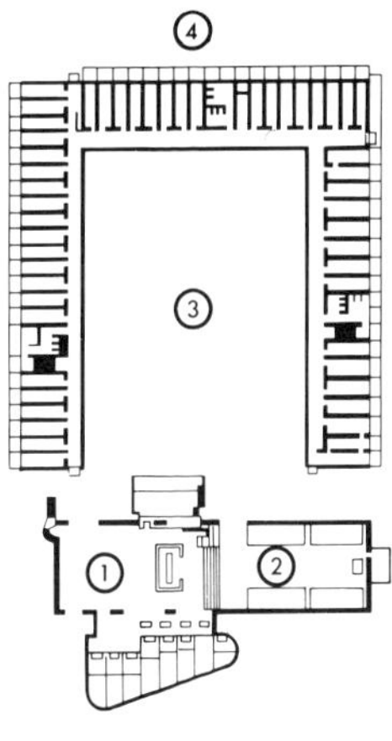

1 Church
2 Choir
3 Cloister
4 Cells

the produce of their lands. In daily life, prayer, reading and manual work had equal importance; thus, apart from their religious devotional role, monasteries became centres of scholarship and monks applied educated minds to the physical problems of farming, forestry, apiary, carpentry, building, and, among many other activities, to preserving and developing the theory and practice of architecture. By prudence and hard work as well as endowment, monasteries became prosperous. Increasing emphasis upon art and elaborate liturgy and intellectual pursuits in the Benedictine Order led to reform movements by the late eleventh century. The most influential was the Cistercian Order (White Monks) established at Cîteaux in Burgundy in about 1100. It was profoundly influenced and expanded by St Bernard who arrived there in 1112.

Cistercians became a major influence in the Church and had a strong influence in England and Wales where there were 53 Cistercian abbeys by 1153, and from these more abbeys were founded in Scotland and Scandinavia.

Cistercian abbeys, such as Fountains and Rievaulx in England, exemplify the ideal fulfilment in architecture of the rule of St Benedict, and the practice of recruiting lay brothers made the Cistercians a powerful economic force as farmers, often on virgin sites, and developers of waste land. Many Cistercian abbeys were built on a monumental scale, though retaining architectural clarity.

Although monasticism declined in the later Middle Ages and in many countries abbeys disappeared in the Reformation, they had, by then, paved the way for secular institutions – schools, hospitals and charities – which, in the Middle Ages, had been provided by the Church. It is misleading to think of medieval monasteries as retreats from the 'real world'; they were a vital part of it and a major force in the preservation and development of civilisation. This is apparent in their architecture if we look at it realistically.

Educational

For most of history this is an aspect of religious architecture. In the last century education has been progressively secularised, but in historic centres of learning up to c.1914, the chapel, as in the Church of the Sorbonne in Paris, (p. 238) has been the focal point and the major architectural component. The architecture of education in the modern world evolved from the medieval monasteries. In England the Dissolution of the Monasteries in the 1530s by Henry VIII created an educational vacuum which was slowly filled by the grammar and public schools. Residential schools have preserved the functional layout of the medieval monastery. The non-residential school has evolved rapidly in the last hundred years, from single rooms and open halls to the sophisticated complexity of the modern school campus. During this period there has been a growth of state education and a decline in church and charity provision for schooling, the rate of change varying between countries.

The basic elements of a school are the classrooms and the playground, with cloakrooms and toilets; then a hall-gymnasium, library, laboratories, workshops etc. There is a tendency for modern schools to resemble factories, which is unfortunate and results from a functionalist attitude to architecture which does not correspond with modern ideals of education.

The fundamental idea of a college is not a building but a group of colleagues (people 'chosen-together') usually under a master. A college is not necessarily educational (e.g. College of Cardinals) but when it is, living accommodation for the fellows or tutors is the basic element; the students visit it for tutorials. Thus it is possible for students to be dispersed through the town or city and for the actual college to be a small but vital nucleus. This is common in many continental universities where the university 'presence' is not obvious as it is in, for example, Oxford, Cambridge and Durham. In these examples

Northumberland, England; a typical country Board school, well designed and built in stone. The style is faintly collegiate and symbolises the high aims of public education in the early 20th century.

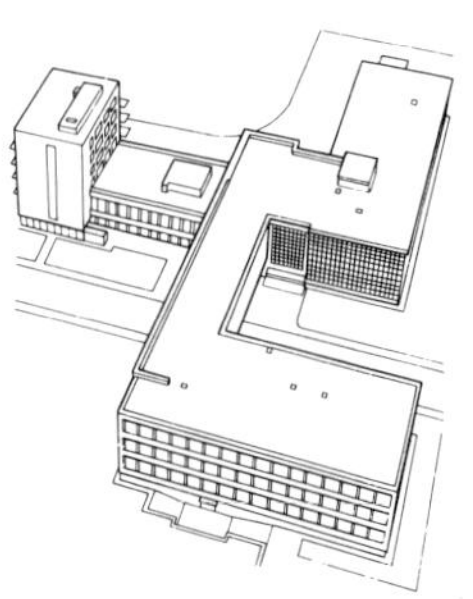

The Bauhaus, Dessau, Germany, conceived in 1919 by Walter Gropius as a school for architects and designers to further the ideals of William Morris and the Arts and Crafts Movement.

the universities are federations of residential colleges in small cities.

What we regard as the typical college derives from the monastic plan and consists of a chapel, hall, library and living quarters arranged round a cloister or 'quad'. This plan has persisted in various styles of architecture until the present day in many Oxford and Cambridge colleges. When the curriculum was extended to include sciences and engineering it was necessary to build laboratories and other features of a modern university outside the collegiate area. Increased numbers of students have also been housed in separate halls of residence. Most modern universities have started with a collegiate plan but where space was available, or where universities were founded on green-field sites the campus plan has been developed by extension of the monastic idea.

Christ Church College, Oxford, an adjunct of the Cathedral (right).

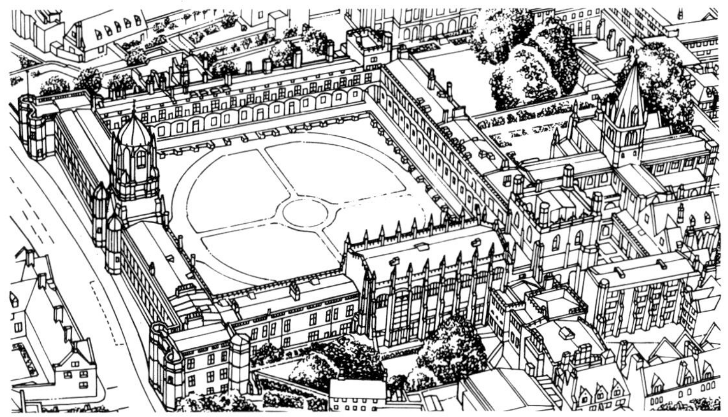

Left Fairlawn Primary School, London; 1960s by Peter Moro. Comfort, convenience, efficiency and durability are subservient to modernist dogmatism.

Industrial

Until quite recently industrial buildings have not been thought of as architecture and the places where people have worked for wages have generally been squalid and ugly. Semi-domestic industries, such as corn-milling by wind- or water-power have participated in the folk tradition of design. The late eighteeenth century saw influences from governmental architecture upon buildings for state industries, especially in France, but the idea of a factory as a subject for architectural design by leading architects is quite modern and reflects the values of a society which recognises its dependence upon manufacturing industry, and takes agriculture for granted.

A tower mill in Czechoslovakia, for grinding corn.

Left The Iron Bridge, Coalbrookdale, England; 1779. A pioneer structure in one of the early centres of the Industrial Revolution. Probably designed by T. F. Pritchard, who did not live to see it completed.

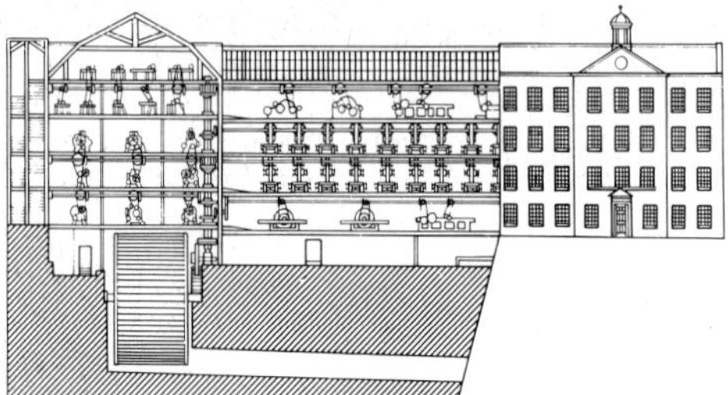

Left Quarrybank Mill, Styal, England; early 19th century. A complicated industrial process is accommodated within the Georgian concept of respectable architecture.

Right The Beam Engine House, Eastney, England; 1887. A respectable façade for pumping sewage – and why not?

Left Boot's Chemical Factory, Nottingham, England; 1930–32 by Owen Williams. Much admired, but unfortunately it became a prototype for housing as well as for factories.

Below The Carl Christensen Motor works, Copenhagen; 1956 by Arne Jacobsen. A modern equivalent of Quarrybank.

Health

In Classical Greece and Rome very high priority was given to buildings for the cultivation of mental and physical health. These included clinics, temples, and theatres, for the Greeks, and an emphasis upon hydrotherapy for the Romans who established spas throughout Europe and equipped them with gymnasia, theatres and other entertainments, as well as hotels for comfortable living. With the advent of Christianity institutional health-care passed almost entirely to the Church, and especially to the monasteries, where the emphasis was on healing by faith. The nadir of architectural provision for the sick probably occurred in the eighteenth century, especially in Protestant countries. Scientific medicine in the last hundred years has enormously improved the curative effectiveness of medicine and surgery but it remains an open question whether modern facilities are more effective than the treatment of the 'whole person' practised in ancient Greece and elsewhere. Modern hospitals have been largely a development of facilities previously provided by Christian charities, but as they have become secular or state institutions they have changed in architectural character, with more emphasis upon the function of curing disease and less upon the treatment of people.

The basic elements of a hospital are reception and consultation, wards and theatres. Services and efficient vertical and horizontal circulation play a very big part in the design.

Reconstruction of the Roman *thermae* at Trier, West Germany. Such health centres were found in many Roman cities, and concentrated upon fitness, cleanliness and preventive medicine.

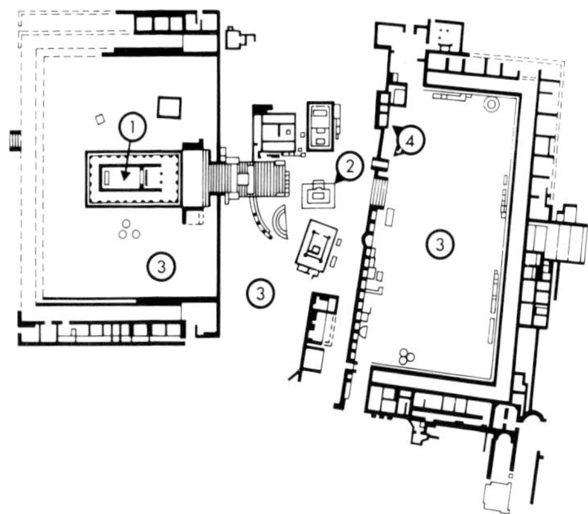

Left Plan of the sanctuary of Asklepios at Kos, the ancient Greek health centre. In the ancient world healing and religion were understood to be related. Art, particularly drama and sculpture, played a part in overall therapy.
1 Temple of Asclepius
2 Altar of Asclepius
3 Terrace
4 Basins

Right The Hospice at Beaune, France; 1443–51 – a refuge inspired by Christian charity but requiring a Christian response. Does the patronal concern for the architectural expression of the institution take precedence over the well-being of the patients? Comfort – yes; but well-being is another question.

Below Royal Hospital, Chelsea, England; 1682–91. A home for old soldiers. The British hospital system has roots in the conscientious care for those who have served their country in war.

Public Buildings

In Classical times there were numerous public buildings for secular use, ranging from gymnasia and public baths to law courts and theatres.

The essence of a public building is that it provides accommodation for numerous people to gather under a roof. This presented a structural problem in spanning a wide floor space and it was sensibly recognised that where many people are gathered there should be plenty of air-space above them and therefore a high roof or ceiling. The perfected Classical solution was the Roman basilica which took two forms: one with a timber roof structure and, more importantly, the cross-vaulted basilica which was the structural prototype from which the major achievements of medieval and Renaissance architecture developed.

From Classical times until the nineteenth century public buildings were commonly paid

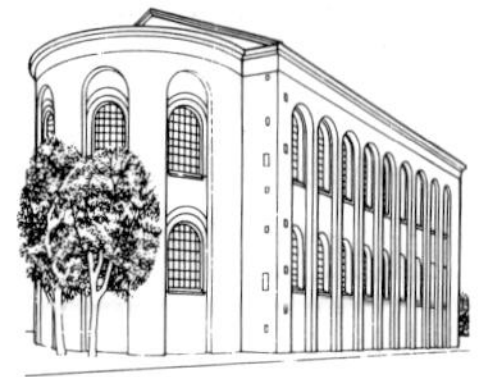

The Roman palace hall (basilica) of Trier, West Germany; now a Protestant church.

The Palace of the Doges, Venice, grew with the city itself from the 9th century to the 16th. A complex ceremonial, administrative and judicial building.

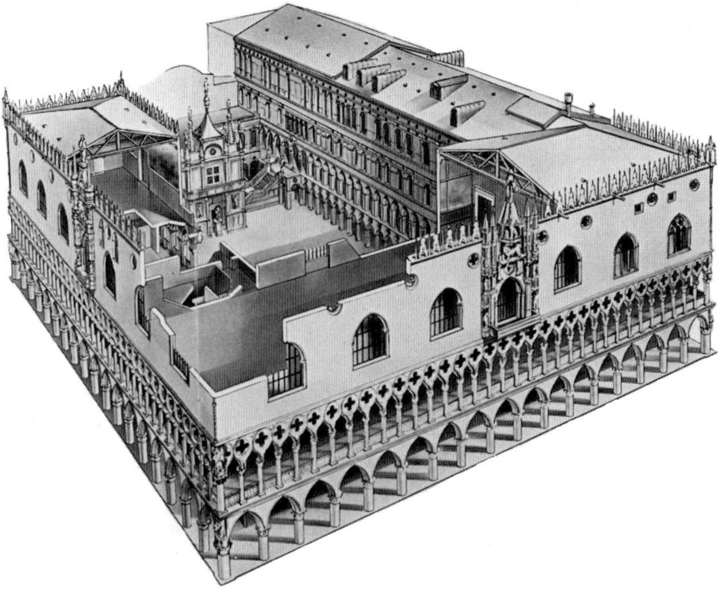

for by wealthy benefactors or privileged groups, such as guilds. These pre-industrial craft trades unions used architecture to establish their prestige over the aristocrats and administrators, and the emphasis was upon quality as a basis for higher remuneration.

In the nineteenth century, art galleries, town halls, museums, barracks, prisons and even workhouses were treated monumentally as public architecture but this coincided with the development of a taxation system, both local and national, which curtailed and eventually almost eliminated private patronage of public architecture as the task of disposing of surplus wealth passed from individuals to committees, and guilds were replaced by trade unions.

Though most settled communities sooner or later provide themselves with a meeting room or hall, civic architecture as we now know it seems to have developed first in city states. The classic instance is the group of buildings round the Agora (market) in ancient Athens, an example followed by the Romans who had, in most towns, a forum, commonly dominated by a temple but mainly used for civic purposes. The open area in the middle was even more important than the buildings which surrounded it and the town square persisted.

In autonomous or semi-autonomous medieval cities, such as Venice and Florence in Italy and the ports of the Baltic such as Danzig (Gdansk) and the mercantile cities of what are now Holland and Belgium, the civic authorities needed not only a meeting hall and offices but a suite of rooms for lavish hospitality and conferences (pp. 300–303). One of the best examples is the Doge's Palace in Venice. Such buildings set the pattern for town halls throughout Europe until the present century when the growth of bureaucracy has led to the proliferation of municipal offices. Civic architecture has generally followed precedents set by kings and princes in their palaces and in Italy the town hall is generally called *palazzo* (as in the Palazzo Pubblico in Siena, p. 188).

Liverpool University Tower; begun 1885, by Alfred Waterhouse. Built of smooth red brick, with hall and splendid staircase in coloured faience. The product of a coal-fired technology.

The Stock Exchange, Amsterdam; 1898–1903, by H. P. Berlage. One of the triumphs of the Arts and Crafts Movement.

Government

There is a natural sequence of development from castle, to royal palace, to modern seat of government. The ultimate in regal seats of government is to be seen in the palaces of Versailles (pp. 234–35), Leningrad and Caserta. The growth of parliamentary democracy necessitated modification of the palace plan to provide a debating chamber or chambers, as at Westminster, or a separate building as in Paris. International institutions follow a similar pattern with a proliferation of offices and committee rooms. Generally state buildings are given a dignified presence and until recently departmental offices (ministries) have tended to look like palaces, even those built in the Modernist style.

Buildings for justice are not always provided by central government but represent the law-enforcing and judiciary role of the state. Law courts present a peculiar problem in planning because the several parties have to be kept separate, and in criminal cases the prisoner is in custody. The usual practice has been to make law courts, as well as prisons, impressive.

In parts of Europe totalitarian regimes have created governmental buildings which use architecture to express the power of the state over people; an interesting if perverted example of meaningful architecture.

Above The Royal Courts of Justice, London; 1871–82 by G. E. Street. Its scholarly neo-Gothic style, like that of the Palace of Westminster, harks back to the medieval origins of the constitution and legal system.

The Reichstag, Berlin; 1884–94 (restored) by P. Wallot. Baroque scale and imperial richness at the heart of the German Empire.

Commercial

Until recently there has been an affinity between civic and commercial architecture. Towns depended for food upon the surrounding country and upon imports of what the locality could not provide. The wealthier citizens who organised a city's economy were almost always the members of its Council, the 'city fathers', and they believed that everyone gained by their own increasing prosperity. Manufacturing, which was mainly inside towns, provided money for food and raw materials, but trade and merchandising also contributed to wealth, as did banking, legal and other entrepreneurial services.

With the growth of industry in the nineteenth century supporting services such as banks and insurance associations proliferated. New industrial towns built splendid town halls in the old tradition, and commercial institutions of all kinds were built in palatial style with the general idea of expressing stability and inspiring confidence. Apart from banking halls, which were sometimes on a grand scale, the internal arrangements were nondescript and façades to main streets were the main architectural expression. Generally commercial architecture has not been innovative though there are exceptions like the splendid nineteenth-century shopping arcades of Milan, Naples and Leeds which prefigure (and still excel) the typical modern shopping centres.

The 'Rows', Chester, England; medieval buildings providing shops on two levels and an upper walkway.

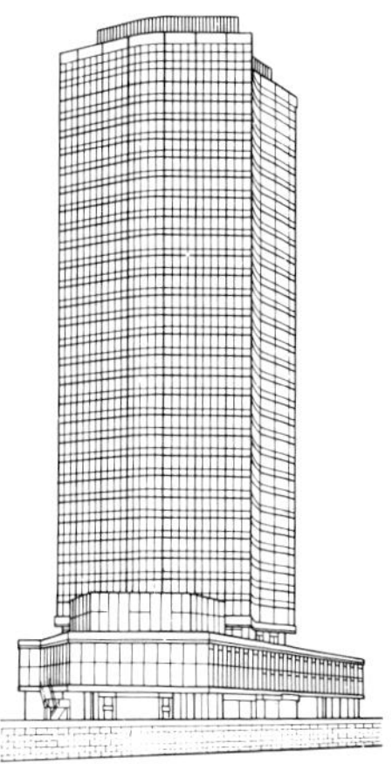

The Vickers Tower, London; 1962, by R. Ward. Pretentious commercialism with nothing much to say except 'I'm big'.

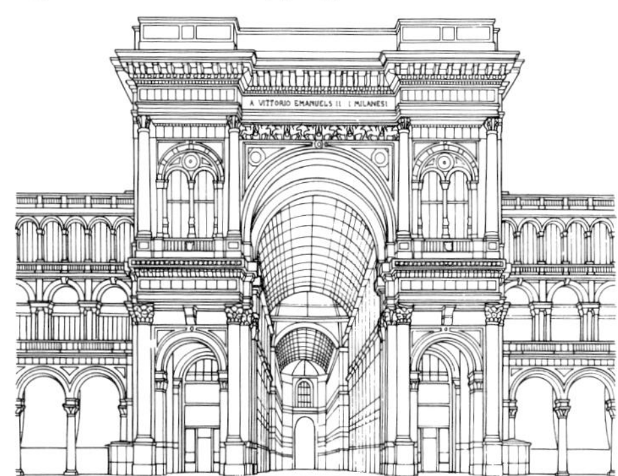

Left The entrance to the Victor Emmanuel Arcade, Milan; 1865–77. The fore-runner of the modern off-street shopping centre.

Folk Architecture

Folk architecture, like other folk arts, is produced by and for the people of a locality, the design usually being done by craftsmen working within a traditional style. It is not unchanging and many influences affect its evolution. Originality is not admired nor called for, except in the solution of a new problem. The use of local materials is almost universal but occasionally imported materials may be characteristic, as on the north-east coast of England where Flemish bricks and pantiles came in by sea.

Arcane architects may influence folk architecture; for example many craftsmen in England learned the Classical way of design from Sir Christopher Wren in the late seventeenth century, and introduced it into the towns and villages of England.

Conquest or colonisation may bring new forms of folk art, including architecture, and in many regions of Europe indigenous folk architecture has been overlaid or modified by ethnic, social and cultural changes. In many places the evolution of folk architecture, visible in surviving buildings, is a fascinating record of history.

Indigenous folk architecture – the architecture of the very first settled communities in the region – has persisted unchanged in some regions and these are of special interest. They may go back far beyond the Christian era, in a few cases as far as the Mesolithic Age. In some places the indigenous tradition is still so strong as to affect the work of modern architects, as in Scotland where there is a persistent sense of the 'spirit of the place' affecting the design of the buildings in which people live.

Modern national boundaries have little or no relationship to the folk styles of architecture but within them there is a growing recognition and revival of regional traditions. Some people see this as the way ahead for modern architecture.

Right A precinct in the Greek island town of Mykonos. Whitewash everywhere.

Right Thatched, stone-built cottage at Rockingham, Northants, England. Thatch is a by-product of the corn harvest, except in marshland areas where reeds are used. In southern countries the fire hazard is serious and the thatch is sometimes covered with mud or mortar and then whitewashed P. 81).

Far right Leuchars church, Fife, Scotland; 12th century. A local development of a style influenced by Durham Cathedral.

Right A 'wee-free' church on the Isle of Skye, Scotland. Derived from the indigenous cottage architecture.

Celtic Fringe

Its main area is the Atlantic coasts and off-shore islands, from the mouth of the Loire in France to the Western Isles of Scotland, including the Channel Islands and the peninsula of Cornwall, West Wales, the Isle of Man and most of Ireland. The architecture more or less coincides with the surviving use of various forms of Gaelic language.

The Celtic tradition is probably the most ancient in Europe. Commodious houses were being built (and have actually survived in the Isle of Lewis) as early as 3000 BC.

The characteristic home was and still is, in the quieter places, a stone-walled cottage with a raftered roof covered with turf, thatch or slates. The single-roomed cottage was improved by adding another room at one end, the 'wee but-and-ben' as it has been called in Scotland. The addition of a barn or byre at either end was the origin of the characteristic linear farm house. A hearth and chimney at one of the gable ends became typical and is probably a style of ancient origin. Cooking was commonly done in a large pot hanging over a turf (peat) or wood fire; a furze oven built into the wall and pre-heated by burning twigs, gorse or brushwood is still not uncommon in substantial farm houses (it produces the most delicious bread). In villages a communal oven was used and some of these are still in use throughout Europe. In these thick-walled houses, built of local stone, 'furniture' such as shelves and cupboards was often built into the walls.

Externally the dry-walling of the houses was slurried and whitewashed with lime mixed sometimes with milk to form the first emulsion paint. This was done even where lime had to be brought from a distance.

Main characteristics of Celtic Fringe architecture include:

Thick, chunky, stone or occasionally earth walls. Gable ends, steep-pitched roofs (40° to 60°) covered with thatch often tied down with rope to corbels at the eaves, or heavily slated roofs resistant to strong winds. The basic house is usually symmetrical with a central door and flanking windows. There is a precinct, usually walled with stone often capped with earth and grass, and, since its introduction from South America in the seventeeth century, fuchsia. Since the eighteenth century the Celtic tradition has been developed in two- and three-storey buildings, usually with sash windows.

Left A Scottish or Irish crofter's cottage, with the thatch tied down by ropes. In the Western Isles there are traces of substantial villages built in this way.

Right A Welsh cottage, with slate roof and a front garden enclosed with a wall.

Below Tintagel Post Office, Cornwall, England; a two-storeyed cottage with dormer windows.

Mediterranean Coast and Off-shore Islands

To understand the origins of Mediterranean folk architecture one must realise that the bare rocks of the mountains bordering the Mediterranean, and the islands, were once covered with trees and that massive soil erosion and desiccation occurred from Roman times onwards. The red bricks of Siena and Verona were made by cutting down trees; so also was lime.

Despite the rocky nature of the terrain, good building stone is hard to come by, though marble can be quarried in many places. Soft sedimentary rocks (tufa) are available but do not weather well. They can, however, be cut with a saw and harden after being quarried. Lime and gypsum (for making plaster) are widely available, also clay for making tiles, and near Naples a natural cement called *pozzolana* was mined by the Romans and used for making a concrete which would set under water.

The Minoans (c. 3000–1400 BC) had framed their buildings in timber and filled-in with blocks of soft rock (gypsum), then plastered the walls inside and out, but this system later gave way to three main types of building, all of which employed rough masonry walls protected from the weather by plaster and/or white-wash.

The first is the bee-hive type of building which requires nothing but stone and consists of ring after ring of stones laid horizontally, or tilted slightly inwards. When a suitable height has been reached the rings are diminished in diameter to form a dome. This is called a corbel or bee-hive dome and is the basic system used in all the great domes until modern times. It is like a half egg-shell when finished and exerts no lateral thrust. The same principle was used in building domes of mud or concrete.

For houses and cottages circular rooms have their disadvantages, and in Europe domical folk architecture has survived in a few places, most importantly in south-east Italy.

The basic Mediterranean house, with walls of whitewashed rubble and Roman tiles covering a low-pitched roof. The windows are small, with louvred shutters.

Trulle, or bee-hive buildings, near Bari, southern Italy. This very ancient domical structure can be built with stones picked up from the fields.

Secondly, the flat-roofed house with walls of rubble and a roof of timber logs covered with concrete and surfaced with floor tiles of burnt clay, or marble in the better houses. There is usually a parapet or railing and a hatch or penthouse giving access and, most importantly, providing convected ventilation to the rooms below. Flat roofs are liable to leak (as modern architects have discovered to their clients' cost) and while they are common to the south and east they give way to the third type, the low-pitched tiled roof along the European coasts where rainfall is greater. Interlocking tiles made of marble were used by the ancient Greeks for such buildings as the Parthenon at Athens, but the same idea became characteristic of folk architecture throughout southern Europe in the simpler form of half-round tiles laid alternately upwards and downwards, the upper curves throwing the water into the hollow gutters made by the downward curves. These tiles, often called Roman, are half-pipes. They are difficult to adapt to curves, splays etc., and are best used on rectangular buildings with gable ends. The character of much Mediterranean architecture results from this fact and even the Classical pedimented temple front is, in part, a reflection of the way in which the roof was constructed. In some places, notably Greece, Yugoslavia and Turkey, tiles were tapered so that they could be used for covering domes.

A typical town house, from Kotor, Yugoslavia.

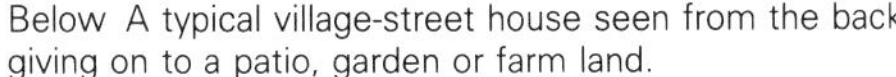

Below A typical village-street house seen from the back, giving on to a patio, garden or farm land.

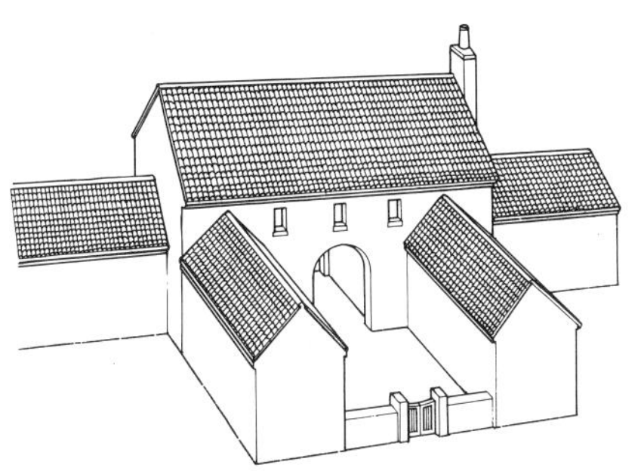

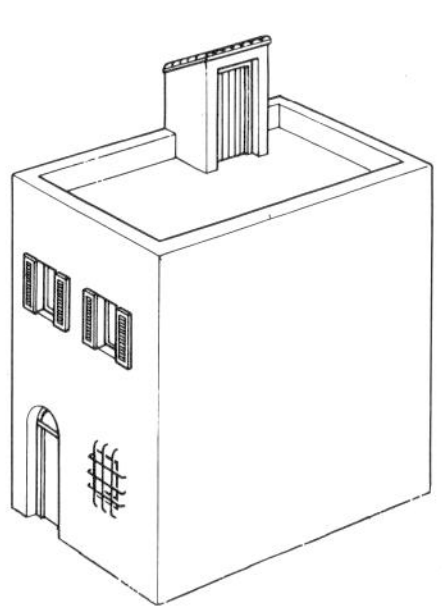

The flat-roofed house is more common on the southern coasts of the Mediterranean. The penthouse gives access to the roof and provides convected ventilation. Such houses often provide evidence of Arab influences.

The typical folk architecture of southern Europe is built with thick rubble walls, usually rendered, stuccoed or colour-washed, in which the windows are cut rather than built. The roofs are of half-round tiles laid to a low pitch, which is adequate where rainfall is low; but these tiles are difficult to keep in place at pitches above 30° and are unsuitable further north without special and expensive precautions such as felt underlays which nowadays make it possible to build Mediterranean-style houses in the north.

Though winter days can be bitterly cold in southern Europe, open hearths and chimneys are rare in the older buildings. The charcoal brazier was the usual means of heating, and old ladies still use bowls of hot charcoal over which they drape their long skirts for the most basic form of central heating.

The peasant costume of southern lands is more comfortably functional than the sunbathing summer tourist may realise. The winter can be bitter and away from the sophisticated cities, in a rural economy, the fact that heat is expensive has always been recognised. According to Classical legend fire

Town houses at Skiathos, Greece (below left) and Dubrovnik, Yugoslavia (below).

was stolen by Prometheus from the gods and they were very angry about it. Man was not to be trusted with fire.

The main characteristics of Mediterranean architecture include thick walls of rubble or brick; low-pitched tiled roofs and overhanging eaves with, or often without, gutters. In low-rainfall areas, flat roofs may be supported on vaults or on timber beams covered with concrete and tiles. Windows tend to be small but, where Arab influence was strong, wooden balconies with pierced wooden shutters and screens are found. Small windows are often barred for security; larger windows have louvred shutters. Doors tend to be emphasised with traditional or Classical surrounds. Buildings are constructed to be cool in hot weather and louvred shutters are common for upstairs windows. Built-in fireplaces and chimneys are rare except in luxurious houses and local heating in winter has traditionally been provided by braziers.

In the eastern Mediterranean domes are common and are expressed externally, especially in churches which, in this area, are commonly very small.

The hill-town of Gattières, near Nice, southern France.

Hardwood Forest

Half-timbered building is common in England and Wales, much of France and Germany, Benelux and around the Baltic. Its character comes from building a complete frame of timber and then filling-in with brick, lath and plaster, stone, or daub and wattle. The preferred timber is oak, which is extremely durable and can be protected against boring insect larvae by tarring. The frames are held together by pegged mortice-and-tenon joints and although they may warp extensively they will not come apart.

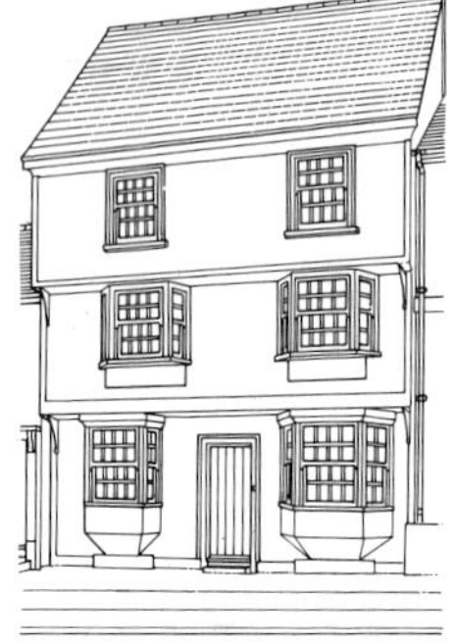

House in Thaxted, Essex, England. The front is stuccoed but the overhanging upper floors indicate a framed structure.

Oak is a delightful wood to work with sharp chisels and planes but is hard to saw. Large beams and wide planks were sawn from trunks of trees but timbers used in framing were often short pieces from the branches, and where longer pieces were needed these were obtained by coppicing which was an essential part of the building trade. Coppicing was done on a 25–30 year cycle and provided fairly straight members which were squared with an adze. Curved timbers for crucks and other purposes were obtained by bending during growth.

Timber-framed structures usually rest upon a plinth of brick or stone. Each storey consists of a rigid frame which supports the floor above, or the roof, and it is easy to corbel the upper floors over the lower floors, thus providing extra floor space which was an important consideration in congested towns. Oak is the ideal timber for carving and in many localities folk architecture was enriched in this way.

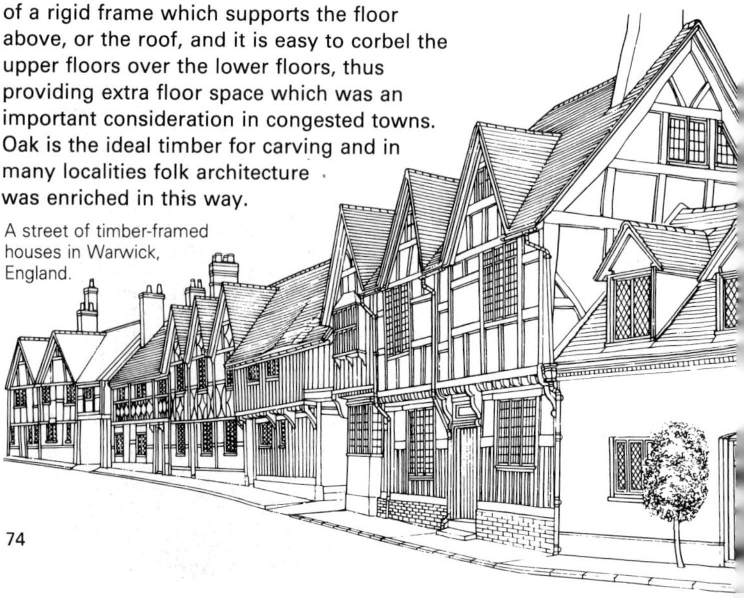

A street of timber-framed houses in Warwick, England.

Left The gable-end of a tall timber-framed house in Rouen, France. It is apparent that some of the windows were introduced later.

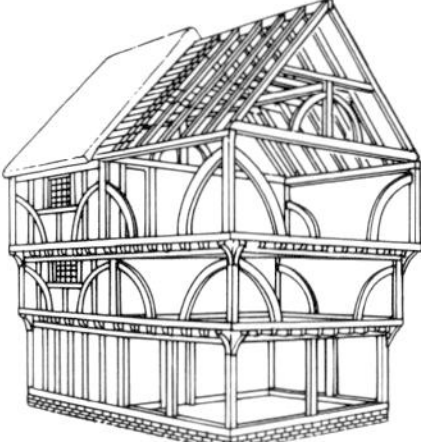

Above A house framed in hardwood, using curved branches as braces.

Below Little Moreton Hall, Cheshire, England; c. 1550–80. Designed and built by master carpenters.

Softwood Forest

Most coniferous trees grow tall, yielding straight logs and poles of soft resinous timber. Pines yield the best 'deals' for carpentry and joinery, whereas larch has properties of durability and is supposed to be resistant to fire. Spruce is springy, and difficult to work with tools. It is best used for masts. These conifers flourish in cool to cold climates with considerable rain or snow-fall.

The basic form is the log hut with logs halved into each other at corners and a roof of horizontal logs, gable to gable, covered with thatch; but this is a crude and restricting system presenting difficulties with doors and windows (p. 18). It is commonly modified with some form of frame and a raftered roof finished with battens and shingles.

An alternative, which is the basis of Norwegian folk building, is to use the logs vertically. In some early structures logs were inserted in the ground as poles or staves, side by side, but a ground-sill forming part of a skeletal frame is a natural improvement, with the staves, generally squared by adzing, attached to the frame. There are many local variations in the treatment of frames and roof trusses, some of them derived from doing in timber what has elsewhere been done in stone and the soft wood lends itself to elaborate coarse carving.

Mediterranean pine tends to be hard and wild in its grain, and due to deforestation (p. 70) there is now little to be had. The ancient building timber was *cupressus sempervirens*. It was abundant in ancient times and the natural shape of its trunk was probably the origin of the Minoan column. It was commonly used for framed buildings which were filled in with soft stone.

Good quality pine, which is now rare, was used in the 18th century for panelling, carved mantelpieces, cartouches etc; also for sash windows and classical external doorways which were commonly painted with white lead. Much pine furniture has now been stripped to show the beauty of the wood.

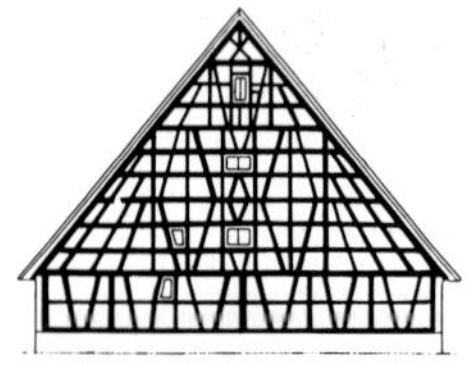

A soft-wood framed farmhouse, at Oberessendorf, southern West Germany.

Decorative painted detail of timber cottages in eastern Czechoslovakia. This kind of decoration is common in folk art, and is found equally on barges and on fun-fair roundabouts.

Right Classical-style houses built of timber, in Bergen, Norway.

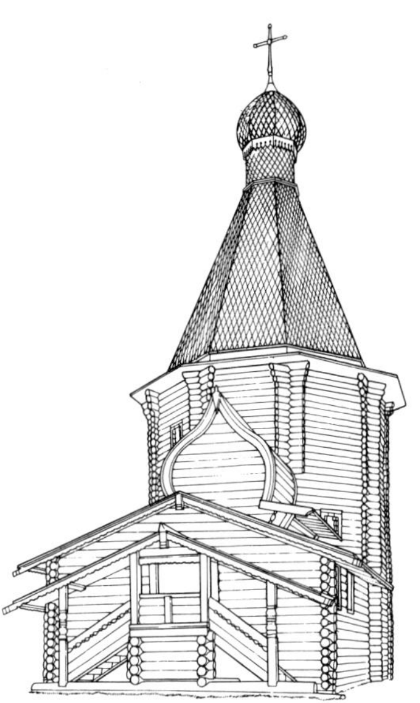

Above Timber cottages with shingle roofs in eastern Czechoslovakia.

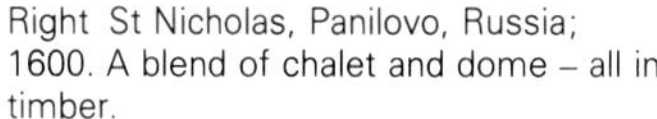

Right St Nicholas, Panilovo, Russia; 1600. A blend of chalet and dome – all in timber.

Above An elaborate chalet-type house in Switzerland, though with a steeper roof than is usual. Decorated eaves are a common feature of chalets.

Right A modern chalet, at Obergurgl, Austria.

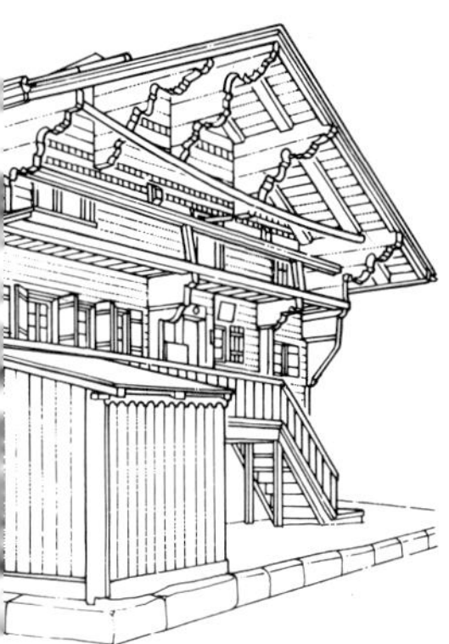

The Old House, Leysin, Switzerland.

Alpine

In Alpine valleys there is a stratum of conifers above the deciduous trees and below the snowline. They grow very big on the lower slopes and diminish with altitude. Stone is also available, unlike the level forests of Germany, Scandinavia and Russia. The climate, though extremely cold at high altitudes at night, is often sunny and warm by day, even in mid-winter. In summer it is hot. Insulation against extremes of heat and cold is a major influence on Alpine architecture.

The chalet form is traditional. It usually has a stone plinth and the walls may be of stone (usually rendered) with wooden windows, shutters, balconies etc., but the dominating feature is the low-pitched roof with very wide eaves. These help to keep snow clear of the building while snow on the roof acts as insulation throughout the winter. Valleys and parapets are avoided and generally the idea is to keep the whole house under the one roof even when it is quite a complex establishment, such as a hotel. Farmhouses, some of which are within the village, have cattle and stores on the ground floor and living accommodation above. Pine trees provide the very long timbers required for the roofs.

Many chalets are constructed of timber but are nearly always on a stone plinth or piers and sometimes, in a few localities, upon stone 'mushrooms', which are said to deter rodents. Internally timber is extensively used for walls. Heating is traditionally by large, tiled, slow combustion stoves using timber as fuel.

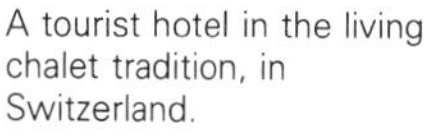

A tourist hotel in the living chalet tradition, in Switzerland.

Mountain and Moor

There are many mountainous and hilly regions of Europe which are not Alpine. They extend from Spain through the central mountains of France to Britain and Norway as well as the Appennines in Italy and the mountains and hills of central Europe extending down into Yugoslavia and Greece. Despite innumerable variations due to climate, culture and materials some general characteristics of mountain architecture may be noticed.

There are three kinds of settlement sites. From every point of view except security, sites in valleys, near rivers, on rich, alluvial soil are best, and major villages or towns are commonly associated with bridges. They may control routes up and down the valleys, and hence the mountain passes as well as the river crossing, and they were often heavily fortified.

In many places towns were built on hill tops, preferably on low hills rising from the valley bottom; the inhabitants went down from the town to cultivate fields and gardens in the valley. Both security and a healthier climate were provided by sites on a hill.

Upland settlements were often simple farmsteads exploiting grazing lands or, occasionally, they were small mining communities. Sometimes upland homes were fortified or at least defensible (eg. pele towers) but generally they depended upon remoteness and their poverty for some degree of safety.

An old coaching inn at Thirlspot, Cumbria, England; built along the contour, with a porch to provide protection from the weather.

Unless built of timber, mountain architecture usually has rubble stone walls and is roofed with local stone if slates or splittable sandstones are available, otherwise with imported or locally made tiles, shingles or thatch. Thatch is not satisfactory where valleys are deep and damp. Roofs are generally steep-pitched except in the extreme south where they are of Mediterranean type.

On sloping sites buildings follow the contours and look out from the slope. One effect of mountains upon people seems to encourage buildings with vertical features, and village church spires are often like needles against the massive background. Turrets and vertical window proportions are common.

On exposed uplands, however, buildings tend to be low with the same precautions against wind found in Celtic Fringe architecture (p. 68). It is a curious fact that mountain villages are usually cleaner than those on flat land, where people become used to mud and bad drainage.

A timber-and-reed hut from the marshlands near Caserta, Italy.

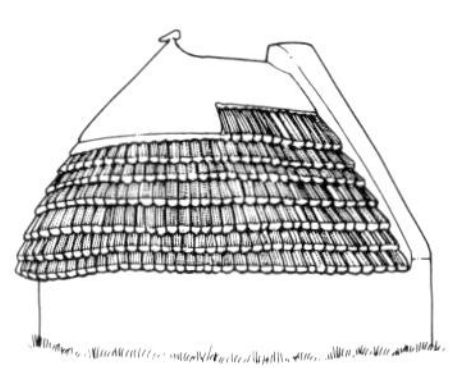

A marshland cottage in the Camargue, southern France, with thatched roof and apsidal end to offer protection against the wind.

Marshland

In extensive marshlands such as the English Fens, the Pripet Marshes of Poland or the Camargue in southern France, foundations are insecure, the only available timber is willow, poplar or other rather difficult materials, and there is an abundance of reeds. The primitive solution is to make structures like baskets, weaving them out of pliable branches and clothing them with a thatch of reeds; it is sensible to select sites which have some stability, such as gravel banks. If such settlements prosper the limitations of wattle construction are such that other ways have to be found and this means importing building materials by water, which has always been the easiest and cheapest mode of transporting them. Channels are found or cleared and the builders come with the materials, bringing their methods with them. Cambridge is a good example of a city built of water-borne materials and strains of architecture.

Stone walls and split stone slates at Stanton, England; typical architecture of the Cotswolds region.

Stone Masonry

Good building stone is rather rare and where it is available it tends to be quarried on a large scale for export from the district. Transport has always been costly, so stone for masonry is at least partly dressed before despatch. Masons at the quarry thus become familiar with contemporary arcane design and have the skills to implement it. As an example, the medieval quarries near Tournai in Belgium produced fonts for export to England.

As a result, folk architecture in the vicinity of a quarry is affected by arcane standards, but craftsmen are naturally conservative and once a local style is established strong influences are necessary to change it. The folk architecture of good stone districts, such as Normandy, the Cotswolds and the Yorkshire Dales, shows a high degree of skill in masonry, a strong local character but also a susceptibility to arcane influences by assimilation without any theoretical basis.

Bricks and Tiles

Kiln-baked bricks, made by hand, were a luxury material in the sixteenth century. Apart from labour and transport there was the cost of fuel, which until the nineteenth century was wood. Until machine-made bricks became available in the late nineteenth century stone was cheaper. Where there was no stone to be had at reasonable cost, local clays were made into bricks, but where timber was available framed construction was preferred with bricks sometimes used for infilling.

Folk traditions in brick, if they developed at all, came late except in a few places where there was an ancient tradition of brickmaking, notably part of the Po valley in Italy where an Etruscan tradition of making terracotta persisted. This is a medium which lends itself to elaborate repetitive ornament.

Tiles were made by the Romans in various forms, from the half-round 'Roman' roofing tile to large flat slabs which were used as building bricks. In the absence of any other durable roof finish, except marble, Roman tiles of burnt clay became, and have remained, almost universal in the Mediterranean region. Further north plain or pantiles were made wherever slate was not locally available. In some areas of plentiful timber and good clay, such as Sussex and Kent in England, tile-hanging became common as a finish for walls.

Houses in Groombridge, Kent, England; a mainly timber style, but with brick, tile-hanging on the walls and weather-boarding (clap-boarding).

Slate and Shales

These are rocks formed from compressed clays and their most important characteristic is that they can be split horizontally, but are difficult to cut and dress on the face except with modern power tools. The finest slates can be split to wafer-like thinness and are used for roofs. Where available they have a notable effect upon the character of folk architecture and the techniques of roofing, sometimes very elaborate, make slate a major influence in building. This is specially evident in northern France.

Coarser slates and shales are used for walling. They are usually laid dry with joints slightly tilted outwards. Traditionally such walls were commonly rendered or roughcast (harled is the Scottish term) in many localities, but in the nineteenth century a style of common architecture was developed, especially in the English Lake District and north Wales, exploiting the beauty of traditional dry-walling.

House in Rouen, France, with slate roof and façade.

Cottages in Langdale, Cumbria, England, built of slate with slate roof.

Dating Folk Architecture

Putting a date on architecture is usually hazardous even when there is documentary evidence. Old buildings have been constantly repaired and modified. Sometimes additions deliberately match earlier work. Sometimes an old fabric, such as a timber-framed house, is up-dated with a Classical brick or stone facade. Sometimes a new owner puts a panel in the wall over a main doorway, with a date and his and his wife's initials, but the fabric may be much older. Gothic window tracery is particularly unreliable and often dates from the nineteenth century. Too much concern about dates and attributions to architects can distract from appreciation and enjoyment of architecture, which is more important. Great buildings should not be seen as historical conundrums. Nonetheless one cannot help being interested in the age of a building, and for major works, such as cathedrals and palaces, some more or less credible information is usually available. This is seldom so with folk architecture.

To make one's own assessment it is best to proceed in the manner of Sherlock Holmes and begin by looking carefully at what is there, in, for example, a small country town. Modernist buildings can usually be dated later than 1925 by their obtrusiveness but during the Modernist period many new buildings have been built in harmony with the established pattern. This practice goes back to the nineteenth century and earlier.

First look at the junction with the ground. Through time the level of streets and pavements rises due to maintenance. If a building starts precisely and tidily at pavement level it is probably recent. If you have to step down into the ground floor, it may be old, more or less in proportion to the depth of the step. Look also at the state of the facing material at first floor level. If it is weathered and worn this also indicates age. Ground floors, especially in shopping streets, are frequently modified, often with a single steel beam to support the whole of the façade above the ground floor. Narrow spans suggest antiquity: very wide spans indicate at least a modern intrusion. If you can enter the building and find low ceilings, genuine oak beams and supports with indications of a timber-framed structure, you may suppose an earlier date for the main structure than is indicated by the façade.

If the façade is in a recognisable style, the question is whether it is Eclectic or earlier, so ask yourself whether it is in the style of the district. A Venetian Gothic façade in Venice might be medieval but in Glasgow or Brussels it is certainly nineteenth-century.

Genuine half-timbered houses, with warped timbers and properly morticed joints, are almost certainly seventeenth-century or earlier. Brick façades are unlikely to be earlier than the sixteenth century, except in the brick areas of Italy. Correct classical façades can be dated with certainty as later than about 1450 in Italy, 1500 in France, and 1600 elsewhere.

Another, and in many respects the best way of dating folk architecture, is to find out the history of the settlement. As far back as the sixteenth century it is possible to identify individual buildings on maps and, as most early maps are dated, before or after that date can be established; but although visits to local libraries may be an interesting variation in the routine of tourism, few people are likely to undertake such serious study, especially if travelling with the family.

In northern Europe, including the British Isles, very little folk architecture survives from earlier than AD 1000 and not much before 1400 except in the Celtic Fringe, where it is impossible to put a certain date upon many settlements. The step down from the outside to the inside is the best indicator. In the west of Ireland, Brittany and Scotland, where penetration from the east was resisted and Viking settlements were not made, a typical crofter's cottage may well be more than 2000 years old in its walls but repeatedly re-roofed. Even if raiders burnt such a cottage the walls would survive and a new roof would have made it habitable again. Signs of fire can sometimes be seen in reddening of the stone.

Much can be learned from imagining oneself to be a primitive but intelligent settler and asking why such a site should be chosen – a natural harbour, good fishing, a shelving beach, a defensible site, good grazing, fertile level land and so on. Nearly 2000 years ago the Roman architect Vitruvius gave instructions for choosing the site of a settlement but long before him men had taken life or death decisions about founding settlements in virgin or captured territories.

In the Mediterranean area we have abundant evidence of early settlement and if there are Roman remains near a village in Provence, southern Spain or Italy the probability is that the site has been occupied ever since. Mediterranean folk architecture differs little from Roman though quality standards declined after the fifth century AD. The foundations and walls of many such houses may well be Roman, and buildings may have been continuously occupied for more than 2000 years. The best way of identifying the origin and development of a folk building is to assess the date of the earliest substantial settlement and work forward. The date of the church is often known and sometimes – as at Montmartre (Paris) – it is known that there was a pagan temple before there was a church. Excavation at many sites has revealed layer upon layer of settlement and sensible people often made use of such walls and foundations as they found when they came. Fortunately for the historian, some sites were abandoned as being unsuitable in changed conditions (eg. Paestum p. 166) and they remain as a record of what they were like at an ascertainable date; but most good sites have been developed and redeveloped many times.

Modern redevelopment, with deep foundations, obliterates all traces of earlier buildings, which is a good reason for recording before demolition and careful scrutiny of the side during excavation.

The Imitation Principle

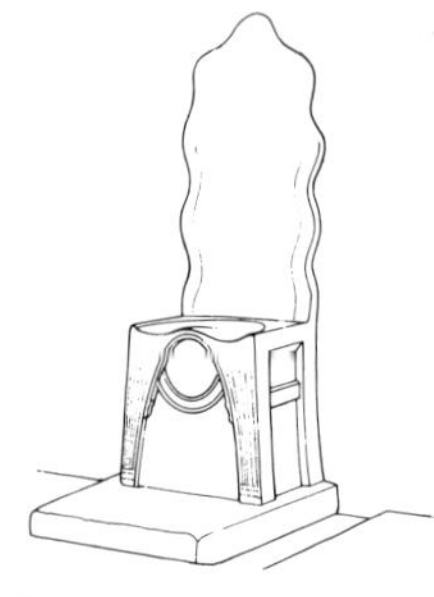

The throne of Minos, Knossos; c. 1500 BC.

The importance of the appearance of architecture is attested through the ages by the deliberate imitation of traditional forms in materials other than those for which they were designed. This is not due to a desire to deceive or to dogged conservatism. Because architecture is meaningful and socially important the established meanings which promote social cohesion are carried forward into new techniques.

An early example is the throne of Minos in the Palace at Knossos. It is made of stone but preserves the legs and rails of a wooden chair. The Greek Doric Order, as used in the Parthenon (p. 101), is one of the touchstones of architectural quality; it is built of marble but the whole of the Order, with its entablature of metopes and triglyphs, originated in timber and the overhanging cornice of all the Orders derived from timber prototypes.

Georgian doorway, converting Classical architecture back into timber construction.

The Orders became the established way of designing in stone under the Romans, and again in the Renaissance period, but when English architects adopted the Palladian way of design they frequently made Classical entrance doorways and mantlepieces out of wood. They thus translated Classical architecture back into the original material – though unwittingly, because the imitation principle did not begin to be recognised as a force in architecture until late in the eighteenth century. Imitation half-timbering in twentieth century gables has been wrongly ridiculed. It is not deception but a valid symbol of continuity in an admired and indigenous tradition. Modernist architecture abounds in imitation, especially in its use of veneers, real and simulated.

The mature Doric Order from the Parthenon, Athens.

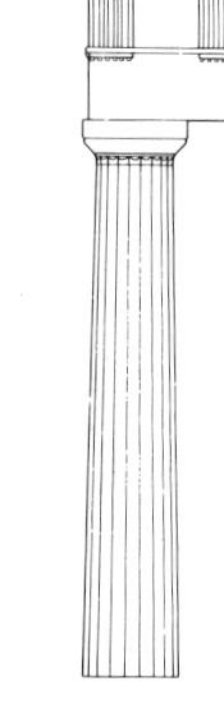

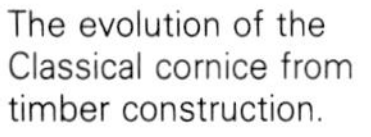

The evolution of the Classical cornice from timber construction.

Imitation Folk Architecture

Long before the Arts and Crafts Movement of the late nineteenth century began to seek a basis for modern arcane design in folk tradition (p. 150), folk-style architecture was being built for sentimental reasons and picturesque effect. The fashion for this kind of building was part of the Romantic Movement but it also received encouragement from the French classical theorist, Laugier (p. 36) who saw the 'rustic hut' or *aedicule* as the basis of all architecture, and from philosophers such as Rousseau.

By the early nineteenth century there were many books, most notably Loudon's *Encyclopaedia of Cottage Farm and Villa Architecture* (1833) which provided rustic designs; and distinguished architects were busy designing in 'peasant' styles for lodges and estate villages. Eclecticism is already evident in these designs which combine features of many different folk styles with fanciful ingenuity. Common architecture of the mid-nineteenth century, in most countries, owes much to this movement and serious professional architects travelled far and wide to fill their sketch books with interesting architectural details. Usually this imitation folk architecture is recognisable by its 'too-good-to-be-true' appearance. It is a valid way of design which has produced some very beautiful buildings and picturesque groupings.

Styles of folk architecture from Loudon's *Encyclopaedia*.

'Swiss' style.

'Old English' villa

'Old Scotch' style.

Settlement Patterns

There is always a reason for choosing the site for a settlement, whether it be a farmhouse or a city. The architecture and layout of the settlement are more easily appreciated if one can understand why it was founded there in the first place. Quite often the reason is obvious.

Paris, for example was an island in the Seine, dividing the river, so that it was easier to bridge there than elsewhere. Founded by a Gallic tribe on the island for security, it was developed by Romans on the southern bank where there was good limestone; it became an island citadel again after the Roman city was destroyed, about AD 280.

Rome is also a river crossing where the Isola Tiburina facilitated a bridge from north to south Italy, defended by Horatius and recently (1983) excavated. Started as a hill town, protected by the river and sustained by the fertile rolling country called the Campagna, it was ideal from the point of view of the original founders. As the Empire expanded, Rome, half way down a mountainous peninsular, became unsuitable as a capital. After it had ceased to be capital of the Empire it retained some economic viability as the site of the martyrdom of St Peter and the seat of the Pope, but when the Papacy went to Avignon it lapsed into ruins. The return of the Popes and then the rise of nationalism restored its economic health. Its survival as a great city depends largely upon mystique.

Edinburgh and Athens began as strongholds in a strategic region with natural citadels on rocky sites and fertile fields around. Such places were geographically destined for greatness.

At the other extreme, some settlements were in the wrong place, or in the right places for a time and then obsolete, usually because of social and economic changes. Mycenae, Delos and Silchester were abandoned. Glasgow, Lille, Liverpool, Venice and Genoa

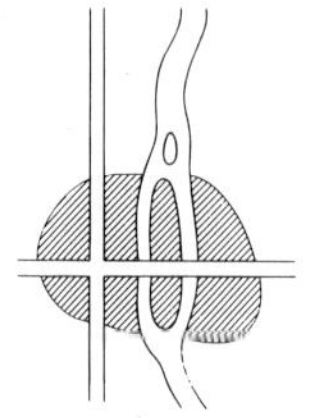

River crossing; as at Paris.

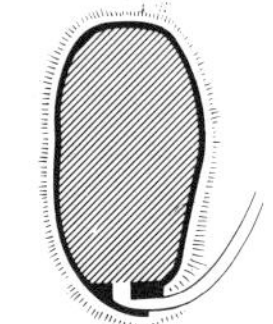

Acropolis; as at Athens.

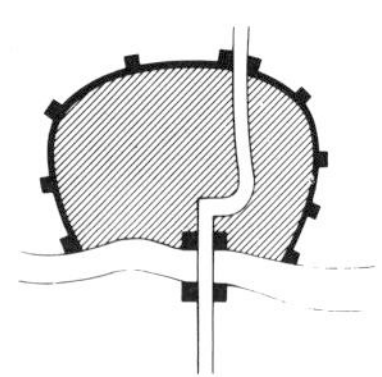

Bridgehead; as at Newcastle-upon-Tyne.

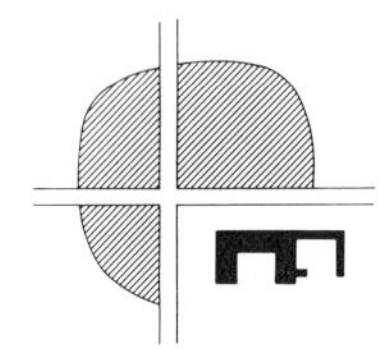

Roman villa (with the villa gone) as at Soissons.

have responded to transient economic conditions, expanded quickly and faced the problems of decline.

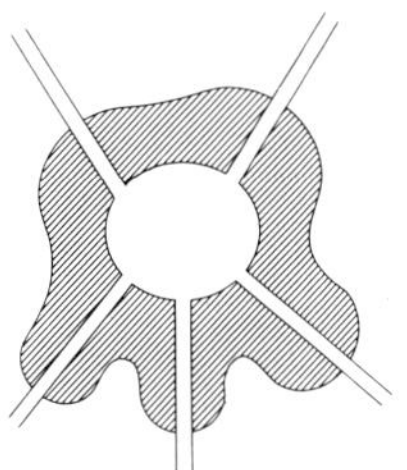
Market at road junctions; as at Rheims.

Crossroads were natural meeting places and developed as markets and fairs. Rheims is a good example. On the Continent many villages started as Roman villas with cottages for the estate workers. The villas have gone but the village survives and the land is still worked under a different social system. Many villages served medieval castles which may now be in ruins. Some served abbeys such as Cluny in eastern France. Some – such as Aosta and Chichester – were developments of Roman towns or camps.

Isolated farms and hamlets can add interest to a journey almost anywhere you may care to stop in open country. Why were they built there and not, say, a hundred metres to the left or right, further up or down the hill?

Planned Towns

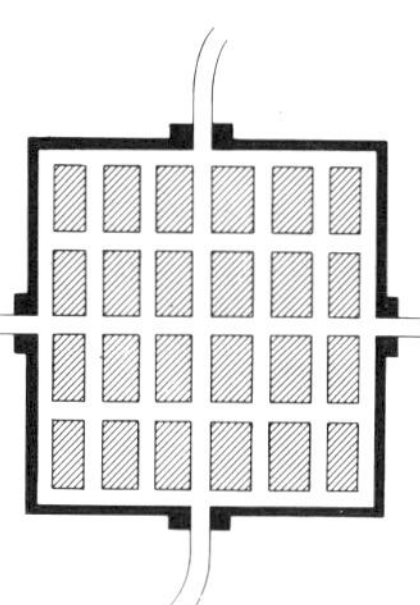
Grid-iron; as at Turin.

Towns have been deliberately planned since Classical times. On new sites the grid-iron plan, commonly used by the Romans, was easy to set out, apparently logical and provided sensible, rectangular building sites. It was used in the Middle Ages for military stations such as Aigues Mortes in France and is still favoured for military camps. Architecturally it has the disadvantage of not providing vistas onto buildings. The roads go past them.

Medieval fortified towns are inherently radial to facilitate the deployment and movement of defenders. When the town becomes too congested the site may not permit an extension of the walls, in which case a suburb develops and this in turn may be walled and linked to the old town.

It was militarily wrong to allow building immediately outside the walls of a town so in many cases a green belt existed, ready to be developed as parkland, as a ring road or boulevard and as a setting for public buildings. The radial planning of Paris was extremely influential.

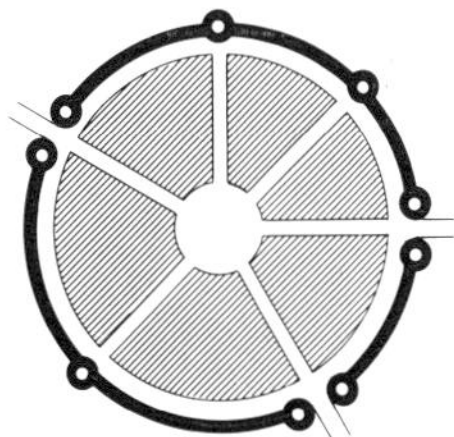
Radial; as at Carcassonne.

With the demolition of defences and the opening up of cities and towns, and their expansion into formerly open country, parks and gardens were created as breathing spaces and pleasure grounds for the citizens.

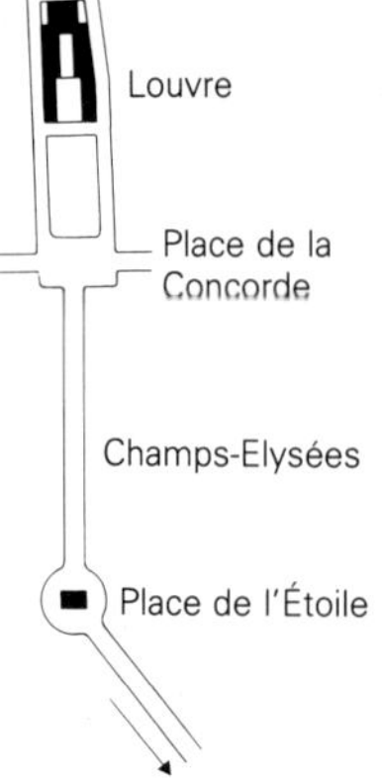

Axial planning at Paris, based on the route leading from the Louvre to the Bois de Boulogne. See p. 236.

Parks and Gardens

The design of urban open spaces goes back to the ancient Greeks who made the essential synthesis of planting, planned paths and architectural features such as parapets, steps, walls and ornamental buildings, as well as relating arcane architecture to its setting in designed precincts. No Classical gardens have survived but their former beauty can be imagined on such sites as Olympia, Epidauros and Hadrian's Villa at Tivoli.

With the coming of the barbarians vast tracts of country were preserved as royal forests, primarily for hunting, but they were also sources of timber and the essential domestic fuel, charcoal. Techniques of forestry were developed, rides or drives were planned through the woods, and hunting lodges constructed. The magnificent continental forests such as Fontainebleau and Compiègne are the result of centuries of design.

Medieval tapestries and illuminated manuscripts show gardens and orchards outside town walls and with the decline of castles and the revival of the country house or villa in the sixteenth century, stately gardens were made as settings for buildings. The relationship of the inside of the house to the precinct again became an important part of architecture.

Sixteenth-century garden design was formal and intricate. Most of the garden flowers and shrubs which we have today were unknown. Flowers were cultivated native species, with an emphasis on herbs. Gardens were very architectural and topiary was much favoured. The Renaissance brought Classical detail and features such as temples and statues for which ever-green hedges provided formal settings.

In the eighteenth century hundreds of new

species of plants arrived from distant lands and this accelerated in the nineteenth. Hybridisation and careful selection produced flowers of unprecedented beauty. The gardener's pallet was immensely enriched and he responded accordingly.

There are four main styles of garden design.

1. The cottage garden which makes a maximum use of small spaces, relying mainly on flowering plants, small lawns, and also growing vegetables. The patio garden is a version of this but architecturally more constrained.

2. The Italian garden, probably of Classical origin, relying mainly on architectural features, cypress trees and hedges, sculpture, fountains and pools. Ideally it provides vistas to and from the house, viewpoints (gazebos) and secluded places for amorous encounters.

3. The grand manner of post-Renaissance garden design which was developed by André le Nôtre (1613–1700) at Versailles (p. 234).

4. The English or Romantic garden. This is informal, picturesque, intimate and gives opportunity for exploiting the beauty of many species in clumps or as single specimens. This kind of garden, though popular on the Continent, really needs grass lawns to be at its best. These are both difficult and costly to maintain in southern Europe, and are at their best in Britain.

Public gardens have generally been on the same lines as private gardens but the need to provide for large numbers of people makes paths much wider and planting is for more generalised effect, to be seen at a distance. This helps supervision to avoid vandalism and misuse. Plenty of seats are needed.

In large private gardens architectural features such as temples often served as formal refreshment places (picnics were a late development), as shelters, or as trysting places. Sometimes the idea of a garden was extended to the horizon with picturesque follies, temples, or monuments. One of the most interesting developments was the Palm House, seen at its best at Kew (p. 25).

Part Two

An Outline of the Background to AD 1100

Stone buildings which we can still recognise as architecture were first made in Europe before 4000 BC. Before that there were timber buildings about which we know little except that timber designs were later imitated in stone (p. 101). If architecture is *significant building* then some of mankind's most notable achievements date from the neolithic and early bronze ages. This period is coming to be recognised as the authentic origin of the legends and folk memories of a golden age to which later Greek mythology gave the name Arcadian.

Until the climate changed for the worse, perhaps around 1500 BC, men lived in self-sufficient communities. They built houses, grew corn and domesticated animals. They hunted and fished and collected crustaceans. Their weapons were simple and designed to procure food. They seem to have had a deep understanding of the order of nature and their architecture was built for communion with and interpretation of natural phenomena and for the housing of their dead. Whether they worshipped any kind of god we do not know, but their social life seems to have had the amiability combined with caution which we still find in groups of animals.

Deteriorating climate with cloudy skies obscuring the instructive heavens, invasive forests, and the incursion of warlike people with bronze weapons put an end to the first age of civilisation in western Europe. The technology of these dimly known neolithic peoples was based upon stone and their architecture was based upon the meaningful disposition of huge stones – megaliths. They seem to have been aware of properties in stone which we are only now beginning to recognise (p. 244).

The Mycenaean civilisation of southern

The elaborate system of bronze age megaliths at Callanish, Isle of Lewis, Scotland, c. 1500 BC (plan): one of the many relics of ancient civilisation along the Atlantic coast of Europe.

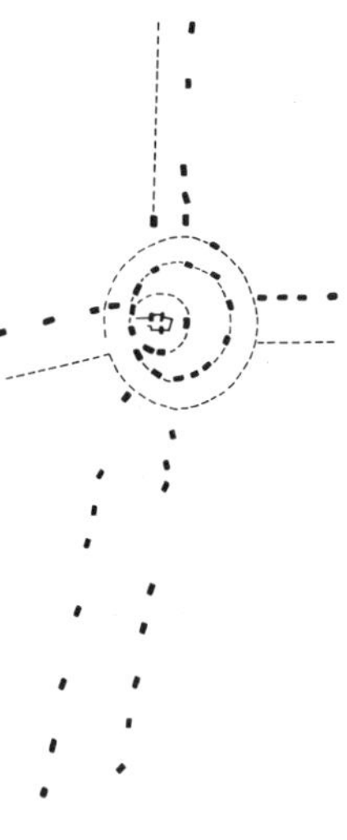

Neolithic house in Skara Brae, Orkney, with built-in stone furniture and covered drains.

Greece came under the influence of Crete where the already ancient Minoan civilisation was in contact with Egypt after 2000 BC. When the Minoan Empire collapsed about 1400 BC some of its architectural tradition was continued in Greece and in particular the column was venerated as a powerful symbol.

After about 1260 BC, new people came into Greece. For about 500 years they probably built in timber and the tradition they brought with them from the forests of Europe was modified by Minoan or Mycenaean ideas. From about 650 a brilliant civilisation emerged in the city states of Greece, the Aegean islands, the west coast of Asia Minor (Turkey) and Greek colonies in Italy and Sicily.

Quarrels within and between city states, especially Athens and Sparta, culminated in the conquest of Greece by Philip of Macedon, after the decisive battle of Chaeronea in 338 BC. Thereafter, his son, Alexander the Great, established by conquest a Greek empire extending as far as northern India. At Alexander's death (323 BC) this disintegrated but Greek architecture flourished in rich successor states. Eventually the western states, as far as Armenia and Assyria, were absorbed within the Roman Empire which itself adopted its architecture from the Greeks, and to some extent, from the Etruscans who had also learned much from the Greeks. Meanwhile the warlike and talented Celtic peoples had irrupted out of Central Europe until they came up against the disciplined armies of Rome.

Rome was founded according to tradition in 753 BC, on a hill beside the river Tiber, which was more or less the dividing line between the Greek city states of southern Italy and the iron-working Etruscans of the north. It was probably a bandit stronghold, as is indicated by the story of the rape of the Sabine women. But Rome needed men, as well as women, to hold what it had established. Instead of being exclusive like the Greek cities, the Romans welcomed recruits and gave citizenship to many of the people they conquered. This, as

Mycenaean (Helladic) seals depicting tree and pillar cults which relate fertility, paternity, trees and columns.

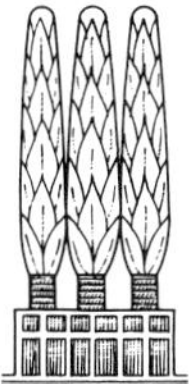

Cypress trees on altar.

Votaries at a Mycenaean column shrine.

Two seals showing the development of the so-called palmate pillars which anticipate the phallic symbol called the *fleur-de-lys*, and the Ionic capital.

much as their discipline and military prowess, enabled them to extend their rule from Scotland to Africa and from Spain to Syria. In all these countries Roman influence has persisted to some extent.

Until the reign of Augustus, (d. AD 14), Roman architecture was probably like that of any other Italian hill town, and according to Suetonius, Augustus boasted of so improving the city 'that he found it brick and left it marble'.

The Romans spoke Latin, originally an Italic dialect with Celtic affinities, and this became the language of scholarship and the basis of most of the western European languages spoken today. In the arts they learned from Greece, and the principles of architectural design as formulated by the Greeks ruled Roman architecture. An interpretation of the work of Greek theorists was written by the Roman architect Vitruvius and addressed to the Emperor Augustus.

Roman imperial architecture flourished until c. AD 330, when Constantine, having become a Christian, transferred the capital of the empire to Constantinople and consecrated that city to the Virgin Mary. The rich and important western provinces of the Empire were then administered from Trier on the Mosel, which, after Rome itself, is the richest repository of Roman art and architecture in the West.

Though the Roman way of civil life continued, the military prowess which had been the backbone of imperial government languished. Barbarian peoples, many of them already educated in Roman ways and in some cases seeking rather to rescue than destroy Rome, infiltrated and invaded across the frontiers. The Ostrogoth, Theodoric the Great, who died in 526, ruled Italy for 33 years from Ravenna and married the Frankish princess, Audofleda, sister of Clovis I, thereby initiating a policy of royal marriages which was to have a profound effect until 1914.

The Franks were the most successful of the barbarian invaders and established a Merovingian kingdom extending from the

The fully-developed Corinthian capital (from the Temple of Jupiter Stator, Rome; founded 294 BC). The thin top member, or *abacus,* was designed to support a lintel.

The Hellenesque capital, from S. Vitale, Ravenna, Italy (526–47). It is derived from the Corinthian style but with an extra abacus *(dosseret)* to support arches.

Rhineland to the Pyrenees. Their kings claimed divine descent from Merovech, son of a sea dragon, and never cut their hair. Clovis I (481–511) fulfilled a vow made in the danger of battle, became a Christian and was baptised by St Remy at Rheims in 506. His son Lothar ruled for 50 years, met death with incredulity in 561 (he did not believe God could let so great a king die) and left his kingdom as personal property divided among his many sons. In the civil wars which followed, the Frankish people were divided to form the nuclei of France and Germany. After prolonged struggle between two fierce widows of murdered kings, Brunhild was defeated by Fredegund, whose issue triumphed and her descendant *le bon Roi* Dagobert (d. 638) was the first notable royal patron of the arts in France.

Meanwhile the prophet Mohammed (d. 632) had established Islam and the Arabs, 'a race of soldiers inspired by religious enthusiasm', quickly conquered all of Roman North Africa, entered Spain and made Córdoba a city second only to Constantinople. The Arabs were heirs to much of Greek civilisation, its philosophy, mathematics and architecture. The threat which they posed to Christian Europe was met by Frankish generals near Poitiers in 732 and they were thrown back to the Pyrenees, but the Arab presence in Spain and its preservation of Greek scholarship was to be profoundly influential in the West.

The Merovingian dynasty in France and Germany gave way to usurpers who were able to provide firm government and meet the Islamic threat. Charlemagne achieved the ambition of many earlier barbarians in re-establishing the Western Roman Empire and was crowned by the Pope in Rome on Christmas Day 800. Charlemagne died in 814 and at the death of his son Louis the Pious, in 840, the Empire was divided among his three sons, a division which eventually consolidated into the countries of France and Germany with a line of small states between them from Benelux to Switzerland.

The slender columns of the Great Mosque, Córdoba, Spain (late 8th century AD), have Corinthian capitals with enlarged abaci supporting round arches. These features are typical of Hellenesque architecture.

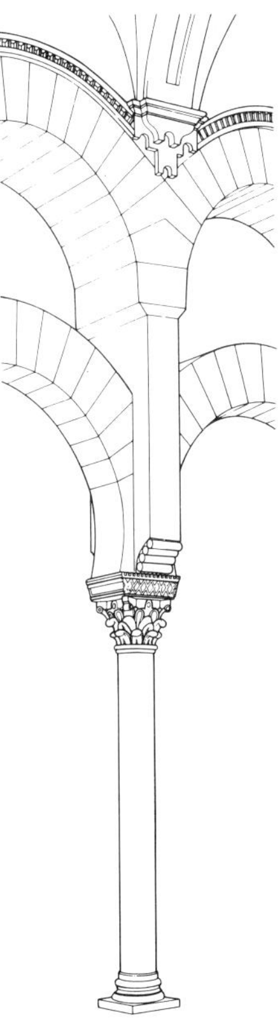

Carolingian architecture was influenced from Constantinople, which was still the foremost city in Christendom and set fashions in art, architecture and dress, much as Paris did in the nineteenth century. The Byzantine city of Ravenna provided accessible examples of architecture and Charlemagne's palace at Aachen (p. 328) had a chapel modelled on S. Vitale at Ravenna.

Britain had been evacuated by the Romans in the fifth century. The Anglo-Saxon peoples who invaded established a brilliant culture which flourished especially in Northumbria to which a Celtic version of Christianity was brought from Ireland via Iona by St Aidan in 635. In the seventh and eighth centuries Northumbrian missionaries carried its culture and Christianity into Europe and Alcuin, Charlemagne's secretary, came from York.

In the ninth century Viking raids devastated much of Britain and France, extending far inland; they led eventually to settlement, redevelopment and trade. From their base in Normandy the Vikings conquered Sicily in 1060 and England in 1066. That the Vikings were superb craftsmen in wood is attested by their ships which were then the best in the world, and they employed marvellous craftsmen in metal and precious stones; but we know little of their architecture until they adapted French ways of building in stone and established what came to be known as the Norman style of architecture in Normandy, Britain, Sicily and southern Italy.

From the end of the Western Roman Empire in 476 to the end of the tenth century, Europe suffered greatly from invasions, plagues, climatic disasters, wars and misgovernment but in these five centuries medieval Europe was created and the modern world foreshadowed. In architecture we call it the Early Romanesque period. Classical principles were not lost; new structural techniques were developed and, above all, new significances were achieved. By the end of the eleventh century the invention of the ribbed vault had made Gothic architecture possible.

St John, Escomb, Co. Durham, England (late 7th century), with tall thin walls typical of Anglo-Saxon masoncraft. Such churches were tall and narrow (compare them with the Scandinavian timber churches, pp. 316–317). Greater size was achieved by extending the length and by adding *porticus* (alcoves) along the sides.

The Idea of Style

The idea that there are styles of architecture is relatively modern – it originated in the seventeenth century. What we now call styles were simply the normal ways of building. Nowadays we recognise that in some places people created kinds of architecture which are characteristic of them and their way of life. We call these styles and in Europe we see them as falling into two main groups, both derived from the architecture of the ancient Greeks. The division began in about AD 330 with the movement of the capital of the Roman Empire to Constantinople. This move was a liberation for Greek ideas about architecture and gave rise to Hellenesque architecture. Later the Moslems adopted the Hellenesque style and spread it to India and Spain

In the Western Roman Empire, the old Roman version of Classical design persisted in what we call Romanesque architecture, as with the rise of Christianity the traditional restraints on the Classical style were loosened.

Romanesque is the basis of all subsequent western architecture, and developed in two main stages. Firstly, as Gothic architecture, which modified Romanesque with ribbed vaulting and increased use of pointed arches. The second stage was the revival of Classical design and rejection of the Gothic achievement. This is known as the Renaissance. It was essentially a short and restricted phase of Italian architecture but it sent shock waves throughout Europe. Various national and local interpretations of the Classical idiom were often identified as styles. Then came the Gothic Revival, Neo-Classicism and Eclecticism, all recognisable but relatively ephemeral styles. Nineteenth-century architects became obsessed by the idea of 'style', and this persisted into Modernism, with its idea of 'the modern style'.

Main architectural styles now recognised

Minoan
before 1200 BC

Helladic
Mycenaean
before 1200 BC

Classical
Hellenic
Greek
7th-4th cent. BC
Hellenistic
later Greek
Roman
derived from Hellenistic

Hellenesque
Byzantine
from AD 330
Islamic
from c. AD 630

Romanesque
from c. 500

Gothic
from c. 1144

Classical
Renaissance
from c. 1400
Baroque
from c. 1600
Rococo
from c. 1750

Eclectic
based on any or all above styles and other exotic styles
from c. 1760
Neo-Classical
Neo-Greek
Neo-Gothic

Modernist
c. 1919–69

Post-modern
a currently accepted but enigmatic description

The Great Styles of Architecture

Classical

The Classical style came into being in the sixth and fifth centuries BC, but it inherited an awareness of sacred geometry which was much older (p. 94). The fundamental element in Classical architecture is the column with entablature, as we can see in the Lion Gateway at Mycenae. The entablature consists of the ends of two lintels and the eaves of the roof which they support. It implies the existence of a colonnade but, whereas neolithic architects identified the trilithon (p. 34) as the fundamental architectural form, Classical architecture concentrates, in its theory, upon the single column. Thus the basic form, the element which architects used for designing, was the support, right through from the ground to the roof, not the span.

Temples and important secular buildings were surrounded or fronted with columns. Important temples had columns all round and consisted of a walled building (the *cella*) within a colonnade. This may have preserved, in a civic setting, the principle of a built shrine within a sacred grove of trees.

The Greeks developed two distinct systems of columnar design which are called the Doric and Ionic Orders. By the fifth century these Orders were the embodiment of rules which, though they did not altogether exclude architectural individuality, confined it to decoration and sculpture, within the framework of a strict architectural discipline based upon geometry, and rules of proportion derived from it.

The Doric Order developed in Greece and southern Italy while the Ionic Order emerged and was typical of the coasts of Asia Minor (Turkey). In the mercantile city of Athens, with its economy based upon oil, silver and shipping, both the Doric and Ionic Orders attained their most perfect form in the Parthenon and the Propylaea on the Acropolis.

1

2

3

4

5

6

1 Helladic Lion Gateway, Mycenae (c. 1250 BC); compare with the seals on p. 95.

2 Column shrine from Knossos (before 1450 BC).

3 Fully-developed Minoan-type column, from the 'Treasury of Atreus', Mycenae (c. 1325 BC).

4 Minoan-Helladic cornice design in stone, expressing log-ends.

5 The Parthenon, Athens, built by Ictinus and Callicrates between 447 and 432 BC and with sculpture decoration by Pheidias. It represents perfection within the limitations of the Doric Order.

6 The Erechtheion, Athens (421–405 BC and later). Begun 11 years after the Parthenon, it shows a lively inventiveness and adoption of the Ionic Order, more slender and flexible than the Doric.

Both the Doric and Ionic Orders had been created for what we would now call liturgical rather than practical architectural reasons and both presented design problems at the corners of a building. The Doric Order was also far too thick for many practical purposes.

According to the Roman architectural writer Vitruvius, a Corinthian architect, turning his back upon tradition and the sanctities, invented a new Order which had the slenderness of the Ionic and the four-equal-sidedness of the Doric. We still call it the Corinthian Order and it became the basic Order of Roman architecture, after Rome had destroyed Corinth as a city in 146 BC because of its independent and insurrectionary spirit, sold its people into slavery and consigned its artistic treasures to Rome.

Under and after Alexander the Great (r. 336–323 BC) Greek artistic achievements and methods were spread through the Middle East, giving rise to an architectural style which we now call Hellenistic. This was adopted by the Romans who conquered the countries which had been part of Alexander's Greek empire.

In the time of Augustus (d. AD 14) a rather obscure Roman architect called Vitruvius Polio wrote a book, *De Architectura*, and dedicated it to the Emperor. In it he tried to tell the architects of his time about the sacred principles of arcane architecture as understood and practised by the Greeks; but Roman architects in that boom period, when imperialism was laying lucrative commissions at their feet, were beginning to explore the possibilities of the arch and the vault, which were alien to Greek theory.

In the next three hundred years (to c. AD 300) Roman architecture accommodated the arch, round vaults and domes within the framework of Greek post-and-lintel theory. Thus, the structural arches and vaults of the Colosseum and many other buildings were actually framed in post-and-lintel Orders of architecture which were unnecessary (see p. 107). This practice persisted for monumental

The Lysicrates Monument in Athens (334 BC), an early example of the Corinthian Order. This Order may have been invented in bronze and challenged masons to imitate it in stone.

architecture up to the Arch of Constantine, Rome (AD 312) although in minor buildings the use of the column as the main support for arches (not as a frame) gained in popularity. This was the precedent for Hellenesque and Romanesque architecture.

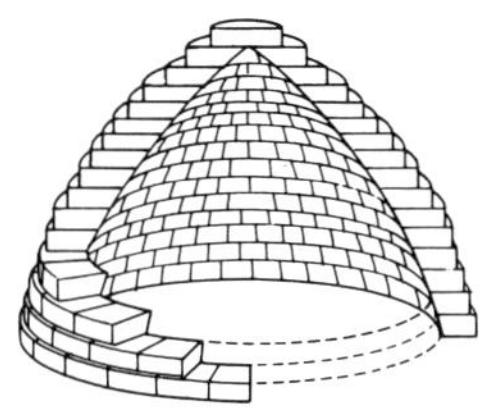

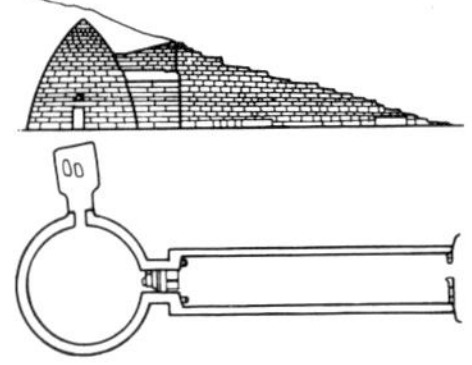

Above Corbel dome construction with concentric rings of stone, shown in plan and elevation in its most monumental form in the 'Treasury of Atreus', Mycenae (c. 1325 BC).

Hellenesque

When the Emperor Constantine the Great moved the capital of the Roman Empire to Byzantium in 330, renamed it Constantinople and consecrated it to the Virgin Mary in 332, there was no longer any reason for continuing the form of architecture which had come to symbolise Rome.

In the new capital, at the meeting point of Europe and Asia, people spoke Greek rather than Latin. Rome had imposed an antiquated Greek style of architecture but the Greeks, along with other peoples of the Middle East, had been exploring new possibilities in architecture and especially the idea of the corbelled dome as it had been used at Mycenae nearly two thousand years earlier, rejected by Classical Hellenic architects but retained in the folk architecture of the Levant. This had been developed in the successor states of Alexander's Greek empire.

Suddenly the regional tradition became the official imperial style and for two amazing centuries there was an outburst of building palaces for the new bureaucracy and churches for Christianity, the new official religion.

The Hellenesque style is sometimes called Byzantine but this term limits it to Christian architecture while, in fact, after the Mohammedan conquests of the seventh and eighth centuries, many of the most splendid buildings were mosques, monasteries and palaces built, mainly by Greek architects, for their Arab employers. The Arab version of Hellenesque came to Spain in the seventh century and exerted an important influence upon the development of western European architecture, especially during the Gothic period. The Levantine (Middle Eastern) regional style from which Hellenesque

Below Two solutions were developed in Hellenesque architecture to the problem of placing a circular dome over a square:

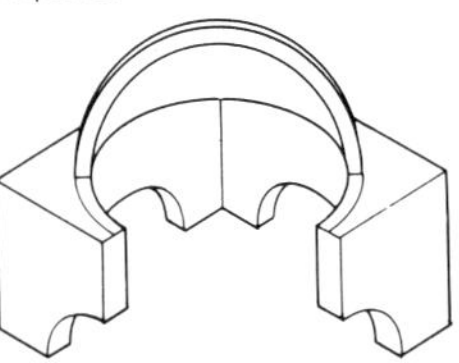

The squinch

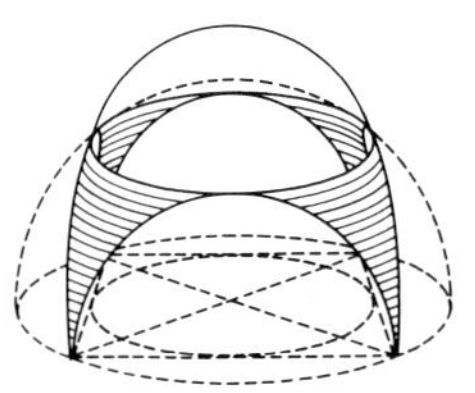

The pendentive

architecture arose was based upon the round, corbel-domed house built of stones or mud; and the great structural invention (date unknown) which made Hellenesque architecture so exciting as a medium of design was the pendentive. This was a triangular segment of a domical surface which made it possible to support a round dome on a square base. The major achievement in Christendom was the Church of the Holy Wisdom (Hagia Sophia) built in the 530s for the Emperor Justinian by two Greek architects, Anthemius and Isodorus. This was, in effect, a reconciliation of the idea of a basilica with a domical system of roofing. Like most compromises it embodied weaknesses which were made good by large external buttresses at a later date. The magnificent architectural conception, which still rides over the city of Istanbul, was perfected a thousand years later by the Turkish architect Sinan the Great (the only architect ever to earn that title along with Alexander, Constantine and Alfred). Sinan was probably a Greek taken as a child into the school for training Janissaries, the élite corps of the Turkish army. He became their Chief Engineer and may be compared with the English Surveyor-General, Sir Christopher Wren, for the quality and quantity of his buildings and because both men invented new ways of using domes (p. 163).

The Eastern Roman Emperors established a base in Ravenna where they had an *exarch* (Greek for governor). They also had a base in Sicily for the re-conquest of the West and when in AD 800 Charlemagne re-established the Western Roman Empire (Holy Roman Empire as it came, rather dubiously, to be called) he looked to Ravenna for an imperial style of architecture in which to build his palace at Aachen.

The Muslim version of Hellenesque architecture influenced Europe via Spain. The Christian version influenced regional and folk architecture in all the European countries, spreading at an early date up the Danube trade route to Scandinavia. It was established

Right The Church of the Holy Wisdom (Hagia Sophia) built in Constantinople (Istanbul) between AD 532 and 537, the supreme achievement of Christian Hellenesque architecture
Plan:
1 Atrium (destroyed)
2 Outer narthex
3 Inner narthex
4 Central space
5 Exedras, which in effect make the central space a rectangle
6 Apse
7 Aisles with spacious galleries above
8 Bapistery
9 Treasury.

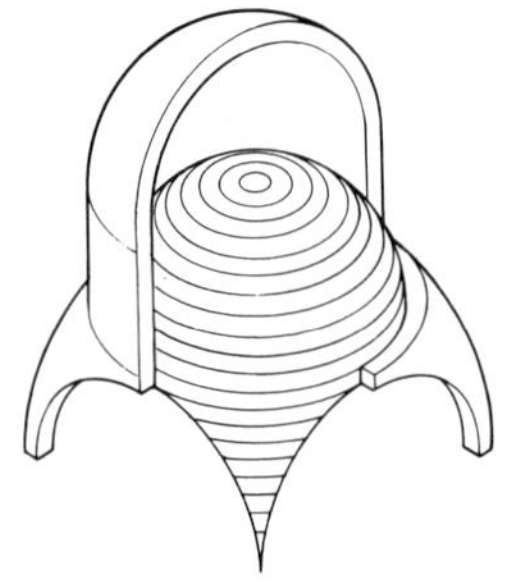

Diagram of the dome construction at Hagia Sophia, with the dome set directly on the pendentives without a transitional drum (compare this with the lower illustration on the previous page).

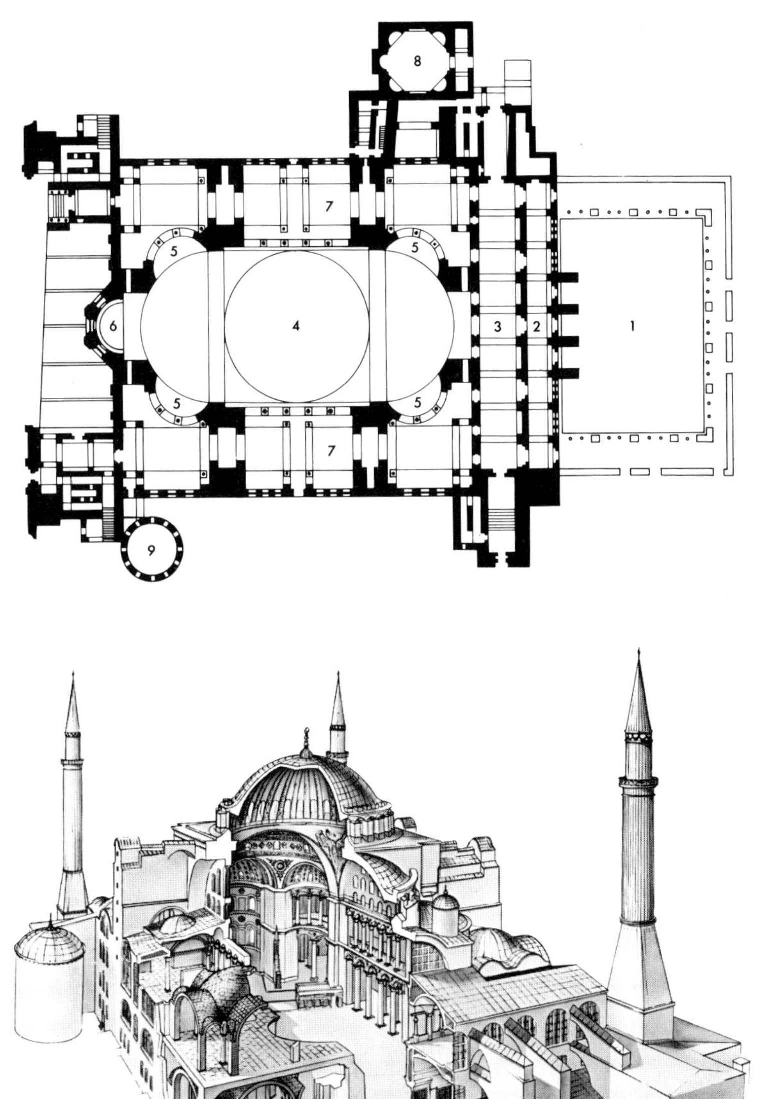
8
7
5
5
6
4
3
2
1
5
5
7
9

in northern Italy in the sixth century and inspired St Mark's Cathedral in Venice in the twelfth century (p. 180), but it also permeated the Alpine valleys and spread through the mountain regions of central France to Périgueux and Angoulême (p. 111).

Hellenesque influence upon Celtic, Irish and Viking art is evident but its extent is controversial.

The horseshoe arch and the pointed arch were both used by Hellenesque architects, the latter certainly long before the development of Gothic architecture in the West in the 12th century.

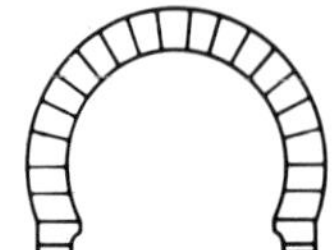

Round horseshoe arch

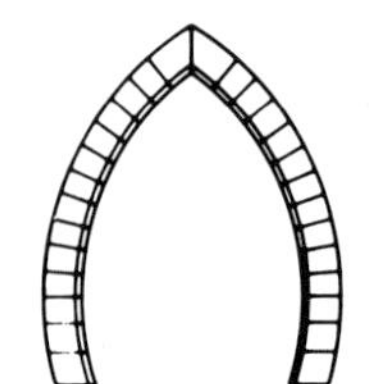

Pointed horseshoe arch

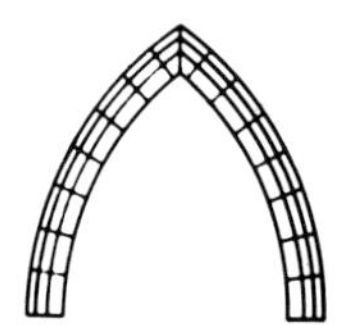

Pointed arch (normal Gothic arch)

Romanesque

Romanesque is the style of architecture that evolved in the West, mainly to provide the churches which replaced pagan temples. Christians required buildings in which to gather together as they had done secretly in houses during the persecution. The Roman house plan, with its main room entered through a courtyard (*atrium*) and a porch or ante-room (*narthex*), was reflected in buildings made purposely for public Christian worship. During the persecution, a table had been placed opposite the entrance door for the ritual meal (*eucharist*); and this became the normal position for the holy table or altar, whereas the sacrificial altars of pagan temples had usually been outside, in front of the temple which was constructed as a house for a statue of the god. This idea of a sanctuary crept into Christian practice with the altar as its central feature instead of the statue.

The simple house plan was unsuitable for worship by large crowds of people so the Church adopted the architectural form of the basilica, which had been used for places of assembly and courts of justice. An apse had usually provided the setting for a throne or rostrum and this also was adopted by Christians as the setting for the holy table.

As more and more people became converts to the new religion the sacrament of baptism became a great public event, held at regular

Below A typical Roman town house plan, the home of a relatively prosperous middle-class family. The earliest Christian worship in Rome was conducted illegally in such houses, and one may see them as the origin of the simple church plan. The main room (1) thus becomes the chancel; the atrium (2) the nave, and the entrance (3) the narthex.

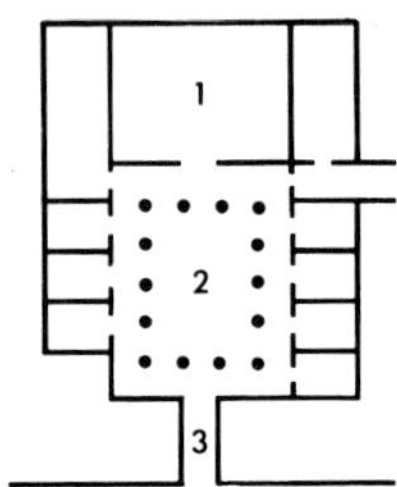

intervals, and special buildings were required in which the font was the central feature. The Roman idea of a domed building with a colonnade all round, which had hitherto been used for many purposes, and especially for the hot room (*caldarium*) of Roman baths, was adopted by Christians for the ritual bathing of baptism. Many important examples of separate baptisteries survive, the most famous being at Parma, Pisa and Florence.

The religious complex at Pisa exemplifies the full development of the Romanesque church, with bell tower (*campanile*, the famous leaning tower) to proclaim the hours and summon to worship; with a separate baptistery at the west end, so that baptism symbolically preceded admission to the church; and on the north side the *campo santo* or burial ground (p. 52).

Romanesque architecture grew out of late Roman architecture and in the early days columns from temples were often reused to build the colonnades and arcades of Christian churches. Where such secondhand columns were not available they were imitated as well as possible, using local materials.

Latin, the international language, became the language of the Church and many of the clergy belonged to ancient Roman senatorial families. Respect for Roman architecture persisted but apparently, even in those days, the only book about architecture was Vitruvius' *De Architectura*, of which many copies were made and used in monastic libraries.

The Black Gate at Trier exemplifies the late Roman imperial architecture which is at variance with the principles of Vitruvius. He knew little about vaults and arches and so, in the wide gap between his academic theory and current building practice, design was free to develop without inhibitions.

Develop it certainly did, and between AD 500 and 1100 the architecture of Western Christendom was invented and all the major functional problems were solved by Romanesque architects.

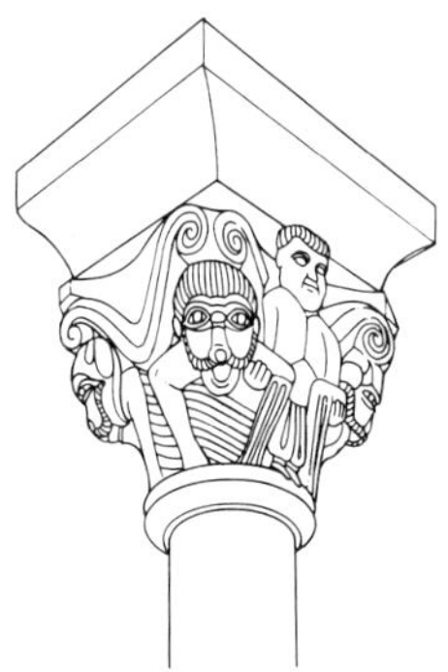

Above The French Romanesque capital, retaining the basic Corinthian form. It is similar to the Hellenesque capital, but with more emphasis on sculpture. From St Michel de Cuxa, Languedoc-Roussillon.

Below The Porta Nigra (Black Gate) in Trier, Germany, built c. AD 300, in effect as a barbican (see p. 45). Trier was capital of the Western Roman Empire. The arch is used within a framework of posts and lintels, as it was in the Colosseum (1st century AD).

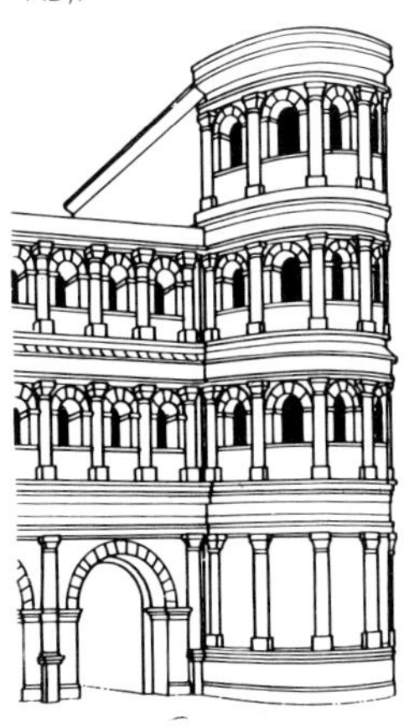

Despite the troubles and tribulations, the plagues, famines, climatic changes, invasions, movements of population, social changes, decline of slavery and rise of serfdom, wars and the threat of Islam, the Romanesque period was the most inventive and creative in all architectural history, its nearest rival being the twentieth century.

Creative change is often the response to a challenge and in the ninth century this came from the fierce and predatory Vikings who burned the timber-roofed basilican churches, forcibly suggesting the desirability of fire-proof construction. When they settled in places like Normandy and Sicily they did in fact build vaulted churches themselves. The idea of protecting religious buildings from the fiery wrath of man led, in the end, to the creation of Gothic architecture.

To vault a basilican church in stone it had to be narrowed and if a simple barrel vault was used the interior had to be dark. Any vault exerts a lateral thrust which has to be resisted, so buttresses became more important and the crucial invention of the ribbed vault opened the way for a new kind of architecture, based upon the Romanesque plan.

To appreciate Romanesque buildings one must recognise that the Classical column, however altered, supports the entablature, which may be the substructure of a timber roof or the beginning of a vault. In this respect, despite its inventiveness, Romanesque looks back to Rome. The Romanesque column may support a lintel, an arch or the beginning of a vault but in each case it remains *the* fundamental element of architecture.

This is not to belittle Romanesque architecture: it may be a good idea to preserve the separateness of the support from the superstructure. It certainly makes architecture easier to understand, just as punctuation makes writing easier to read.

In the early days, indeed up to the Viking invasions of the ninth century, the Roman basilican plan was used even as far north as

Autun Cathedral in Burgundy (c. 1120–32), in the fully-developed Romanesque style. (see also p. 255).

1 Pointed barrel vault
2 Transverse arch
3 Pointed Romanesque arches
4 Modified Corinthian pilasters with sculptured capitals
5 Pilasters superimposed, anticipating the vertical mouldings of Gothic architecture (see Amiens, p. 226)
6 Arcaded triforium, with round arches
7 Clerestory (restricted, like the triforium, by the barrel-vault construction)
8 Eastern apse (altered)
9 Classical Baroque reredos (a common addition to French medieval churches).

Hexham in Northumberland where, in about 675–680, St Wilfrid built what was considered, at the time, to be the finest church north of the Alps; it was destroyed in 876 by the Danes but the crypt still exists (p. 260). Crypts were often built to house the relics of a saint and were retained, unaltered on that account, when the rest of the church was rebuilt. Visitors are frequently charged a fee for entering a crypt, but it is well worth paying because the crypt is not only the earliest part of a church but often architecturally the most interesting, and religiously the most holy.

After the turmoil of the Viking invasions, which extended to Italy and Sicily, down the Danube to Constantinople, across the North Sea to all parts of Britain, along the coast of Europe, round Brittany and up the River Loire into the very heart of France, there was a great period of re-building to which the Norsemen, now converted to Christianity, made a vigorous contribution. They created a variety of Romanesque architecture in Normandy, Sicily, southern Italy and England which is called *Norman*. It is interesting, especially for the British tourist, to find the familiar style of Durham and Norwich cathedrals or Romsey Abbey not only in Normandy but in Ancona (S. Maria di Portonuovo), Bari and Trani on the east coast of Italy (p. 174–6).

The end of the first millennium seems to mark a sudden upsurge of confidence in European civilisation which may, in part, be due to the fact that many people in the late 900s were fearful of the Day of Judgement, predicted for AD 1000; this may be compared to our own preoccupation with the possible holocaust of nuclear war, the ultimate crime of governments against life on Earth. The new confidence engendered by the fact that 'it didn't happen' is reflected in the marvellously inventive and exciting architecture of the eleventh and twelfth centuries. It was during this period that the *chevet* was developed. This Romanesque invention was exploited to the limits of possibility in stone construction

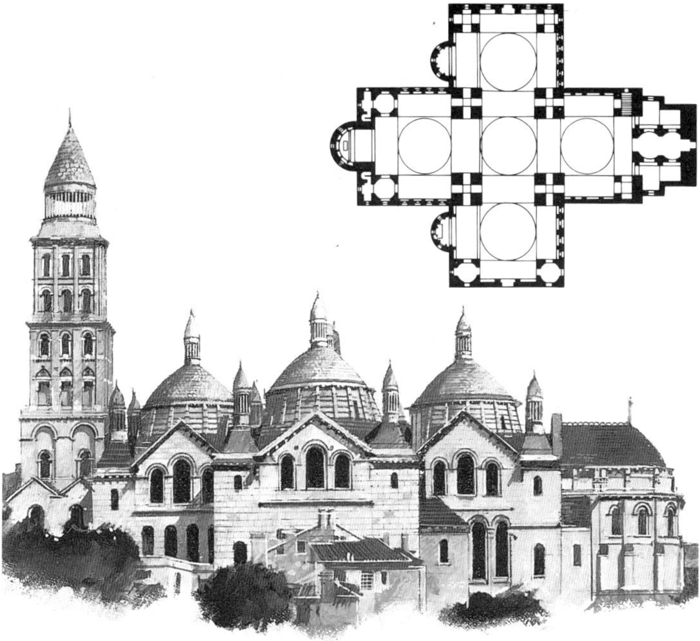

The Cathedral of St Front, Périgueux, France, built c. 1120–73; a Romanesque cathedral with a typical Hellenesque plan, very similar to that of St Mark's, Venice. The dome is carried on pendentives which spring from slightly pointed main arches.

by Gothic architects. It consisted of an aisle (ambulatory or walk-way) wrapped round an apse and giving access to radial chapels. Structurally it provided a conical system through which thrusts from the vaults, and sometimes a central tower, were carried down safely to the ground.

A dominant characteristic of Romanesque architecture is that the column, with base, shaft and capital, was almost universal, though sometimes reduced to a vestigial pilaster strip on outside walls. Vaults were also of the Roman type, either barrel or cross vaults, but at the end of the eleventh century Romanesque architects at Durham built what are probably the first ribbed vaults over a major church. This Romanesque invention made Gothic architecture possible. It was a revolution in structural thinking about building in stone.

Romanesque architects preferred the Roman round arch but also used pointed and horseshoe arches (p. 106). The austere character of Romanesque churches, as we now see them, is misleading. Originally the walls and columns were covered with paintings; and sculpture, which is one of the glories of Romanesque architecture, was also coloured in many cases.

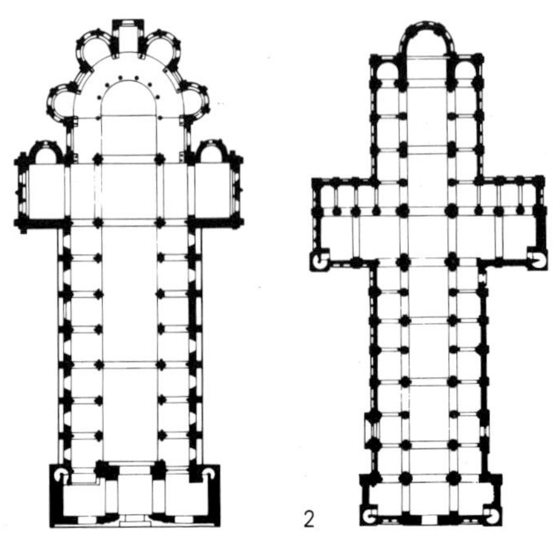

Left Comparative church plans:
1 St Austremoine, Issoire, France (12th century). Its barrel-vaulted structure was conservative, but by taking the aisle round the apse and so giving access to a cluster of chapels, it helped to establish the major French invention in church design, the *chevet*.
2 Durham Cathedral, England, mainly 1093–1133. The original plan, shown here, was a cruciform development of the basilica, terminating in an apse (which was later replaced by an eastern transept, the Chapel of the Nine Altars). Durham was conventional in plan, but revolutionary in structure.

Durham Cathedral, a combination of superlatives, and the final resting place of St Cuthbert of Lindisfarne. Its features include: pioneer ribbed vaulting; the most massive Norman columns, with incised patterns; 'early English' rose window; the reredos (Neville Screen), late 14th century by Henry Yevele, architect of the nave of Canterbury Cathedral.

St Austremoine, Issoire, France. The aisle is taken round the apse, which opens into it with columns and is surmounted by a half-dome. The chevet thus created makes it impossible to have a large east window, and gives the effect of broken-up lighting. It is worthy of note that both the French chevet and the ribbed vault (as at Durham) were Romanesque inventions.

Castles

The late Romanesque period coincides with the establishment of feudalism, a system of land tenure based upon service to an overlord. The threat of Islamic conquest of Europe via Spain had been met by the military invention of the armoured horseman (knight-in-armour), the prototype of the twentieth-century tank; and in the Middle Ages the struggle was turned back upon the heart-lands of Islam by the crusaders (after whom one of the most famous Second World War tanks was appropriately named). To keep a knight-in-armour required a large economic support system which feudalism provided, by the grant of estates of land in return for knight-service and support troops such as archers or infantry.

Some kings held their dominions together; but powerful dukes, counts and barons, who had contracted to provide numerous knights and retainers, often got out of hand, revolted or quarrelled among themselves, sometimes even for succession to the crown. They needed headquarters from which to operate, to which they could retreat if necessary, and in which they could secure their families; hence castles. These also played a part in local government and subjection of the populace. From Scotland to southern Italy and from Bohemia to the Atlantic coast of Spain, castles were built like a rash of pimples, starting with a fortified mound (motte) or a tower on a hill, and developing into the complex military installations of the sixteenth century.

Below Continuity within defence needs: the Romanesque castle of Porchester, Hampshire, England, was built in 1160–73 in one corner of the old fortified Roman camp.

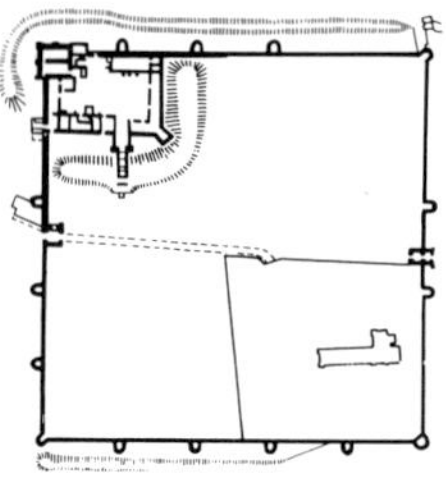

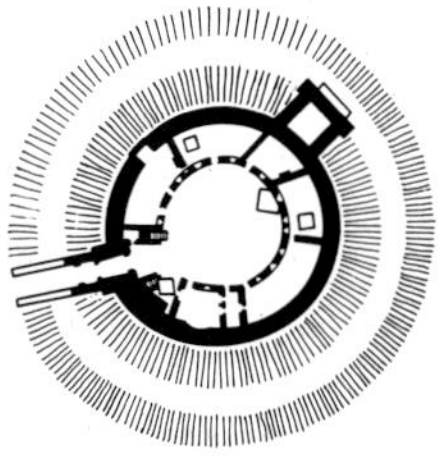

Above The castle of Restormel, Cornwall, England, is of the motte-and-bailey type; its gateway is 11th-century and its shell keep on the motte is 12th.

Right Caernarfon Castle, Gwynedd, Wales, built in 1283–1323. It has a very powerful residential gatehouse, leading to a huge bailey, which is surrounded by individually defensible towers.

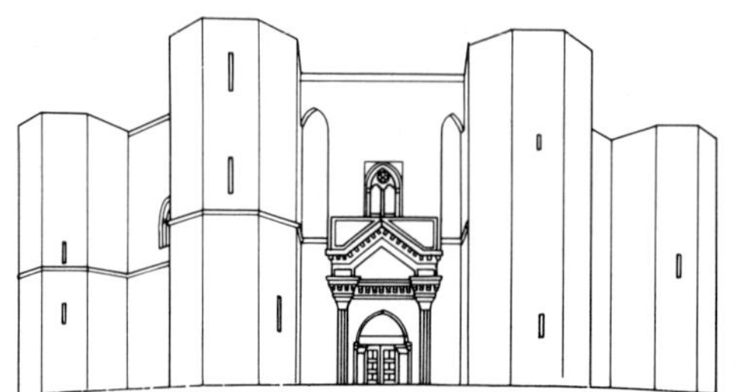

Left Castel del Monte, Andria, Italy, built in white marble by the Emperor Frederick II (r. 1220–50). A palace rather than a castle, its decoration shows a deliberate attempt to revive Classical architecture long before the Renaissance.

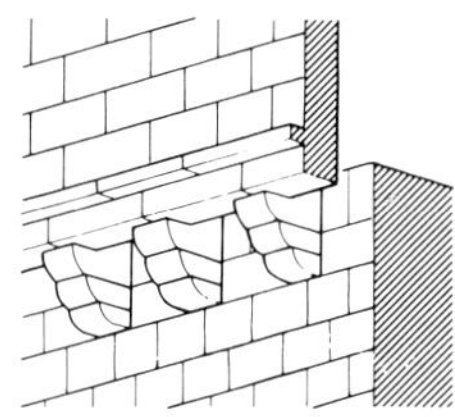

Above Machicolation, a means of building out from the castle walls permitting the defenders to protect the base of the walls from above.

Below A corbelled 'garderobe' ('lou'), a convenient variation on the theme of machicolation.

Castles were the architectural expression of a militarised secular society supported mainly by a subject population of agricultural workers: peasants in many parts of Europe, slaves, serfs or villeins working on manorial estates in others. It was an almost illiterate society, but the nobility could read heraldry and carried their pedigree on their shields.

As might be expected, military architecture was not very inventive and even the fully developed medieval castle, such as Caernarfon, had few advantages over a Mycenaean stronghold of 1200 BC which had a better barbican and far better living accommodation (p. 45). The most important innovations were, firstly the corbelled battlements (machicolations) which facilitated protection of the base of the walls and, secondly, the development of the gatehouse as the owner's or constable's quarters in case of revolt and assault from *within* the castle!

Left Sirmione Castle, Lake Garda, Italy, built of brick in the 13th century. More a pretentious residence than a military stronghold. It has a defended harbour.

Below left Harlech Castle, Gwynedd, Wales, a gatehouse castle built in 1283–90 with architectural formality and axial symmetry.

Below The 13th-century cloister of the monastery of Benevento, Italy; the cloister, which was placed between the church and the living quarters of the monks, has become symbolic of the monastic way of life. The style here is essentially Hellenesque, and owes much to Islamic influence, though usually called Romanesque or Lombardic.

Monasteries

In parallel with feudal society, and in some legal respects participating in it, was a literate religious society based upon the Christian Church. This was reflected most importantly in monasteries, which were religious communities, more or less autonomous within the rules of their federation which was called an Order. The most important for Romanesque architecture was the Benedictine Order with headquarters at Cassino (Italy) though its most important architectural influence was exerted from Cluny in Burgundy.

In monasteries were preserved the civilised values which the illiterate warriors defended. Monks provided all the social services from hospitals to hotels, set standards in farming, forestry, apiary and the whole range of rural industries. They preserved and copied books, fostered the arts and gave education to boys and girls who aspired to the way of life based upon religion.

It should be noted that at the same time Islamic religious communities in Spain were performing a like service and so too were the Jews who were scattered throughout Christendom and Islam.

Medieval 'Architects'

Nowadays an architect is a professional man or woman with pretentions to inheriting the role of the artist-architect created in Italy during the early Renaissance period (p. 130). From the fall of the Roman Empire to the Renaissance the word architect was seldom used and it has been suggested that master masons were equivalent to architects in the Middle Ages. Recent research (especially the work of the Australian scholar John James) has demonstrated that major achievements of medieval architecture, such as Chartres Cathedral, were the work of various teams of masons, each with its own master and recognisable ways of working. Who then was responsible for the overall conception? We do not know, but in the case of abbey churches and cathedrals it seems improbable that the clergy did not play a large part in deciding what was to be built. We know that some specialised in theology and some (St Thomas Aquinas for example) in the then closely related subject of philosophy, some in farm management and some in librarianship and book production, so it is not unreasonable to suppose that some brethren studied architecture; and we know that they could refer to libraries which included at least *De Architectura* by Vitruvius (p. 102).

In secular architecture, especially the design of castles such as the Tower of London, Norham Castle on England's frontier with Scotland, the castle at Andria which was built for Frederick II in southern Italy or Caernarfon Castle, the seat of the first English Prince of Wales, it seems highly improbable that the design was left entirely to a master mason. English documents show that masons were actually conscripted to work on military buildings and this implies, what we already know from other sources, that officials called Clerks of the Works and later Royal Surveyors, precursors of the office of Surveyor General (held by Sir Christopher Wren) had a major part in deciding what was to be built. In monastic communities a 'clerk of the fabric' would be responsible for maintenance and at least for minor new buildings. Confusion arises today because we expect there to have been an architect in the modern sense, but the evidence suggests that throughout the Middle Ages, the professional role of the modern architect was taken by a clerk of works who also paid the workers and co-ordinated the different trades. Master masons, carpenters, smiths, plumbers and glaziers, with their teams of skilled and unskilled men, worked to contract within the tradition of their craft organisations, undoubtedly contributing in detail to the design of the building. Occasionally an abbot or bishop claimed credit for the design and Abbot Suger certainly had a major role at St Denis in Paris, but the general picture is of a group within which there were defined functions, a very close involvement of the craftsmen in the design process and, most importantly, the building owners and their agents were much more aesthetically aware, better informed and concerned for the beauty of the building than are most modern clients and estate agents. It is partly the fault of the patrons (or clients, as architects call them) that so many modern buildings are ugly.

Chartres Cathedral, France, dedicated to the Virgin Mary but on a site that was probably a cult centre in pagan times. Vestiges of a Romanesque church remain, but the Gothic cathedral was conceived in about 1194 and was to have had nine towers. Over a period of construction lasting some 65 years there was a series of modifications and compromises, as the design evolved under a succession of master masons. Chartres is famous for its sculpture and its stained glass – the work of artist-craftsmen contributing as members of a remarkably harmonious design team. (See also p. 228).

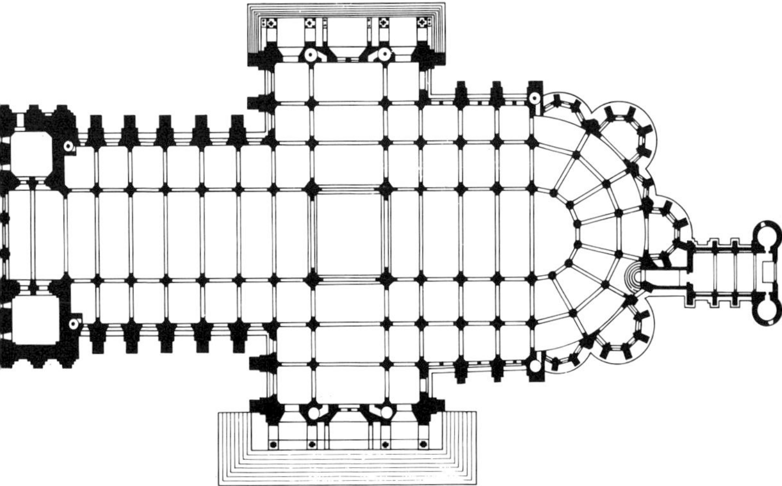

Left Lincoln Cathedral, England, containing traces of an earlier Romanesque church, but mainly built from 1129. Lincoln was an intellectual and economic power-house in the 13th century.

Right The monastery church of S. Francisco at Assisi, Italy, 1128–53. Its design combines Romanesque and Gothic elements. The interior is decorated by Giotto and others.

Right The west front of Orvieto Cathedral, Italy (1310–30, and later to 1580) embodies Romanesque and Gothic ideas, with brilliantly-coloured mosaics and sculpture – a *tour-de-force* of medieval artist-craftsmen.

Far right A carved pillar from the Abbey Church of Souillac, France, 1130–40, typical of the lively sculpture of the Dordogne region.

Gothic Architecture

The name Gothic to denote an architectural style originated after the revival of Classical art and architecture during the Renaissance and was a term of abuse, since the whole medieval achievement was regarded as the outcome of the barbarian invasions. Among the invaders were the Goths who acquired much of Italy, southern France and Spain; but Saxons, Franks, Germans, Burgundians, Lombards, Gepids and even the Huns were all lumped together and called 'Goths'. The architecture of their descendants, some fifteen generations later, and represented by Chartres, Siena or Salisbury cathedrals, was called Gothic and seriously considered, by most cultured people in the eighteenth century, to be barbarous and totally without merit. Such is the power of mythology over minds! But by the nineteenth century it was commonplace to see Gothic as the architecture of Christianity and the Renaissance as a revival of pagan values; this was an equally misleading ideological interpretation of history.

Most guide books, and even serious histories of architecture, identify Gothic with the use of the pointed arch and see Romanesque and Gothic as two distinct and different architectonic systems, with a so-called 'transitional style' between them.

In fact, Gothic was the consummation of the long and amazingly creative Romanesque period. The pointed arch had been known for many centuries and studiously avoided because medieval, like Renaissance, builders regarded the circle and semi-circle as perfect forms. The pointed arch was imperfect but its structural advantages were enormous, most of all because, by varying the pointedness, the tops of arches over different spans could be kept level. The really important difference between Romanesque and Gothic architecture was the Romanesque invention of the ribbed vault, which was originally used with round arches.

In timber-framed structures, from as early as 1500 BC in Crete, the structure had consisted of a timber frame filled-in with any suitable non-structural material, from gypsum blocks to wattle daubed with mud. Carpenters built the frame and then it was filled-in to provide insulation.

Until the end of the eleventh century masons built solid walls and their way of producing a fireproof roof was to take the walls up-and-over. Probably in the first century AD the Romans realised that two round vaults could intersect at right-angles, a fact which had been known to moles, rabbits, and mice for quite a long time and, presumably, to human miners but in those days, as now, there was little opportunity for feed-back from one branch of knowledge to others.

The visitor to Durham Cathedral should be aware that when he looks up at the vaults of the chancel, and its aisles, he is seeing the first architectural fruits of the greatest architectural revolution in history. There, in the ribs of the vault, the idea of separating the structure from the enclosing walls was first

Comparison of the relationship of height to span in pointed and round arches. The pointed arch clearly gives much more flexibility in design.

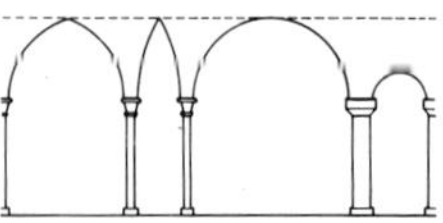

The barrel vault (1) and the cross vault (2). The cross vault isolates the intersection of two barrel vaults, normally at right-angles.

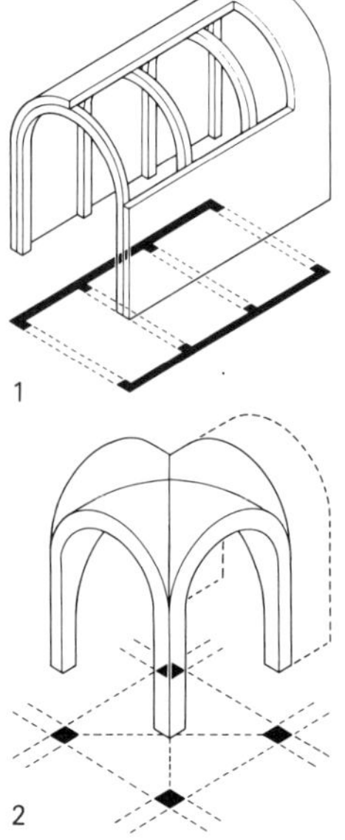

The nave of Laon Cathedral, France, 1160–1225, is transitional from Romanesque to Gothic. The pillars of the nave are still complete Orders with capitals and abaci, above which rudimentary superimposed columns rise to the ribs of the vaulting.

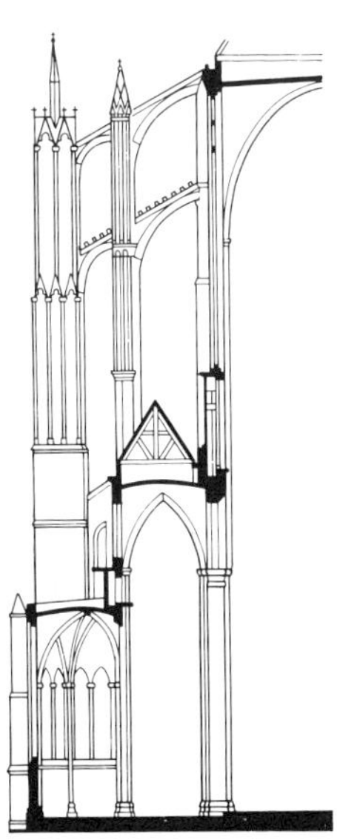

Half section of the 14th-century chancel at Beauvais Cathedral, France. The highest vault in Europe, it is supported by a series of flying buttresses.

exemplified on a major scale. Once this had been done the traceried east windows of York Minster and Gloucester Cathedral became possible. So did the aetherial structure of Beauvais and the fan vaults of King Henry VII's chapel at Westminster Abbey; and so did the marvels of modern structural design. The strange thing is that carpenters had been isolating the structure for ages, but when the master masons took to the idea and worked it out in stone, the sheer difficulty of doing it led to the inventive explosion which is embodied in the great cathedrals.

Once the structure had been conceived in terms of lines of thrust (p. 17) the old idea of the column supporting a load became less important. For example, the roof of the chancel of Beauvais Cathedral is only partly supported by the columns of the arcade beneath. The main load goes at an angle, down through the flying buttresses. So it was that the capital of a column ceased to be a cardinal feature of architecture; the Orders became obsolete and eventually the ribs of the vaulting were carried right down to the ground, inside the building. This, though, was really a decorative expression of the structural form of the building and the real work was done by the flying buttresses, carrying the load over the aisles to the main buttresses, which were structurally at right angles to the axis of the building, thus freeing the whole of the side walls between them for non-structural infilling; this was done with stone tracery supporting stained glass.

Italian Gothic, at S. Petronio, Bologna (1390–1447). The planned east end was never built.

Above The fully-developed chevet, at Le Mans Cathedral, France (1217–54).

Below York Minster, the largest English medieval cathedral, surmounted by 15th-century towers.

1

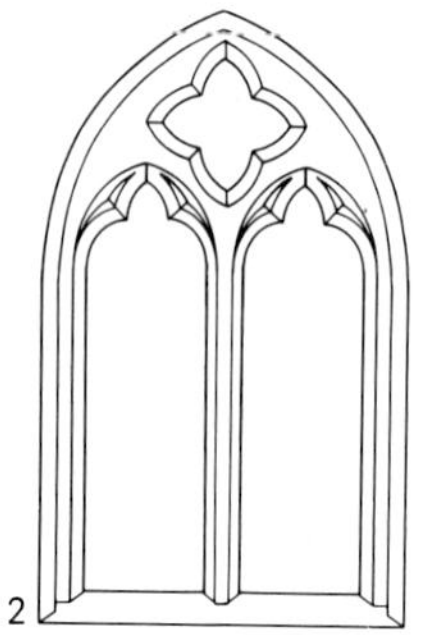
2

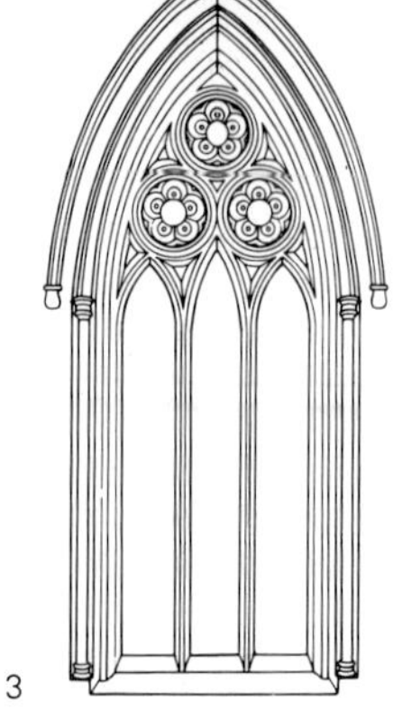
3

That is the structural story but structure is not an end itself: it serves a purpose, functional or aesthetic or, in most cases, both. From the village church to great monastic churches and cathedrals, the church building was conceived to be the house of God. The early basilicas were practical buildings where Christians and others could be taught the gospel and worship God, but increasingly, and especially in abbeys, the actual church building became an act of worship in itself, continuously renewed with embellishments and additions. By the twelfth century, and within the sturdy discipline of Romanesque construction, light was being used as an element in the architectural expression and eventually the slender structures of Gothic architecture made it possible to enclose a space and transfuse it with coloured light, mobile with the movement of the sun and seen by medieval people as creating, within the church, the atmosphere of heaven. If we look only at the solid parts of medieval churches we miss the enormously important element of light manipulated by coloured glass and tracery, and the enclosing darkness of vaulting, interpenetrating spaces, parallax and perspective. Certainly, stained glass windows depicted and instructed, but they did much more than that, and because they conditioned the light by which the church was seen, and transfused it with the substance of sacred pictures, they were a very important

Tracery
The origins of tracery can be seen in the grouping of three simple arched (lancet) windows (1). In the next stage (2), two arches are linked by a cusped quadrilateral made up of the heads of four arches. The cusp (possibly a Muslim idea) is the key to the development of tracery. It is the unsupported (pendent) junction of two arches; its most extreme form is found in the pendants of fan vaulting. Geometrical tracery (3) is an elaboration of single curves. The reverse curve (known as the *cyma recta* – the line of beauty) led to the emergence of curvilinear and flamboyant tracery (4). Typical French flamboyant (or flame-shaped) tracery (5). Rectilinear (or Perpendicular) tracery provided a vertical support for the intrados (inner curve) of the arch (6 and 7). It anticipated the ultimate rejection of the arch in favour of the lintel, which accompanied the secularisation of architecture.

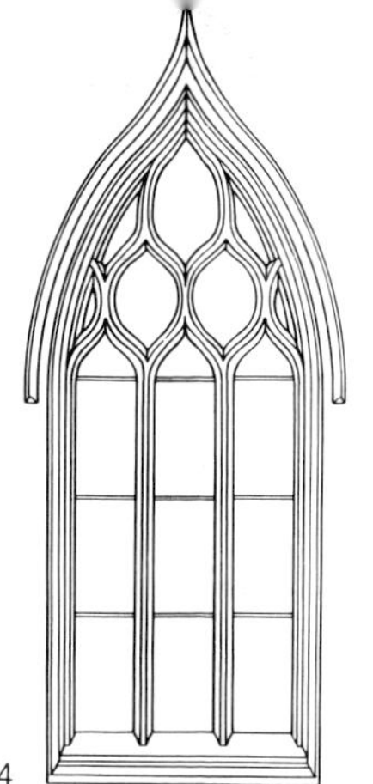
4

5

6

part of the architectural and religious conception.

Gothic architecture evolved principally in England and northern France, the area corresponding fairly closely with Viking penetration (ninth to eleventh centuries), where the consequent need for rebuilding encouraged the masonry business. Relations between France and England were close and often hostile, with English kings claiming sovereignty of France, and French spoken at the English court. The main difference between French and English Gothic probably arose from the fact that the great French churches were mostly built inside walled cities on congested sites. They tended to be higher and more economical in the use of land than English churches which were in smaller and more open towns. Whereas French Gothic became more elaborate, English Gothic from about 1350 became more austere and rectilinear, with a strong emphasis on vertical lines which has suggested the name 'Perpendicular' for the fifteenth-century style.

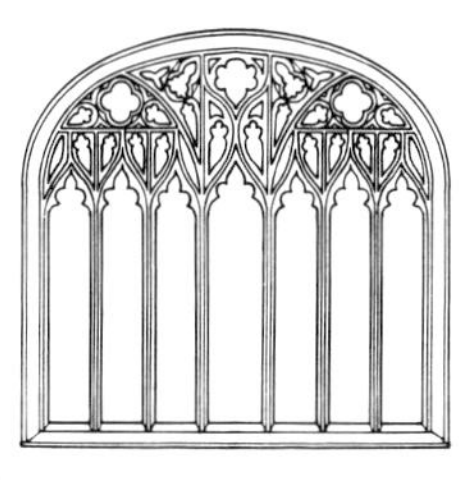
7

Gothic architecture developed in other countries with marked variations due to their different traditions. (See especially Italy, Spain, Germany).

To appreciate Gothic architecture one must realise that it was part of a way of life, very different from our own, based upon religion and chivalry. Architecture was not just a matter of building in stone. Beautiful though these structures may be, they were incomplete without their furniture, the work of smiths in iron, silver and gold, sculpture in wood and stone, glass, ceramics, tapestries, gardens, tents and pavilions, heraldry, harness and, not least, the vestments of the clergy, the costume of the nobility, the robes which were the perquisite and uniform of officials, the simple clothing of the simple people. It was certainly a more cleanly age than that which followed.

Ideally medieval society and a very large proportion of its economic resources were devoted to expressing man's duty to God. Despite the pageantry of heraldry and chivalry, the splendid rituals of the church, the delight in beautiful books, arts, costume and manners, the life of the aristocracy was austere, with physical comforts despised. Food was more plentiful than it had been since the fall of the Roman Empire and much of the vigour of the age came from the use of protein-rich beans.

No society which existed over many centuries can possibly be summed up in a few sentences, but, as a corrective to the modern over-emphasis of the cruelty, dynastic squabbles, militarism and oppression of the age, the rhythmic, orderly and aspiring architecture of the great and lesser churches reflects the other side of the coin, a society trying to live by high moral standards in the service of God and a moral discipline, sometimes harshly enforced but accepted even by kings.

A commemorative brass of Sir Peter Courtenay (d. 1409), from Exeter Cathedral, England.

The decay of medieval civilisation is often attributed to the revival of Classical art and culture, despite the fact that Greek philosophy had been well known in the monasteries and the dates do not really fit the theory. A more plausible explanation is the growth of commerce and the financing of wars by commercial bankers, making money earn money by usury. What was, much later, to be called the capitalist system struck at the roots of the medieval way of life.

Above Sculptured figures of the south portal, Chartres.

Left The chancel of Norwich Cathedral, England, with later Gothic tracery and vaulting growing out of Romanesque substructure.

Renaissance Architecture

Early Renaissance architects were well aware that they were participating in the revival of Roman civilisation. For many centuries Italy, the heart-land of the Roman empire, had been subjected to division and foreign domination, but many men had dreamed of restoring the greatness of Rome. In the Church this had almost been realised, only to be snatched away by the transfer of the Papacy to Avignon (1309–76). At a secular level Cola di Rienzi was proclaimed Tribune of Rome in 1347 to restore the prestige of Rome, but when he failed the mob turned enthusiasm into fury and burned his body on a fire of thistles.

In the universities and the merchant guilds of the Italian cities, and even among the nobility (mostly of barbarian origin) who had come to live in the cities, the revival of Classical art and learning (rather than the Roman way of life and political system), was more successful. It did indeed initiate a new culture throughout western Europe:

The creative idea was that, after the fall of Rome, Europe had surrendered to barbarism, which for Italians was represented by Gothic architecture in such buildings as the Palazzo Vecchio in Florence (p. 183). Attempts had already been made, notably by the Emperor Frederick II (r. 1220–50) to re-establish the Roman way of design (p. 116) but he was rejected as a foreigner and a heretic. The break-through came in about 1403 when a young Florentine artist, who had disappointed his father by not becoming a lawyer, set off for Rome with an even younger sculptor who was his close friend. They were called Filippo Brunelleschi and Donatello. They studied and measured Roman architecture in Rome, then returned to Florence to set up in business as sculptors and architects (in that order). Donatello became one of the greatest sculptors of all time. Brunelleschi forsook sculpture for the practice of architecture. His greatest work was the dome of Florence Cathedral though this has little to do with the Renaissance, being more the product of a

S. Lorenzo, Florence, Italy, 1421–60, designed by Filippo Brunelleschi and completed after his death in 1446 by A. Manetti. It adopts the traditional basilican form, and uses the Latin cross extended with side chapels and further chapels in the apse. The crossing is topped by a dome on pendentives. The airy and controlled feeling of the interior expresses the aims of Renaissance architects.

powerful, ingenious and practical intellect devoted to the solution of an apparently insoluble structural problem. It may indeed be regarded as the final achievement of Gothic architecture in Italy. But in smaller works for the Church and for the nobility, Brunelleschi produced the first true Renaissance architecture.

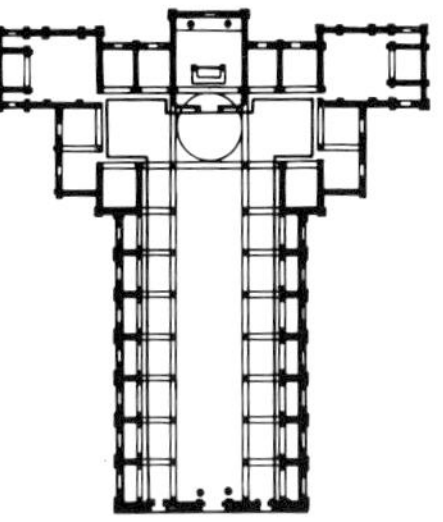

Brunelleschi relied partly on memories and measured drawings of buildings in Rome, but also on Romanesque buildings nearer home, which he almost certainly thought were Roman originals. This fortunate mistake brought a vivacity and tenderness into his version of Classical architecture which was not entirely lost even by his more academic successors.

The major intellectual phenomenon of fifteenth-century architecture was another Florentine, an aristocrat brought up in exile in northern Italy. He undertook the enormous task of extrapolating from *De Architectura*, by Vitruvius, whom he considered a semi-literate workman, to discover the true principles of Classical architecture as expounded by the Greeks. He was called Leon Battista Alberti (1404–72) and his book, *De Re Aedificatoria (Concerning Architecture)* is the first modern statement of architectural theory. It has affected almost all architectural thinking to the present day. Palladio popularised it and Le Corbusier adapted it to suit his own ideas about the nature of modern architecture.

Alberti was a scholar who had the advantage over most of his kind in being also a practising artist. Serious students of architecture, amateur or professional, should see the Palazzo Rucellai in Florence, S. Andrea at Mantua, and the façade of S. Francesco at Rimini, in which Alberti created the academic prototype for Renaissance architecture in Europe and America. This is not to say that he was a great architect like Sinan, Michelangelo, François Mansart, or Sir Christopher Wren,

Above and opposite above Renaissance architects saw a proportional relationship between architectural forms, such as the Ionic column or ideal church plan, and the human figure. Francesco di Giorgio, c. 1482.

Below The unfinished façade of S. Francesco, Rimini, Italy (1446–50). Alberti remodelled this medieval church in a style based closely on Roman models.

but he did define the intellectual foundations upon which Renaissance architecture was to be built.

Contemporary with Alberti was Francesco di Giorgio who worked with Piero della Francesca at Urbino. Like Brunelleschi he interpreted and developed Classical and Romanesque architecture. Thus we can see two separate ways in which Renaissance architecture was being designed in the fifteenth century: the one according to rules derived from the ancients and supposed to be consistent with the order of nature as made by God and therefore immutable. The other may be called evolutionary, though that word did not exist at that time in its present meaning. The evolutionary way, deriving from Brunelleschi and the medieval tradition, referred back to the ancients but allowed for creative artistic innovation. It is this which makes Renaissance architecture one of the great styles, distinct from Classical, and not a sub-style like those which followed it.

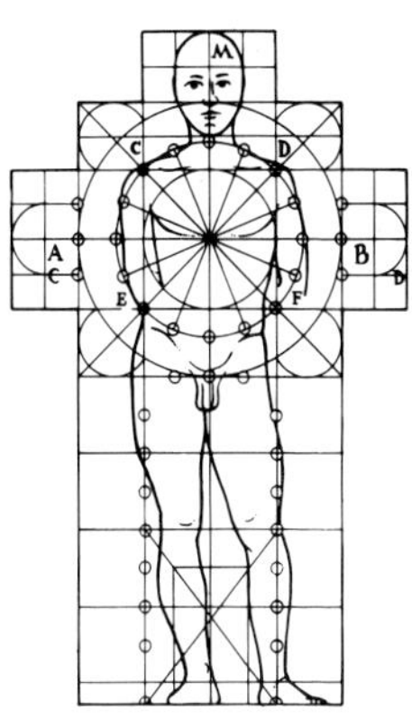

Below Pythagorean musical theory illustrated by F. Gafurio, 1492. The relation between dimensions and musical harmonies discovered by Pythagoras was thought to indicate proper proportions for architecture.

Left Palazzo Rucellai, Florence, 1446–51, by Alberti. The first 'stylar' building of the Renaissance, with a façade of superimposed Orders of architecture; this use of a different Order for each floor of the building reflects the design of the Colosseum.

Donato Bramante (1444–1514) came from Urbino and began his architectural practice in Milan, in a free Renaissance manner derived from the medieval architecture of Lombardy; but in 1499 he moved to Rome where opportunity abounded. In Rome he followed the old maxim and designed in the Roman style, his epoch-making building being the little round temple in the courtyard of the Franciscan monastery of San Pietro (1502) on the supposed site of St Peter's martyrdom. This is a very sensitive and un-Roman design, though it did conform to the most important principles laid down by Alberti, and it established an admirable precedent for the development of Renaissance architecture in Rome. It also established Bramante's reputation and in 1506, following the deliberate demolition of the superb Romanesque basilica of St Peter on the orders of Pope Julius II, Bramante began to build the present St Peter's (p. 190) to an ideal centralised plan (round or within a circle). Ideal it was and totally unpractical for the liturgy of the Catholic Church. It was modified by his successors including Michelangelo and finished with the present Baroque façade by Carlo Maderna in 1612. Raphael, who was Bramante's nephew, Antonio da Sangallo, and Peruzzi, all worked in Bramante's office and, as Sir John Summerson has said, Bramante's importance lies in 'his exposition of the essential logic of Roman architecture as the basis for a new classicism adaptable to the needs and spirit of his age'. He can be seen as a prototype of the successful modern architect who gives opportunities to talented young men in his office. Bramante certainly had some of the most brilliant assistants in all history.

What is called the High Renaissance style prospered in the first quarter of the sixteenth century. Despite its enormous influence and prestige there are very few buildings which exemplify it, even though it embodied the ideals upon which European Classicism was to be founded.

Right Detail of the Basilica at Vicenza, Italy, begun in 1549 by Palladio who invented this combination of Classical columns and arches to reface a medieval building with wide structural bays.

Right The Loggia del Capitano, Vicenza, 1571, by Palladio.

Below The Tempietto, Rome, begun in 1502 by Bramante.

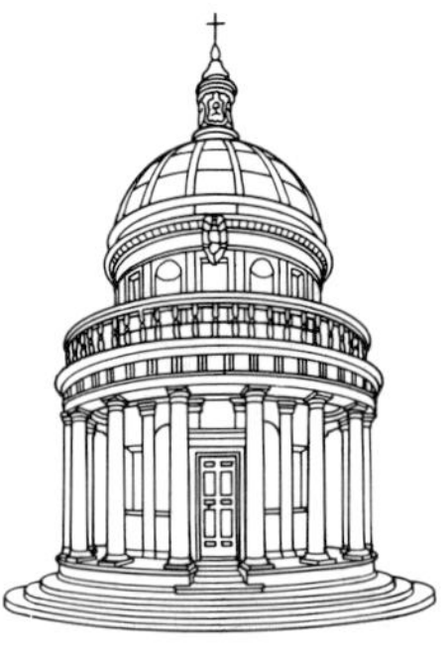

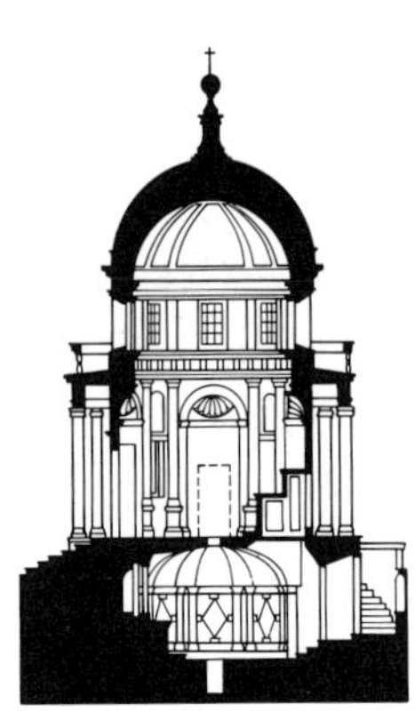

The great theorist of the sixteenth century, Andrea Palladio (1508–80) formulated and exemplified Alberti's rules in an illustrated book which was to become an architectural 'bible' in Britain. But while recommending the rules as a way of guiding less talented people than himself. Palladio roundly stated that, as a great artist, he himself would override the rules when his own inspiration justified breaking them. Thus, in Palladio's own work the two attitudes – immutable rules and stylistic evolution – were fused.

The sixteenth century was a tumultuous and tremendously creative period throughout Europe. It was a very uneasy age, not only torn by wars and the Reformation, but with its assumptions challenged by humanism, the emergence of science, the discovery of America (1492), an explosion of international trade, banking, notes of credit, and capitalism. Feudalism had declined with the growth of mercenary armies, and the ideal of service gave way to the pursuit of advantage.

The greatness of an age depends largely upon its capacity to recognise, admire and encourage the outstanding talent which is probably always latent in any community but seldom allowed to flourish. The splendour of the Renaissance in Italy certainly does not derive from political institutions, which on the whole were appalling, nor from any sort of social justice of the kind which we now espouse, but from a consensus of belief in excellence, whether of birth or breeding, of inspiration or skill or of practical success. It is often called the age of humanism but it is necessary to remember that, as far as we can tell, all the great artists of the Renaissance combined with their interest in humanity a belief in God. Italian humanism was the very opposite of atheism in that, especially in the writing of Alberti and the poetry of Michelangelo, there was a reconciliation of the pagan gods with Christianity. One could respect what Apollo stood for and still be a Christian. This was an essential fact of Renaissance art.

Patronage came mainly from the Church and the nobility. The Church in Italy generally followed the precept of Pope Pius II (Piccolomini r. 1458–64) who is reported as saying, 'It is indispensable nowadays for the Roman pontiff to be rich. Splendour and wealth are important for one who commands'. Challenged by the Reformation after 1517 the Catholic Church responded with ever more glorious architecture and became the principal patron of the Baroque manner in the late sixteenth and the seventeenth century.

Palazzo Strozzi, Florence, 1489–1539, designed by Benedetto da Maiano and completed by Cronaca. Its fortress-like rusticated exterior is topped with a huge cornice proportionate to the whole height of the building. Inside is a Classical arcaded *cortile* or courtyard and balconies, onto which the rooms open. The principal rooms are on the first floor, the *piano nobile*.

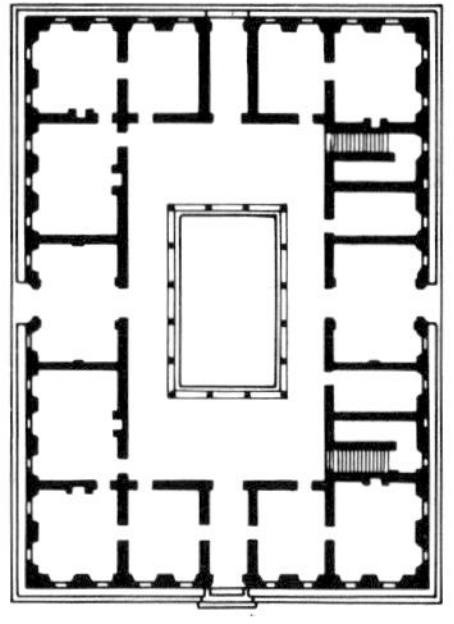

Aristocratic patronage included large contributions to church building and decoration but mainly took the form of palaces built in cities. These sought to show the owners' awareness of fashionable trends in the arts but security required almost windowless ground floors, with strong grilles on the narrow slits which lit the servants' quarters. The main accommodation, the *piano nobile*, was on the first floor but still with somewhat reticent windows in the outside walls. Most *palazzi* had a courtyard (*cortile*) with open colonnades or arcades on all floors to give access to the rooms. Bedrooms were on the second floor and sometimes included suites for junior members of the family. The top floor, under the rafters, was sleeping accommodation for servants and guards. Where possible, there was a garden beyond the *cortile*, a plan that echoed the typical town house of wealthy, ancient Roman families as well as the street-farmhouses which are characteristic of the Italian folk tradition (p. 71). The Italian *palazzo* was and still is a family home.

Italians quickly tired of 'correct' design and their ebullient spirit first broke the rules 'for kicks' in a style which has recently come to be called Mannerist. To appreciate this architecture fully you need to know the rules, and participate in the fun of defying them. One of the most amusing examples is the Palazzo del Tè at Mantua.

Having broken the rules Italian architects, encouraged by papal policy during the Counter-Reformation, passed joyously to the Baroque which until recently has been thought to be decadent. In a purely academic sense it was, but it was also an ideal style to provide scenery for the courtly ceremony and military pomp of the seventeenth century.

It is, however, a mistake to think that Baroque was wanton and undisciplined. On the contrary, Baroque architects delighted in complex geometry in domes, ellipses, and a counterpoint of curves which matched the musical style of the time. The best Baroque buildings are as intellectually complex as the

The Palazzo del Tè, Mantua, Italy, 1525–35, by Giulio Romano. This Tea House, originally in an extensive pleasure garden, is a humorous architectural folly, deliberately disregarding the rules of Classical architecture. See also p. 26, and the palace of Echternach, p. 305.

fugues of J. S. Bach, and the organs which were designed for churches in the Baroque period set a standard for these instruments which is again being recovered after a period of decadence in the nineteenth century. Music and architecture meet in such great Baroque organs as that at St Bavo, Haarlem, in Holland (p. 304). Music, resounding through the enclosed space of a church, was part of the overall conception, just as plainsong and coloured light had been in Gothic architecture.

'The Renaissance', like all births, happened at a time and place. The place was Italy but the confinement, so to speak, took a long time. In architecture it may have begun in 1400 with the competition for the Baptistery doors at Florence, which Brunelleschi failed to win and so set off for Rome to study ancient buildings. It was complete at the death of Bramante in 1514; but Renaissance architecture did not reach Britain until the mid-sixteenth century and then in a very crude form. Not until Inigo Jones (p. 277) began to build a Palladian villa at Greenwich in 1615 did truly Classical architecture come to Britain, by which time it was out of date in Italy. In England the Palladian style flourished until after the middle of the eighteenth century. It was 'Renaissance' architecture but long after the Renaissance.

Renaissance architecture spread quite slowly from Italy to other countries yet other aspects of Renaissance culture flourished generally much earlier.

The gateway of the Château of Anet, France, built in c. 1552 by Philibert de l'Orme, writer of the first free-thinking theory of architecture (*L'Architecture*, 1567). De L'Orme broke the rules of Classicism with serious intent to achieve progress in French architecture and to create a national and rational style. To a large extent he succeeded but he received scant recognition from later academic architects and the public.

The concept of 'the culture of the Renaissance in Italy' dates from the nineteenth century and comes from a book with that title by Jacob Burckhardt published in 1860. It is arguable that the efflorescence of achievement in the visual arts in Italy owes much to the fact that northern Italy was the first country to develop a money economy by financing other people's wars; that it had the most complex genetic mix in Europe; that it had an age-old tradition of sensuality; that it became the religious capital of Western Europe in the fifteenth century; that it was divided into many city states, from papal to republican; and that it had an invaluable system of training craftsmen by apprenticeship to a master who commonly combined artistic talent with business acumen but worked within a guild system which, unlike modern trade unions, guarded standards of quality. Call it culture if you like, but it was rooted in practicalities, and above all in giving good value for money to the Church and the wealthy patrons who valued and respected craftsmanship and excellence of performance. Almost anywhere could have a Renaissance if it wanted it.

The Palace of the Emperor Charles V at Granada, Spain; built 1527–68, thus begun in the year in which Charles's troops sacked Rome. This shocking event marked the end of the High Renaissance faith in an orderly rational world. This palace was intended to be a Spanish version of pure Classicism, but, though fairly correct in detail, it shows the restlessness which overtook European culture in the 16th century.

What was achieved in Italy set a standard which is still valid. The architecture of all western countries stems to a great extent from the Italian achievement in the fifteenth and sixteenth centuries.

The other side of the coin was a ruthlessly élitist society which gave no quarter to its enemies and was committed to the survival of the fittest modified by a Christian obligation of charity to the weak, as in the parable of The Good Samaritan, and elimination of the wrong-doer, as in the parable of The Sower.

The physical characteristics of Renaissance architecture are simply stated. Greek architecture was ignored and virtually unknown. Renaissance architecture used the elements of Roman architecture in a modern context and, as the context changed, so the interpretation of Classical precedent developed. The Orders of architecture remained fundamental to all architectural design.

In each of the countries to which Renaissance architecture spread it was re-interpreted under the influence of established traditions even when, as in France, it was introduced and practised by Italian architects. The purest Italian style was developed in Britain in the eighteenth century.

Wollaton Hall, Nottingham, England, 1580–88, designed by Robert Smithson (c. 1536–1614), the architectural counterpart of Shakespeare and the greatest architect of the Elizabethan age. Like Shakespeare he had a sense of history, a smattering of Classical knowledge, a feeling for composition and a dynamic confidence in England and English ways.

Styles Derived from the Great Styles

Baroque

Baroque was a development of Renaissance architecture. It served a changing way of life and less austere taste, flourishing most in the faithfully Catholic countries – Italy, Spain, Austria – but appealing less to the religiously divided French and hardly at all in Protestant England, though the term English Baroque is used by art historians in order to misfit such architects as Wren into a European category.

Baroque architecture is vigorous, curvilinear, three-dimensional and deliberately grand. It incorporates painting, sculpture and all arts and crafts of decoration as part of its own nature.

Vierzehnheiligen Church, in southern Germany, built by Balthasar Neumann in 1744–72, creates a dynamic and ambiguous internal space through a chain of overlapping ovals separated by three-dimensional transverse arches. Its rich and dramatic decoration complements the plan, to express the Counter-Reformation notion that the Church should echo, in Baroque design, the power and magnificence of God over against the austerity of Protestantism.

Rococo

Rococo is a refinement of Baroque and flourished especially in France under the feminine influence of *salon* society during the 'Age of Reason'. The fashion for elegance pervaded most of Europe and a widening awareness of the rest of the world is reflected. Chinese, Indian and other exotic styles were interpreted in terms of fashionable sensibility. In England especially, growing awareness of the Gothic achievement encouraged so-called *Gothick* as a Rococo style.

Rococo art is sensitive, elegant and made with exquisite craftsmanship. It was the art of a society which generated the ideas from which revolutions came – to destroy it; but to say that these revolutions were reactions against Rococo and the society it represented is simplistic and misleading. The sensitivity and curiosity led to new ideas about the way people should live, and how society should be arranged to reduce poverty and human suffering. They are reflected in sensitivity to beauty in architecture and decoration.

The Cupola Room, Heaton Hall, Manchester, England, built in 1772 by James Wyatt with Rococo decoration by Biagio Rebecca. Rococo designers used many styles – Oriental, Etruscan, Gothic and others – but always with delicacy. Modelling was in low relief and painted decoration was common. Generally Rococo was somewhat cheaper than Baroque.

Classical Revival (Neo-Classicism)
In the reign of Louis XIII (r. 1610–43) the French minister Colbert established academic institutions for the study and practice of the arts. The magnificence of the court of Louis XIV (r. 1643–1715) gave abundant opportunity to artists and craftsmen, provided that they had gone through the hoops prescribed by the authorities. The establishment of academies almost inevitably led to a reappraisal of Renaissance ideas. The Italians, it seemed, had failed to understand the true principles of Classical architecture and French academicians made this good by reference to Greek as well as Roman sources. A new purity of style became obligatory and both Baroque and Rococo were rejected, though they survived and flourished in interior decoration. The aim of Neo-Classicism was to purify the Renaissance tradition and in Britain and Germany this led architects, and still more their patrons, to turn to Greek architecture and encourage the idea that Roman architecture was only the decadent form of Greek. The struggle of Greece for liberation from the Turks in the early nineteenth century, and Lord Byron's part in that struggle, boosted a version of Neo-Classicism which was based entirely upon Greek architecture.

The Panthéon, Paris, built 1755–92 by J. G. Soufflot, and originally known as the church of St Geneviève. Its plan is a Greek cross and represents a return to the theory of the High Renaissance, recalling Bramante's plan for St Peter's, Rome, and S. Maria della Consolazione, Todi (p. 188). The Panthéon is representative of academic Neo-Classical architecture, and the desire of scholars to restore what they believed to be the purity of ancient Classical design.

Eclectic Architecture
Eclecticism is the practice of choosing elements from various systems of thought in the formation of an acceptable doctrine. It has been used mainly in the study of philosophy but is equally applicable to architecture. In the eighteenth and nineteenth centuries the expansion of global trade brought western people into contact with older civilisations which had architectural systems quite independent of the Classical and Gothic traditions of Europe. It was natural that expanding awareness of other cultures should be reflected in architecture. Eclecticism became a fact rather than a doctrine, and in Britain, especially, a synthesis of world styles of architecture was acceptable.

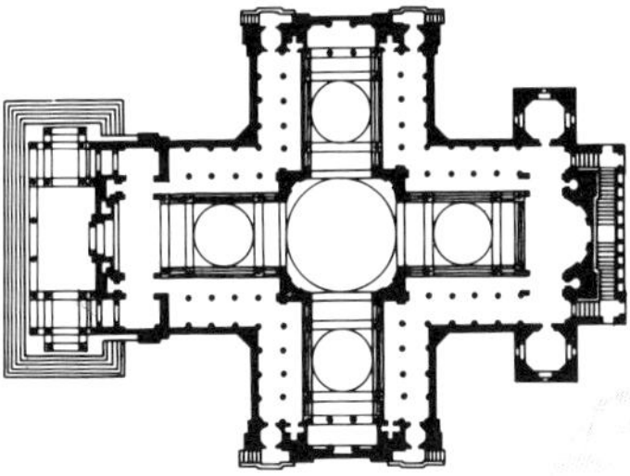

Victorian Eclectic architecture was not just the revival of one architectural system but a synthesis and re-interpretation of world architecture. It could put an Italian Romanesque bank alongside a Venetian Gothic insurance office with perfect confidence and an admirable sense of harmony in scale.

It was in the important quality of scale that Eclecticism produced the most widespread influence on European architecture, with a mixture of elements from early Florentine, Venetian Gothic and Renaissance or Romanesque arcading and an oriental overallness of pattern which became characteristic of street architecture from Italy to Scandinavia.

In monumental architecture Eclecticism produced a fusion of styles which was often the result of careful historical study, especially at the *École des Beaux Arts* in Paris where Eclecticism became the basis of a new Grand Manner. Paris, with its established academic system, became the main centre of architectural education and development, attracting students, many of them already experienced architects, from many different countries.

The Grand Manner should not be confused with Baroque and the name Edwardian Baroque is based upon a misunderstanding both of Eclectic and Baroque architecture. In London, three examples of the Eclectic Grand Manner are The Central Hall, Westminster, the Victoria and Albert Museum and the Ritz Hotel. In Paris, three outstanding examples are The Opéra, St Augustin and the Basilica of le Sacré Coeur on Montmartre.

In the social and cultural climate of the late nineteenth century it was possible to see this Eclectic architecture as the natural consummation of all human achievement in the art of architecture. Perhaps it was.

Eclecticism provided training and employment for an immense number of artisan craftsmen who enjoyed a high degree of job satisfaction but were not well paid. It could not have existed without them.

Cardiff City Hall; 1897–1902, by Lanchester and Rickards. It is typical of the Romantic splendour with which 20th-century architecture began. Mainly Classical in detail, it owes much to *Beaux-Arts* influence.

The Basilica of the Sacré-Coeur, Paris, built 1875–1919 as an act of national expiation, and designed by Paul Abadie. Though dramatically exploiting its hill-top site, it is a scholarly Eclectic design in the Hellenesque tradition, reminiscent of St Front, Périgueux, which he remodelled (p. 111).

Gothic Revival

This was mainly an English contribution to the development of European architecture. In England the Gothic style had never died out and is represented in the work of Wren and Hawksmoor, in the seventeenth and eighteenth centuries, as a somewhat crude survival of the great tradition. It also persisted in domestic building, especially in stone districts such as the Pennine valleys and the Cotswolds. But the Revival was something new; not a continuation of medieval architecture but a re-birth (like the Renaissance) in which Gothic became an alternative style to Classical. The word 'style' suddenly came into discussion and criticism of architecture and opened a long period of historicism in design. Historical study became necessary for the practising architect as a basis for designing in historical styles, especially Gothic.

The Gothic Revival began in the mid-eighteenth century as a charming version of Rococo (p. 143) and was more used in decoration than in structure. It was an aspect of what has been called the Romantic Movement but it also had ethical and religious motivation. Gothic was considered to be a Christian style, as opposed to Classical which was pagan in origin. From the early eighteenth century until well into the twentieth the Gothic style was almost obligatory for the enormous number of churches which were built in growing industrial towns. In the 1860s new churches were being consecrated at the rate of one-a-week in England.

Strawberry Hill, Twickenham, England, built by Horace Walpole from 1747 to 1763 in Rococo style, and extended by Lady Waldegrave in 1862 in a severe Victorian manner. It thus demonstrates both forms of the Gothic Revival within a single building; it is possible to walk through a doorway from the Gothick style of the mid-18th century to the carefully-studied Gothic of a century later.

An important aspect of the Gothic Revival was a growing recognition of the real values of medieval art and civilisation; this led to the Pre-Raphaelite movement in painting and to the Arts and Crafts movement.

For sheer quality of design, rooted in medieval tradition but, like Brunelleschi's work in Florence, full of vitality and originality, English Victorian churches are an outstanding contribution to the sum of fine architecture. This heritage is at risk because of population movements and regroupings, the collapse of the old social hierarchy of responsibility for churches, and the decline of religious commitment in the conurbations.

The University Museum, Oxford, England, 1855–59, by Benjamin Woodward under the influence of John Ruskin. Gothic architecture was here re-interpreted in the new building material, iron, combined with stone used in a conventional manner though it has a Venetian flavour.

Arts and Crafts

The Arts and Crafts Movement grew around William Morris (1834–96) in England but it was really part of a much wider questioning of historicism and a search for new art forms through a more direct response to and better observation of nature and mankind. It happened to coincide with the growth of socialism and the doctrine of evolution. We have noticed (p. 146) that Eclecticism could be seen as a consummation of achievement: but it was also seen as a triumph of complacency.

Arts and Crafts people decried the debasement of the craftsman to artisan status, executing designs from the architects' drawing board. They abhorred the replication of ornament by machines and industrial processes. Recognising the part medieval and Renaissance craftsmen had played as creative artists, they advocated an architecture based upon craft techniques and the participation of the craftsman in all aspects of decoration.

Though not committed to the Gothic style, Arts and Crafts was a logical development from the Gothic Revival, seeking to get to the aesthetic and religious principles of Gothic architecture rather than the appearances.

The Pastures, North Luffenham, England, built in 1901 by C. F. A. Voysey, one of the leading members of the Art Workers Guild. The emphasis on craftsmanship, on the sensitive adaptation of English folk styles and the search for domestic informality made this style very influential within England.

Art Nouveau

Art Nouveau and Jugendstil were part of another widespread movement which took different forms in various places, notably Vienna, Brussels, Glasgow and Barcelona. Its manifestations in these places have in common a seeking after new proportions, new forms, and decorative motifs without historical connotations. In straining for newness Art Nouveau artists resorted to distortion and exaggeration, especially in portraying the human figure, and there is an element of sickness in the work of many of them. The extension of Arts and Crafts ideas throughout Europe supported Art Nouveau and it is frequently hard to draw a clear line between the two movements.

Art Nouveau is identifiable by its exaggerated linear qualities, distortion of natural proportion and a weird quality of sinister sensuality. A great deal of architecture built throughout Europe between about 1900 and 1914 shows Art Nouveau influence. Art Nouveau recognised the importance of decoration and was more concerned with decoration than with structure, and often made its buildings highly colourful.

The Casa Milà, Barcelona, Spain, 1905–10, by Antoni Gaudí. It is built of stone sculpted in depth – as was the Parthenon (p. 101) in a very different idiom.

Modernism

Modernism rested upon the questionable belief that because 'architecture is the mirror of society' modern architecture should reflect mass-production technology and materialism backed by positivist philosophies which eliminated value judgments. Perversely, Modernism was propagated with puritanical fervour which, like the puritanism of the seventeenth century, rejected all decoration and imagery as evil. The doctrine of pure functionalism – 'useful therefore beautiful' – quickly collapsed because of its manifest absurdity, but materialism, underpinned by Marxism, led to the propagation of an architecture which was purely utilitarian in being designed to satisfy only the physical needs of people. This was one strand in the development of the Modern Movement.

The other strand came from the Renaissance. Modern humanists recognised the abstract qualities in Renaissance art. Painting and sculpture went through a non-figurative stage in which the forms were supposed to have meaning in themselves. In terms of architecture this was interpreted in two ways: either to base 'design' upon structural and functional forms or to turn architecture into large-scale abstract compositions.

Modernism produced more ugly buildings than ever before in architectural history and the basic reason for this is quite simple. There was no concern for beauty and very little for the real needs of people. It takes its place among the totalitarian movements of our age.

In some respects the Modern Movement was beneficial. Although it purported to be a new universal architecture for a new age it now has to be seen as a sub-style derived mainly by reaction against previous styles.

But it must in fairness be said that Modernism has explored new ways of building more than any other movement since Romanesque. It has greatly enlarged the architect's pallet (p. 26) but still has to discover how to create architecture with it.

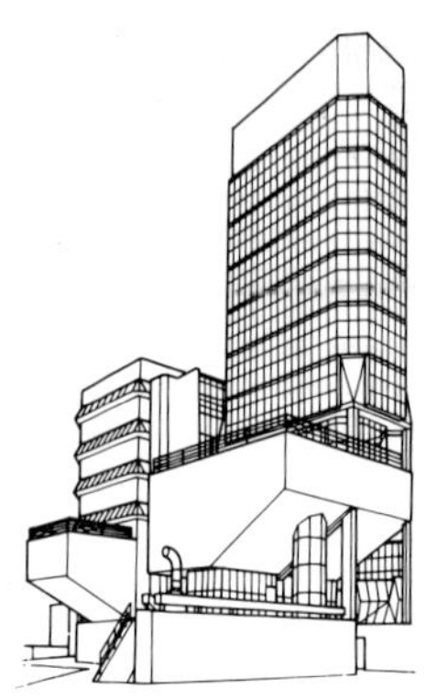

The Engineering Department, Leicester University, England, built by J. Stirling and J. Gowan; 1963. Its complex shapes directly reflect use as form is made to follow function faithfully, according to ideals first proposed in the mid-19th century.

The Swiss Pavilion, Cité Universitaire, Paris: a students' hostel designed by Le Corbusier. Its abstract sculptural qualities aroused great interest and it was much imitated, although the accommodation provided for the students was not entirely satisfactory, the main problem being overheating in summer because of the large south-facing windows.

Regional Styles

The great styles – Classical, Hellenesque, Romanesque – have been interpreted differently in various places. The least variation occurred in the Classical style within the Roman Empire but, even so, there is a great difference between the architecture of a *praetorium* on Hadrian's Wall (across northern England) and the Palatine Hill in Rome.

The great styles vary considerably from country to country but conform to the same principles and have the same characteristics. For example, Hellenesque architecture in Sicily is recognisably the same style as it is in Ravenna, Aachen, Venice or Padua. Gothic architecture in northern France, England, West Germany, parts of Italy and Spain is consistent but in some whole countries, and in regions within otherwise consistent countries, there are variations which merit, by their differences and their special qualities, the name of regional style. For example, in the Yorkshire area of England there are major examples of the Gothic and Renaissance styles (York Minster, Castle Howard) yet in the Pennine dales formed by rivers which are tributaries of the River Ouse, there is a vigorous and beautiful style of stone architecture derived from late Gothic. There is also a regional version of Georgian domestic architecture. Again, in Brittany, which is particularly interesting for its Celtic folk architecture, there is a regional (the Bretons might call it national) style of Gothic architecture and an overflow, so to speak, of hard-wood framed architecture into such places as Rennes and Dinant.

Sometimes a regional style existed for only a short period, but it may still be very important and interesting, as for example in the Anglo-Saxon churches of ancient Northumbria which for a couple of centuries (635–876) was one of the most important cultural centres in Europe. Likewise, the Moorish conquest of southern Spain and the creation, in the eighth century, of Córdoba as a city second only to Constantinople in the western world, established the Islamic version of Hellenesque architecture which flourished until the fifteenth century. Echoes of Spanish Muslim architecture are to be seen as far away as Auvergne in France (Le Puy) and Fountains Abbey in England.

Regional styles differ from folk architecture in that they are employed for larger buildings and designed and built by experts – architects and contractors. The line between folk and regional style is not always clear but although regional styles may appear to be developed from folk architecture they are generally a version of arcane architecture modified by strong local traditions. The manor house, *schloss* or *château* is seldom folk architecture and usually exemplifies a local standard of arcane design.

Below Mediterranean-style houses in Carros, France.

Right Bridge House, Warkworth, Northumberland, England; a regional version of 18th-century Georgian architecture adapted to the local climate and to the available stone.

Below Houses and shops in Colmar, eastern France – a blend of arched construction and plain stuccoed walls with timber-framed superstructures.

Part Three

Greece and the Aegean

We think of Greece, and especially of Athens, as the cradle of Western civilisation in which Classical standards of architecture were discovered; but in fact the Aegean islands, particularly Crete and Thera (Santorini), the coasts of Asia Minor (Turkey) and the Peloponnese were important locations before Athens. After a volcanic eruption of Thera in about 1500 BC which signalled the end of the Minoan Empire, power passed to the mainland Greeks. Mycenae (p. 100) then became the leading city-state, conducting a trade war against Troy which controlled the entrance to the Black Sea. At Mycenae one may see the so-called Treasury of Atreus which may have been the tomb of the legendary hero, Perseus.

To appreciate the original evolution of Classical architecture the ideal sequence of site visits is as follows: Knossos; Mycenae and Tiryns; Olympia for the earliest evidence of the Doric Order in the Temple of Hera; Athens for the consummation of Doric and Ionic Orders, and the beginning and fulfilment of the Corinthian Order in the Lysicrates Monument (p. 102) and the Temple of Zeus. The best Hellenistic sites in Greece are the health centre of Epidauros, with its magnificent theatre, and the Island of Delos which became, under Roman rule, the principal emporium for slaves from Asia. The outstanding architectural relic of Delos is the megalithic shrine of Apollo.

Above The megalithic temple at Delos, the supposed birthplace of Apollo.

Below The entrance to the 'Treasury of Atreus', Mycenae, c. 1325 BC. One of the columns which once flanked the doors is now in the British Museum. See also pp 100, 103.

Above The main staircase of the royal apartments at Knossos, Crete; before 1500 BC. Knossos is the most remarkable example of multi-level planning in ancient architecture.

Left The temple of Hera at Olympia; from c. 590 BC. The wooden columns of the original temple were successively replaced by stone Doric columns. Their design varies with the date of replacement, thus serving as a history of the evolution of the whole Doric Order.

After the conquests of Alexander and the establishment of the Hellenistic successor states, Greece itself slipped into the background of architectural history but the Greeks played an important role in the development of Roman and Hellenesque architecture.

The domical way of building, seen in Mycenaean tombs, permeated the folk architecture of many of the Greek islands as well as mainland Greece and although, as a general rule, arcane architecture has not sprung from folk architecture the amazing eflorescence of domical architecture in Constantinople after AD 330 (pp. 103–5) seems to be an exception to this. Out of arcane Mycenaean tombs came a folk architecture which, though it was not adopted by the in-coming, so-called Dorian peoples, surfaced after fifteen centuries at the folk level. Here it served as the structural basis of one of the great arcane styles, Hellenesque, which flourished in Greece until the country was conquered by the Turks in the mid-15th century.

Since Greece was liberated in 1832 its architecture has followed European fashions, but the old inspiration is not dead. The new science of Ekistics, which is interpreted in many countries as concern for the quality of the environment and the rights of other species to live along with humankind without persecution, has roots in Athens. Ekistics is the study and implementation of how people can live best in communities.

Below The Propylaea to the Acropolis, Athens; 437–432 BC. Literally the 'structure before the gates', the Propylaea serves a function similar to a barbican; while its use of both Doric and Ionic columns to solve the problems of the sloping site is masterly. The temple of Nike Apteros (427 BC) is visible on the right (see also p. 49).

Below right The Hellenesque monastery of Nea Moni, on the island of Chios; mid-11th century. The modest size and use of a dome placed on squinches is typical of this style; the interior is covered in mosaics.

Above The Temple of Zeus, Athens; c. 170 BC – c. AD 130. It is a fine example of Hellenistic architecture in the Corinthian Order.

Below The monastery church at Daphni, near Athens; 11th century. Having a larger dome than most Greek churches, it is a gem of Hellenesque architecture, and has Gothic cloisters built by Cistercians after it was vandalised by the Fourth Crusade in 1205.

Turkey in Europe

The Hellenesque style has deep roots in Greece and the Middle East but its first flowering came in Constantinople (now Istanbul) after AD 330 when the new capital of the Roman Empire was established. Freed from the constraints of the Roman style of Classical architecture, Greek architects in Constantinople and throughout the Middle East began to develop a 'contemporary' architecture based upon the use of the corbel dome. This became the official architecture of the Orthodox Church but also spread into lands adhering to the Catholic Church.

The greatest of all Hellenesque buildings is the Church of the Holy Wisdom, Hagia Sophia, in Istanbul. It became a mosque and is now secularised as a museum but it is still manifestly a religious building. Churches in Istanbul are noted for mosaics, which were the most favoured form of decoration.

The Turks conquered Constantinople in 1453 after it had been fatally weakened and sacked by Crusaders in 1204. As a bridgehead and base on the European side of the Bosphorus, the Turks built the *Rumeli Hissar,* a very splendid castle.

When Suleiman the Great consolidated and extended Turkish power in Europe his chief architect, Sinan (1489–1588), built the Mosque of Suleiman, which is modelled upon Hagia Sophia but shows an understanding of the forces in a building similar to that which made Gothic cathedrals possible. This is one of the most beautiful as well as one of the most intellectual buildings in the world. It is not in the Classical style, but, more than most Classical-style buildings, it exemplifies the ideas of Classicism and in its proportions and quality it is a direct descendant of the Parthenon.

Below The Rumeli Hissar (castle) on the Bosphorus, built by the Ottoman Turks in 1453.

Above The mainly 6th-century church of S. Irene, Constantinople, built in the Hellenesque style that was to be taken over by the Turks 1000 years later.

Below The 4th-century Byzantine 'Golden Gate' to Constantinople, now bricked up.

Above The Blue Mosque or Mosque of Sultan Ahmet IV, built 1609–17 by Sedefkar Mehmet Aga. Its name derives from the predominantly blue tiles that cover it internally. It is built over the palace of Justinian (r. 527–65). It may be interesting that the year after the Blue Mosque was completed saw the introduction of Roman-style Classical architecture into Britain by Inigo Jones; p. 276.

Of the many mosques in Istanbul which derive from the Mosque of Suleiman, the most conspicuous is the so-called Blue Mosque which is also a very beautiful building.

The Palace of the Sultans has romantic overtones and a history of cruelty and intrigue which distract the visitor from the quality of its architecture. An interesting feature of the state rooms is the way conical brick domes were used to provide, by convection, an air-conditioned environment. This is unique in Europe though common across the Bosphorus in Asia.

Decadent Sultans, tyrannised by the dominant women of the Harem and loaded with uncomfortable jewellery, did at least have cool, clean air to breathe, which the modern visitor to Istanbul (or anywhere else) may not find in a modern hotel.

ng into the gia Sophia, 2–37. The endentives, upper aisles and the forty windows in the drum of the dome are visible. The Islamic medallions were added at a later date, when many mosaics were covered over. See also p. 105.

Left and below S. Saviour in the Chora (Kariye Mosque), Istanbul; built in the 11th century and substantially modified 1303–26, in the renaissance of Hellenesque design that followed the collapse of the Latin Empire of Constantinople (1204–61). The interior is notable for its fine mosaics.

Above The Mosque of Suleiman (1551–58). Though built by Sinan the Great for an Ottoman sultan, it can be seen as the supreme achievement of the Hellenesque tradition. Unlike its prototype, Hagia Sophia, it is not a compromise between a basilican and a centralised plan. The essential difference is that the huge dome is buttressed diagonally to the main dome by secondary domes. It is surrounded by a complex of monastic buildings.

Right The interior of the Blue Mosque. Built in mature Ottoman style, the combination of colour, proportion and abstract decoration creates a vast outward-looking prayer-hall, essentially different from the contemporary Christian (Baroque) building, which tried instead to contain heaven on earth.

Italy

To understand the architectural history of Italy one must realise that, since about the time of Julius Caesar, the country has in a sense been turned upside down. Socially, economically and culturally the south was then pre-eminent. Now it is the north.

Along the southern shore, in Sicily and on the west coast at Paestum and Naples there were prosperous Greek cities. Paestum rivals Athens for the splendour of its Doric temples (p. 27). Though not built with the refinements possible in marble they have a rugged strength which is perhaps more representative of the character of the ancient Greeks than the Parthenon (p. 101) which is unique in its sophistication.

The state of Rome was culturally set between the Greek colonies of the south and the Etruscans who had settled in what is still called Tuscany and in the Po valley.

Ancient Rome was a city-state. It extended the concept of citizenship into the territories it conquered, from the Levant to Spain and the Sahara to Scotland. It was fundamentally an urban society based upon military service and an aristocracy who qualified by public service and derived their wealth from the holding of land. Poets idealised military duty and rural simplicity – combining rugged vitality with an idyllic way of life based upon slave labour.

The consequent high value of cultivable land tended to keep cities compact. Until recent times even Rome relied upon gardens, orchards and farms in the immediate vicinity. Corn (in bread and pasta) vegetables (especially in *minestrone*) olive oil, salads, wine and cheese have been staple items in the Italian diet since Roman times, with economical use of meat in a great variety of sausages.

Population growth and the increasing redundancy of the free poor led to squalid congestion in urban slums which has persisted into modern times. The growing need for defence, from the fourth century AD onwards, led to town walls; these gave a military as well as an economic reason for preserving an agricultural system which could be worked from inside the towns.

From the fall of the Western Empire in AD 476 until the unification of Italy in 1860–70 the political history of the peninsula is exceedingly complex and impossible to describe here but the basic pattern needs to be understood.

The great age of Roman architecture was from about 27 BC to AD 330 when Constantinople became the new capital of the Roman empire. Rome itself, sacked by barbarians and deprived of economic and political importance, languished until the fifteenth century.

With the fall of the Roman Empire Gothic and Lombard adventurers took over the countryside and gradually replaced the old villas with castles which they could defend against their neighbours; but the cities, which were sometimes republican, sometimes under a count or duke and sometimes led by a bishop, increased in power and defended themselves with walls. The craft industries were within cities and craft guilds were powerful. Banks likewise were in cities and Italy led the world in breaking the taboo against usury.

The alien aristocracy gradually succumbed to the lure of the cities and moved from their uncomfortable castles, first into towers (p. 48) within the cities and later to *palazzi* (town houses).

To a large extent the Italian Renaissance was a 'spin-off' from the commercial acumen of the nobility who learned to adapt from a rural economy in an increasingly dessicated country to exploitation of an urban economy based upon craft industries, and the marketing of country produce such as oil and wine.

Italy was divided, from the twelfth to the fifteenth centuries, by allegiance to the Guelph (Church) or Ghibelline (Holy Roman Empire) parties (a division central to the story of Romeo and Juliet), but superimposed upon this division was the antagonism of France to the Empire. An infinite complexity of alliances and intrigues resulted in many little wars and city-states had to be alert and energetic to survive and retain their privileges. The two great seaports of Genoa and Venice, both republics, competed in trade throughout the known world until the Mediterranean lost commercial predominance to the Atlantic countries in the sixteenth century.

From the fifteenth century the Renaissance of Classical art and the rise of humanism, together with the firm establishment of the Papacy in Rome, gave Italy a leading cultural and religious role in Europe. This to some extent compensated for its declining economy.

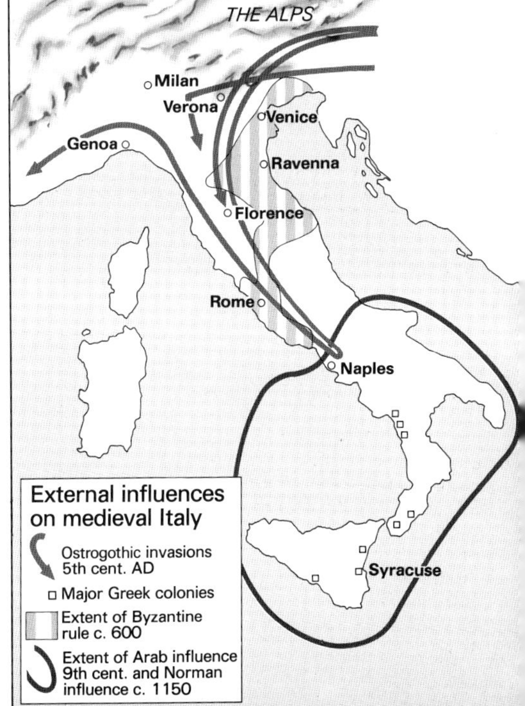

The invasion of Italy after the Roman period. Arabic, Spanish, Norman and Byzantine influences in the south were culturally as important as the better-known Gothic and Lombardic invasions.

Left Massive polygonal masonry in the walls of Alatri, central Italy. It resembles stonework at Mycenae (p. 100), and is not uncommonly found in the lower parts of the walls of Italian hill-towns.

Below The Greek 'Basilica' of Paestum; c. 535 BC. It has early Doric capitals with a large overhang to reduce the span of the lintels.

Right The temple of Fortuna Virilis, Rome; c. 40 BC. A typical temple of the Republican period, it has an Ionic porch with attached columns along the side (a form known as prostyle peripteral).

Above The Basilica of Constantine, also known as the Basilica of Maxentius, in the Roman Forum; AD 310–313. Its concrete arches, coffered by placing boxes on the shuttering to save material, enabled huge areas to be spanned.

Right S. Maria degli Angeli, Rome; the central hall of the Baths of Diocletian (AD 302) restored as a church by Michelangelo in 1563, and giving a good indication of the original lavish appearance of the baths.

Left The Arch of Trajan, Benevento; AD 114. It is built of Greek marble.

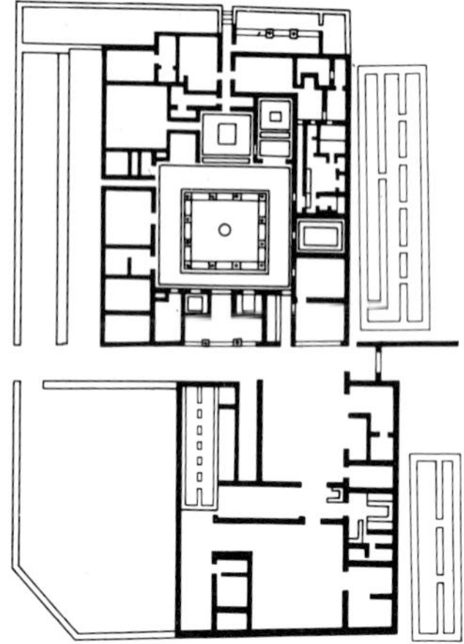

Above Plan of the villa at Francolise, southern Italy, built around an arcaded *atrium*. This kind of plan was used by Roman gentleman-farmers for their villas throughout the empire.

Right The partially restored Corinthian columns of the temple in Brescia erected by Vespasian in AD 73.

Below The Roman amphitheatre of Verona, built in c. AD 290. Structurally it resembles the Colosseum which was built some 200 years earlier, and it accommodates 28,000 spectators.

Italian Folk Architecture
From the foothills of the Alps to Sicily Italian folk architecture is of Mediterranean style. It is, in fact, the basic architecture from which the Classical tradition sprang and has changed little since early early Roman times. Whatever the local stone may be, it is used for thick rubble walls, with small windows of about 1:1½ or 1:2 proportion. and stuccoed. Sometimes windows are round-arched. Arcades along streets and as loggias are common. Interiors are lofty and cool, often with vaulted ceilings. Roofs are low-pitched and covered with half-round (Roman) tiles. Gable ends are usual. Towers, belfries, turrets etc, are usually a natural extension of the structure and have a charming simplicity, especially round Lake Maggiore and Lake Como, but almost every unspoiled hill-town has picturesque towers or turrets, often with a hipped roof, which is quite difficult to construct with Roman tiles. Maturity in folk design seems to have been achieved in the Romanesque period and great architects, especially Brunelleschi (p. 130), derived inspiration from it.

Etruscan funerary urns, such as may be seen in the museum at Tarquinia (100 km north of Rome and a 'must' for students of architecture) show the prototype of the pro-style Roman temple. Thatched huts are still built of branches and reeds in the fields and vineyards to this design, although they are becoming rare.

In towns, almost blank walls are presented to the streets but behind the entrance, which is commonly large enough to admit a cart or carriage, there is often a spacious courtyard house. Many country towns and villages

Left Roofs of Roman tiles and brick walls dominate the character of Siena, and many other Italian towns.

Below Rezzato, near Brescia; a typical Italian village street with houses backing directly on to farmland.

Right The village church at Monterosi, north of Rome. The Baroque style is congenial to Italians and has often, as here, been incorporated into folk art and architecture.

Below Sirmione, on Lake Garda; houses adjoining the castle. With brightly painted walls, they are typical of the common architecture of northern Italy.

Below A complicated three-way bridge at Commacchio, near Ravenna – common architecture of great ingenuity.

Above A modern *fattoria* or farmhouse near Foggia, not very different from a Roman villa.

Right Medieval canal-side buildings in Venice.

Below right A coastal farm near Manfredonia, showing a probable Arab influence, including a chimney for smoking fish.

Below The Alpine village street of Sauze Doux, its utilitarian aspects reflecting those of Rezzato (p. 169).

Above A typical Neapolitan farm, constructed of rubble and concrete. The vaults of its façade recall the Roman Basilica of Constantine (p. 167).

present an urban façade to the main roads but behind this there are farms extending as narrow strips into the countryside.

In some districts, mainly north of Rome, brick is the common material. Sometimes it is stuccoed but commonly bricks are exposed. They are of Roman type, as used for castles, city walls, churches and public buildings. In Lombardy there is a tradition of moulded clay decoration – terra-cotta – going back to pre-Roman times.

South-east Italy shows Arab influence in house design and a very ancient form of corbel-domed house *(trulle)* has persisted along the south-east coast (p. 70). *Trulli* are still being built, especially in the developing vineyards to house grape-pickers. The south-east also shows Arab influence in the design of houses with vertical walls. Often these have flat roofs and the typical mono-pitched ventilating shaft, sometimes combined with a staircase or ladder in larger houses. The Emperor Frederick II (r. 1220–50), who was King of Sicily from 1198 and admired Muslim culture, established Arab communities in this region especially at Lucera near Foggia. Though these were massacred after his death Arab influence in architecture persisted and was more influential in other parts of Italy than Christian historians have sometimes been willing to admit. In guidebooks 'Lombardic' is often a euphemism for Islamic.

A particularly interesting style of farmhouse flourished in the Naples region. It consists of parallel barrel vaults, reminiscent of the basilicas of ancient Rome, and was economical of timber.

North of the Po valley there was plenty of timber and a very interesting transition is made from Mediterranean to Alpine style folk architecture. English influence was strong there in the eighteenth and nineteenth centuries and much of what appears to be folk building was in fact affected by the English Romantic movement and the cult of the picturesque, but it is no less admirable on this account.

The eastern part of the Alpine region has long been disputed territory and shows strong Austrian characteristics in its folk architecture.

Romanesque

While England and France were developing the Gothic style in the twelfth century, Italy was producing an exquisite form of Romanesque architecture which culminated in the Cathedral of Pisa. This style remained faithful to the Classical Orders and proportions but, by abandoning the cornice and exploiting the late Roman idea of springing arches from Classical capitals without an intermediate element, by preferring the round arch, by adopting ribbed construction and combining it with domical construction (as at Ancona) and by absorbing the Hellenesque achievement of surface decoration, the Italians of the great age of medieval civilisation achieved an architecture rooted in their own traditions.

In the fourteenth century this led on directly to the Renaissance. It is a pity that the out-of-date architectural judgments which pervade so many of the guides to Italy debar tourists from fully appreciating the most glorious period of Italian architecture. Its development happened almost entirely in church architecture.

Despite the enormous ideological influence of the Renaissance in Italy, the supreme achievement of Italian architects is to be seen in Romanesque architecture. It did, indeed, provide much of the inspiration, and a link with Classicism, which enabled Renaissance architecture to be born.

Ancona Cathedral; 1128–89. The dome and its substructure incorporate three different architectural traditions: Hellenesque in the pendentives, Romanesque-Norman in the columns and arches; and Gothic in the ribbed dome.

Below The Old Cathedral of Brescia, a round, domed building of the 12th century over an earlier church. Despite design and liturgical difficulties, round churches have continued to fascinate architects.

Above and left S. Maria di Portonuovo, Ancona; 1034. Ancona saw the union of the Romanesque and Hellenesque traditions, and this church is a fine example of Romanesque.

Above Trani Cathedral, built in 1094 over a 7th-century crypt. It is an example of Apulian Romanesque. Its *campanile* was added in 1230–39.

Left S. Zeno, Verona; 1070. One of the great Romanesque churches of Italy. The porch with Classical columns carried on the backs of animals is a common Romanesque motif in Italy. The bulky load carried on thin columns suggests Hellenesque influence, which was strong in north-east Italy.

Left The interior of S. Nicola, Bari; 1085–1132. This church was influential in the spread of the Romanesque in southern Italy.

Right The round 5th-century church of S. Andrea, Perugia; with a Gothic doorway.

Right S. Caterina, Pisa; 1251–1330. Just as the Classical temple had an enclosure of columns, many Romanesque churches in west central Italy were enclosed in tiers of columns and arches, often, as here, in multi-coloured marble. Later, Alberti would revert to columns with lintels, discarding the arch as an unstable design element.

Left S. Maria in Trastevere, Rome; basically 7th century but with many later additions. It is a perfect example of a fully developed basilican church, with transepts, apse, and fine mosaics.

Below The Cathedral of Prato, Tuscany; 12th to 14th centuries. The external pulpit (1440–42) was designed by Donatello and springs from a bronze capital. The *campanile* dates from 1413.

Above S. Ambrogio, Milan. Founded by St Ambrose whose body is preserved in the crypt. Rebuilt on its present plan c. 850. Rebuilt and vaulted in the 12th century. See also p. 8.

Above S. Apollinare in Classe, Ravenna; 534–39. A Hellenesque basilican church on the site of a temple of Apollo! The circular *campanile* was probably built at the same date, one of the earliest in existence.

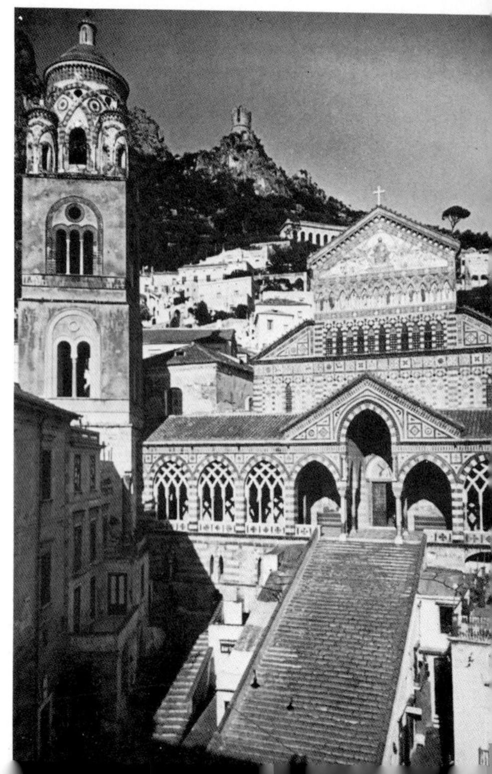

Right Steps and façade of Amalfi Cathedral; 13th century. Its Hellenesque style shows Arab influence, perhaps imported *via* Sicily, and the cloister is almost pure Arabic. The façade has been restored.

Hellenesque

From early times Greeks have influenced Italian architecture. Both the Etruscans and the Romans learned from the Greeks and when the Greek city of Byzantium became Constantinople, and capital of the Roman Empire in AD 330, the old Classical tradition persisted in the West and evolved in Romanesque architecture. But the Greeks had made a fresh start and their new architecture flourished in Constantinople and throughout the eastern parts of the Empire. With the fall of the Western Empire the Byzantine emperors tried to regain Italy and Sicily. Thus Hellenesque architecture pushed into Italy from the south but more importantly from the north-east. There the Exarchate (vice-royalty) of Ravenna became, in the time of Justinian (r. 527–65), a major centre of Greek culture extending its influence to the Atlantic and the North Sea.

Ravenna is the best place to see the pure Hellenesque architecture of the sixth century. Its principal characteristics are: the use of domes, the use of a *dosseret* (an additional abacus) over the capital of a Classical-type column, to support an arch in a thick wall, and the use of mosaics as decoration for large wall surfaces and vaults. The linear design of these magnificent pictures in marble, glass and tile, influenced medieval painted wall decoration and stained glass and, through such artists as Giotto and Botticelli, Renaissance art.

At Ravenna there are two very important prototypes for European architecture. One is the domed, circular church of S. Vitale; the other is the basilican church as at S. Apollinare in Classe and S. Apollinare Nuovo.

Islamic influence in Sicily, south and east Italy also brought Hellenesque ways of design, though the Italians play this down.

S. Lorenzo, Verona; 12th century. In Romanesque style, it re-uses Roman materials such as columns with their capitals adapted to carry arches of brick.

Left S. Vitale, Ravenna; 526–47. It is a masterpiece of spatial design, consisting of two concentric octagons. Its carved capitals and 6th-century mosaics depicting Justinian and Theodora are remarkable.

Right St Mark's, Venice; 1063–85. In plan it is based on the now-demolished Church of the Apostles in Constantinople. Internally its rich mosaics, marble, bronze work, sculpture, gold and silver make it an artistic treasure house as well as a church.

Below S. Antonio, Padua; 1232–1307. This great pilgrimage church blends Hellenesque design (its seven domes were inspired by St. Mark's in Venice) with Gothic elements, such as the chevet.

Italian Gothic

Pointed and horseshoe arches, ribbed and domical vaults, and slender supporting structures were all part of the Romanesque style in Italy. That the Gothic style flourished in castles, city walls and secular buildings in some cities may be partly due to French and Austrian potentates and trading connections; but Italians have a flair for fashion, not least in the Church, and Gothic decoration was enthusiastically adopted and adapted by Italian artists. Many Gothic churches are fundamentally Romanesque but enriched by the opportunities and stimulus of the Gothic vision. The epitome of Gothic design in Italy is Siena Cathedral with Orvieto a close second.

Venice has a splendid Gothic church – SS. Giovanni e Paolo – which is missed by most visitors to St Mark's, but the Venetian Gothic (which was to inspire John Ruskin in the nineteenth century and gave birth, amongst other buildings to St Pancras Station in London) was devised for places. It is an amalgam of Hellenesque, Romanesque and Gothic ideas developed mainly as an architecture of façades, which northern Gothic certainly was not.

Generally, the Italians absorbed and learned from the essentially alien Gothic style, taking from it what suited them.

Above The Palazzo Vecchio, Florence; 1298–1314. The fortified façade and high tower epitomise the municipal government of many medieval Italian city-states.

Above right S. Anastasia, Verona; 1290–1481.

Right SS. Giovanni e Paolo, Venice; 1260–1385. One of the major Gothic churches in Italy, its widely-spaced, slender columns in the nave are linked by wooden ties. These were commonly used in Italian churches to perform a similar function to flying buttresses in France. The church contains the tombs of the Doges of Venice.

Left The Palazzo della Ca d'Oro, Venice; 1424–36. Built by the architects of the Doge's Palace, it is in typical Venetian style, combining complex arcading and tracery with decorated masory and a roof of Saracenic origin.

Right The early Renaissance façade (1491) of the Carthusian monastery church, Certosa, Pavia; 1396–1497.

Far right Interior of the Certosa: memorable, wholly Gothic in character, and Classically re-interpreted in the west front.

Left The Palazzo Pubblico, Siena; 1289–1309. It is built mainly of brick. The tower, of the mid-14th century, is the highest in Italy, and its machicolations are an unfunctional stylistic feature.

Below Palazzo del Municipo, Perugia; 1293–1443.

Left and below Siena Cathedral; 1226–1380. Its vertical Gothic design is contradicted by its black-and-white marble stripes. Its west front, by Giovanni Pisano, is ornate and sumptuously decorated. The interior is a remarkable spatial experience.

Renaissance

At the beginning of the fifteenth century *(quattrocento)* Renaissance architecture involved a rejection of Gothic and a return to Classicism. The father of the movement was Filippo Brunelleschi (1377–1466) who is credited with the invention of perspective and went with the sculptor, Donatello, to study and measure Roman remains in Rome itself shortly after 1400. As a result he restored the use of correct Classical Orders. Then another Florentine, Leon Battista Alberti (1402–72) re-stated and developed the Classical theories of Vitruvius.

Alberti established design on a foundation of science as then understood, and said that beauty was dependent upon designing according to principles which were inherent in the way the world was made. The basis of design therefore was a set of rules ('discovered not devised' as Alexander Pope put it in the eighteenth century). Until the 1520s this orderly view of architecture held the field and gave rise to what we call High Renaissance architecture; but after the troops of the Emperor ran amok in the streets of Rome in 1527 and with the Reformation developing throughout Europe, the tidy relationship of cosmology and theology which had inspired Alberti gave way to what art historians call Mannerism.

Below and below right S. Maria dei Miracoli, Venice, built in 1481–89 by Pietro Lombardo. It was one of the earliest Renaissance works in Venice, and one of the most beautifully detailed buildings in the world, especially around the steps to the chancel.

Right The Palazzo Antinori, Florence; c. 1480. It shows extreme simplicity within the Tuscan tradition of formidable aristocratic urban buildings.

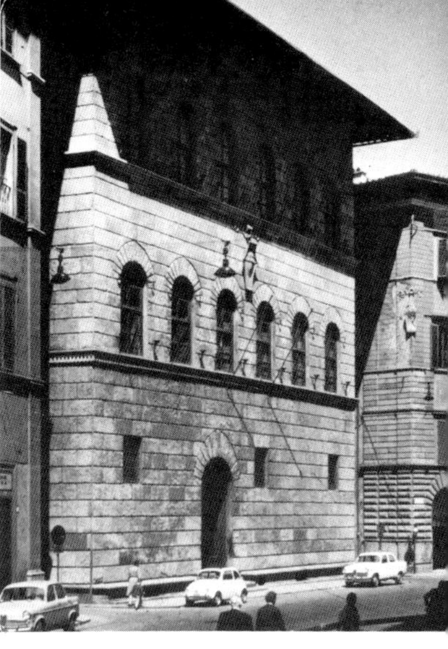

Above Carefully-observed Classical detail in the Pazzi Chapel, Florence, built by Brunelleschi in 1429–46. See also p. 8.

Above The Palazzo Pandolfini, Florence, built c. 1520–27 to a design by Raphael, anticipates Palladio. It has a symmetrical two-storey façade but is approached by a door in a one-storey wing behind which there is a garden.

Left The Palazzo della Cancelleria, Rome; 1486–98. It was the first major Renaissance building in Rome; architect unknown.

Above and right S. Maria della Consolazione, Todi; 1508–1604, by Cola da Caprarola with Peruzzi as consultant. A unique realisation of the High Renaissance ideal centralised plan.

Below The Cortile of the Palazzo della Cancelleria, Rome; 1486–98.

Above and below The Palazzo Farnese; 1515–45, by Antonio da Sangallo followed by Michelangelo and others. The huge cornice, in defiance of Alberti's theories, is proportional to the height of the whole building.

Above Casa Pollini, Siena; c. 1527, by Peruzzi. A sensitive interpretation of traditional architecture on a site where Classical formality would have been inappropriate.

Left S. Maria della Pace, Rome; 1500–1657. The semi-circular porch was built by Pietro da Cortona in Baroque style.

Mannerism and Baroque

The Palazzo del Tè (1525–35) at Mantua, which deliberately thumbs its nose at Classical rules, symbolises the loss of faith in systems of value, but you need to know the rules to appreciate the jokes. This is generally true of Mannerist art, sophisticated and cynical (but see p. 138) and quite different from Baroque which was quickly established by the Counter-Reformation after about 1560. The Baroque proclaimed the power and magnificence of the Catholic Church and, for the discerning, its fundamental structure was embodied in the profound geometry of Baroque buildings by Bernini, Rainaldi and Longhena.

Baroque was a joyous architecture which suited the Italians and was adopted for palaces, public buildings, gardens and parks. Gradually it lost its intellectual basis and became a popular idiom, and a folk art of Baroque decoration swept Europe and America, as can be seen in the picture frames of national galleries and the decoration of carts, roundabouts, barges, saloons, and bar parlours. Even the 'modern movement' in Italy was affected and, apart from the few text-book examples, shows a riotousness of fancy though impoverished by a modern prejudice against gilding.

Baroque restored to Italy the grandeur and vulgarity of Roman art which had been lost in the Christian austerity of Romanesque, Gothic and the High Renaissance.

Above and above right St Peter's, Rome; 1506–1626. A work of many hands, including Michelangelo, who designed the dome and amended Bramante's original centralised plan from a Greek to a Latin cross. The nave was extended and the west front completed by Carlo Maderna, and the piazza colonnades by Bernini.

Right Il Gesù, Rome; 1568–84. Its architects, Vignola and della Porta, developed Alberti's ideas in the scrolled façade and the unified ground-plan, with transepts no wider than the aisles.

Right Palazzo Massimi, Rome, by Peruzzi; 1532–36. Its curving façade and Doric portico are important departures from Classical models.

Left The Spanish Steps, Rome, by A. Specchi and F. de Sanctis; 1721–25. A masterpiece of Baroque town planning, with subtly-designed planes, curves and levels.

Below S. Maria della Salute, Venice; 1631–82 by Baldassare Longhena. Though Baroque in detail, its octagonal plan imitates S. Vitale at Ravenna.

Below The Trevi Fountain, Rome; 1732–62 by Salvi Pannini.

Above The Piazza del Popolo, Rome; laid out in the early 19th century and extending from twin churches by Carlo Rainaldi (1611–91). The piazza is the main entrance to Rome from the north, and gives a powerful sense of having arrived.

Right The Sanctuary of the Madonna di Vico, at Vicoforte, near Savona; 1590–c. 1790. It has a magnificent Baroque dome, oval in plan, and is the mausoleum of the House of Savoy.

Left Waterfall in the grounds of the royal palace of Caserta, near Naples; 1752–.

Left The Scala Regia in the Vatican, built by Bernini in 1663–66, with dramatic false perspective and light effects.

Right Syracuse Cathedral, with an imposing Baroque façade. The interior comprises a Greek temple to Athena adapted to Christian use in the 7th century.

Rococo and after

It is difficult to distinguish between later Baroque and Rococo in Italy. The main characteristic of Rococo is a delicacy of detail, exemplified in great freedom of style and emphasis on surface decoration rather than architectural, three-dimensional form.

From Etruscan times, the Italians have excelled in lavish and inventive decoration executed with great skill. Often the greatest pleasure is to be experienced by looking at details rather than the whole. Rococo art in Italy rewards careful study and general impressions of it are not enough. (Admittedly this could also be said of any great period but it is essential for Rococo.)

In the eighteenth century foreign influences, especially French, extended the range of available motifs beyond the design capacities of the traditional artist-craftsmen, and the profession of the drawing-board architect, often trained in Paris, further widened the gap between design and execution. Gothic Revival and Art Nouveau influences contributed to the growing stylistic chaos, which was suddenly arrested by Mussolini and the imposition of a Fascist style: brutal, domineering and devoid of decoration other than emblems of the regime and symbolic sculpture.

After World War II Modernism swept Italy as an exuberant fashion. A few buildings exemplify Modernism at its most intellectual and austerely Classical, especially some by Pier Luigi Nervi (p. 35).

Right The late Baroque Church of Ronciglione, central Italy; 1671 by Vignola.

Above The Borsa, Genoa; in the pompous Classical style of the early 20th century with Art Nouveau influences.

Left The Galleria Umberto I, Naples; 1887–91, by Emanuele Rocco.

Below The Galleria 25 Aprile, Cremona, 1935; in the brutalised Classical style of the fascist era.

Left 1 Via Repubblica, Pesaro; 1902–07 by Giuseppe Brega in flamboyant Art Nouveau style.

Below A small house at Marotta, Apulia, 1962 by Sergio Marchetti, and epitomising the brash experimental and often exciting approach to domestic design of modern Italian architects.

Spain and Portugal

The present political designation of the two countries of the Iberian Peninsula has little relevance to the history of Iberian architecture. The Pyrenees are a formidable range of mountains which seem to be a natural frontier between Spain and France, but the mountains begin again south-west of the River Ebro and stretch out like the fingers and thumb of a hand to the Atlantic coast. Strung out along two thousand miles (3200 kilometres) of coastline there are communities which look outwards to the sea and backwards to the mountains. One such community, by accident of inheritance long ago, is a separate country, Portugal, and the river Tagus that runs out of the heart of Spain reaches the sea through Lisbon in Portugal.

Hispania was a Roman province which flourished in the first to third centuries and then declined and fell to barbarians in the fifth century. There are extensive vestiges of Roman architecture, the most impressive being bridges and aqueducts.

At the time of the barbarian invasions, the Visigoths passed through France into Spain leaving strong Visigothic elements in the South of France. The Visigoths were Arian Christians, not Catholics. They built in a Romanesque style but apparently favoured the horseshoe arch. They were not left in peace to develop this idea because in 711 the Muslims crossed the Straits of Gibraltar and conquered most of the peninsula except for a small strip along the northern coast, which remained Christian.

The Muslims made Spain and Portugal one of the most prosperous and civilised regions in the world. Córdoba was their headquarters and it became a city of half a million people, second only to Constantinople, in the ninth century.

Throughout the country what we would now call an environmentalist approach to social and economic problems produced a system of irrigation which vastly improved the fertility of the country and its prosperity because, in those days as always, the true basis of prosperity, in any ecosystem, human or othewise, is food.

The Great Mosque at Córdoba is the principal monument from the early Muslim period. It shows

Spanish history has been dominated by the attempt of Castile to act as a centralising authority on the individual regions of the peninsula. Visigothic conquest following Roman domination did not eliminate indigenous cultures, which still persist, especially in Portugal, Catalonia and the Basque Country.

The position of Spain as the heart of the Hapsburg Empire and the Counter-Reformation in the 16th century under Charles V and Philip II brought cultural influences from Italy, Austria and the Low Countries, at a time when great wealth was being imported from the Americas.

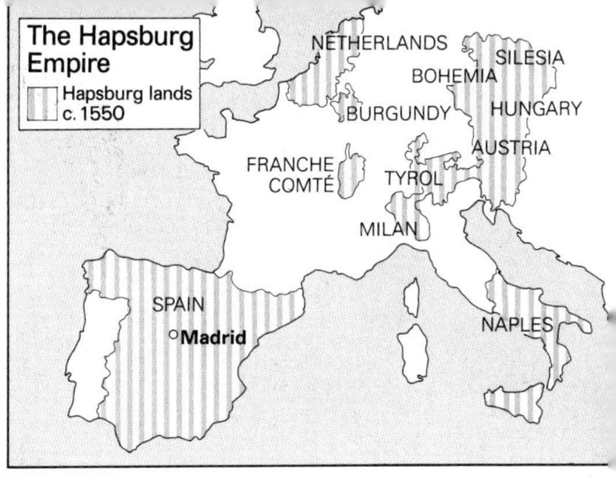

a highly creative attitude to design and it appears that the architects, while working in a mainly Hellenesque idiom, incorporated Roman and Visigothic ideas.

The virility and tolerance of the Muslim caliphs gave way to persecution of Christians under Mohammad I (r. 852–886). This was partly due to the intolerance of Christians themselves. The Christians moved northwards as Muslim power receded towards the south after the defeat of Muslim forces by the Carolingians in France in 732. These Christians took with them Arab ways of building and the name Mozarabic is given to their style of architecture which was built in the ninth and tenth centuries.

Faced with the Christian re-conquest of Spain, which was not complete until almost 1500, the Muslims formed a political union with Morocco from which came a different style of architecture. It was more like that of the main middle-eastern centres of Muslim culture. This style is called Maghribian because it originated in the Maghreb (north Africa). It is more decorative and colourful than early Muslim architecture but less adventurous structurally. The outstanding achievement was the Alhambra Palace at Granada. This was begun in the twelfth but was mainly built in two stages in the fourteenth century. It is the best example in the west of the delightful integration of buildings, gardens and landscapes which is a feature of the best Muslim architecture throughout Islam. After Muslim power in Spain ended with the conquest of Granada in 1492, many Muslims remained in the reconquered territories and built in a style, derived from their own tradition, called Mudejar. The style lasted until it was overtaken by intolerance and the Renaissance but it served to pass on concepts of space, proportion and feeling for the relationship of structure to decoration which became inherent in Spanish and Portuguese architecture at all levels and in their colonies around the world. Christian Spain, like southern Italy, owes more to the Arabs than most of the inhabitants care to acknowledge.

As in England (pp. 261–3) so in Spain, there were two stages of Romanesque architecture. The first was Visigothic and only relatively minor buildings have survived. The site of the Visigothic cathedral of Córdoba is under the Mosque.

Above The Roman bridge at Alcantara; AD 105–16. Its widest spans, over the river Tagus, are some 27 m (90ft).

Right S. Juan de Baños de Cerrato, Palencia; AD 661. A well-preserved Visigothic building of three aisles, it has marble pillars supporting horse-shoe arches and a timber roof. Its plan (below) shows its external colonnade, resembling a Classical temple.

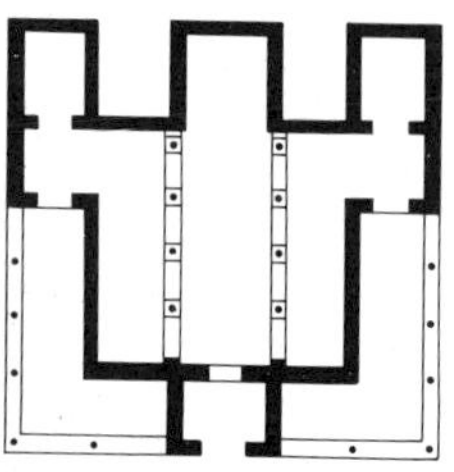

Left S. Maria de Naranco, near Oviedo; 848. A barrel-vaulted church on two floors, though without a sanctuary.

Below The 7th-century church of S. Pedro de la Nave, Zamora, built in the form of a Latin cross with small slit windows.

Right S. Cristina de Lena, Oviedo; c. 905. The screen between chancel and nave is shown here. The building develops the barrel-vault with transverse arches.

Left and below The Great Mosque, Córdoba, built from 785 by Abd ar-Rahman incorporating Visigothic elements to a style probably derived from Damascus and Kairawan. Its multitude of doubled red-and-white arches support a large flat roof, while in the mihrab or sanctuary more complex scalloped arches support a dome built up on interlocking ribbed arches.

Below Plan of the Alhambra, or fortified palace of the Nasrid dynasty, in Granada; mainly 1338–90. Unlike Christian castles of the same period, but similar to the palace of Minos at Knossos (p. 157), it is a complex of elegant buildings enhanced with courtyards, fountains and gardens: (1) Hall of Ambassadors, (2) Court of Alberea, (3) Baths, (4) Hall of Two Sisters, (5) Court of the Lions, (6) Hall of Abencerages.

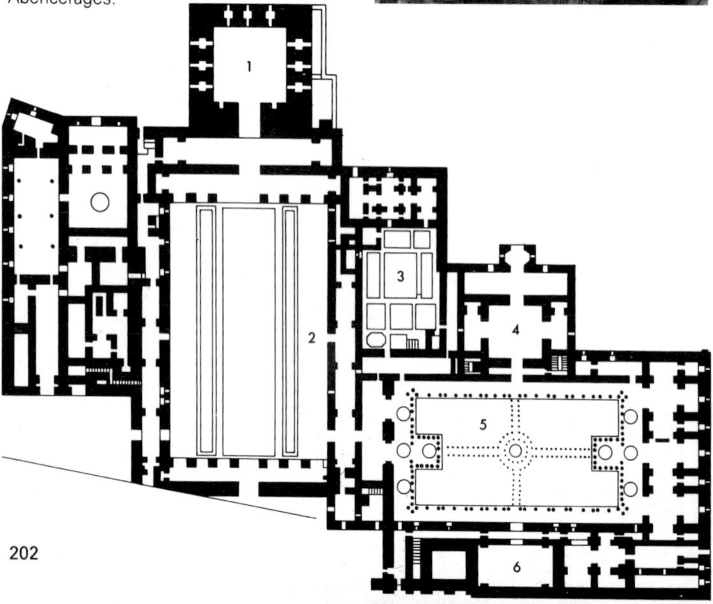

Above The Court of the Lions in the Alhambra. Notice the use of corbelled as well as voussoir arches. Much of the elaborate decoration of the vaults is achieved by corbelling, sometimes to achieve stalactite effects.

Left The Casa de Pilatos in Seville, from the 15th and 16th centuries. Built in the Mudejar style which incorporated many elements of Islamic decoration, its debt to the Alhambra, especially in the stucco work and the tiling of the arcades, can clearly be seen.

Left The Sinagoga del Transito, Toledo; 1360–66. It inherits the Muslim traditions of intricate decoration. Both Muslims and Jews were expelled from Spain around 1500, impoverishing the country commercially and architecturally.

Below The Alcazar, Seville, was begun in the 12th century as a Muslim palace, but after Seville's reconquest by the Christians in 1248 it was partially reworked in a similar, Mudejar, style. This picture shows the dormitory area.

Above S. Maria la Blanca, Toledo; c. 1360. Originally built as a synagogue, its decorated horse-shoe arches and gold strapwork create a rich effect.

Right The cloister of S. Juan de Duero, Soria, a Templar church of the 13th century. Its unusual interlinked arches are another example of the Mudejar style.

Spain and Portugal in the Middle Ages

After the Muslim period, later Romanesque came into Spain as a complete system, introduced by the Benedictines. The style had already evolved in France, Provence and Lombardy to produce regional variations which also passed into Spain.

The most important influence was from Cluny in Burgundy, along the pilgrim route to the shrine of St James (Santiago) at Compostela. Though much altered by later Baroque additions and embellishments, this cathedral of Santiago de Compostela is a fundamentally Romanesque building with the fully developed Cluniac plan. The Portico de la Gloria resembles Vézelay and Autun in Burgundy (pp. 255–6) and it may be noted here that a secular relationship with Burgundy was the origin of Portugal becoming a separate country. In 1097 it was given as a county by Alfonso VI of Castile to Henry of Burgundy who married his illegitimate daughter, Teresa.

At the north-east corner of the peninsula, in Catalonia, the abbey of Ripoll achieved great renown as a centre of scholarship. Gerbert of Aurillac, the mathematician, worked there from 967 and Arabic numerals were introduced to Europe through the school at Ripoll. How important this was for the future of architecture may be judged by trying to do a long-division sum in Roman numerals: MCCXXXVIII divided by DCXXIX for example (answer, in Arabic figures 1·9682034).

As in Germany (pp. 324–7) Romanesque was a congenial style which persisted in many places. Gothic came from France, to a large extent under Cistercian influence, but even though French architects were commonly employed by the Cistercian Order, Gothic changed when it moved into a warmer climate than England and northern France where it was born. High-pitched roofs, in particular, are alien to the prevailing southern low-pitched roofs with tiles so, as in southern France and Italy, the Gothic style was by its nature exotic. Though there are some lovely Gothic buildings in Spain with well-thought-out plans and beautiful details, the full magic of Gothic church architecture is not achieved in Spain and Portugal.

Gothic castles are a very different story. Centuries of strife, family quarrels and dynastic rivalries made Spain a land of castles and the terrain provided splendid sites for them.

Much had been learned from the Arabs who were ingenious military engineers. In the eighth century they had reached the Bay of Biscay and they were gradually forced back over a period of seven centuries. When Christian kingdoms were established, the nobility retained immense power and the traditional oath of the Aragonese nobility to their king was, *We, who are as good as you, swear to you who are no better than we, to accept you as our king and sovereign lord, provided you observe all our statutes and laws, and if not, no!*

If the castles have a proudly independent look and if, when more settled times came, many nobles chose to make them more comfortable rather than build palaces, it is not surprising.

Right The Cathedral at Zamora (1152–74) has high barrel vaults and a curious lantern dome over the crossing with corner-turrets. This style has Hellenesque affinities.

Above and below right S. Martin de Frómista, a church on the pilgrimage route from France to Santiago de Compostela; 11th century. The French Romanesque style was introduced to Spain along this route.

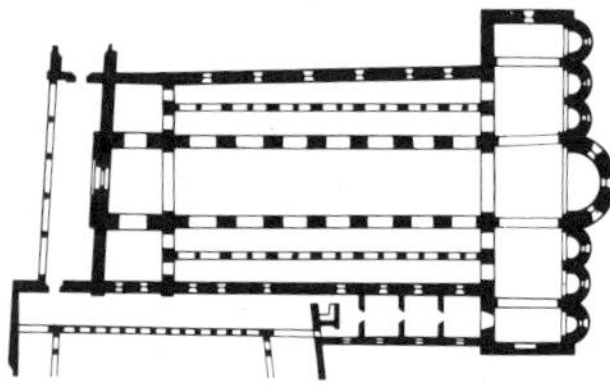

Above and left (plan) S. Maria, Ripoll; built c. 1020–32. An important centre of learning, its cosmopolitan community is reflected in an eclectic architecture.

Opposite Portico de la Gloria, Santiago de Compostela; 1075–1128. One of Europe's great pilgrimage centres, the plan and structural conception with the great barrel vaults and chevet are French.

Left and below (plan) The monastery of Poblet, Catalonia; late 12th century.

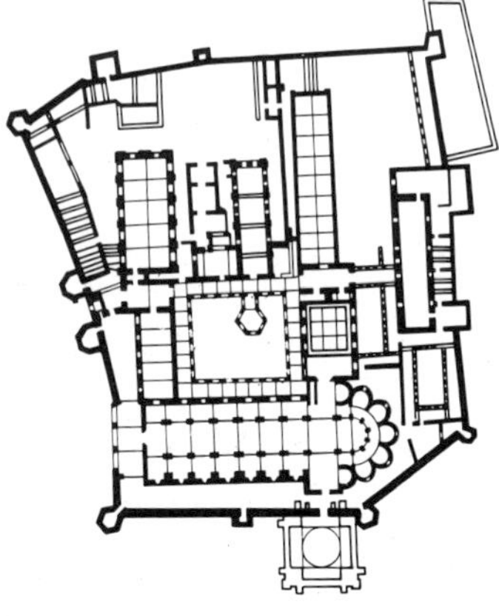

Above Segovia Cathedral; begun 1522 and said to be the last great Gothic cathedral built in Europe.

Right Burgos Cathedral; 1221–1457. The *cimborio* or lantern above the crossing, the decoration here exemplifies the richness of the late medieval Plateresque style.

Below Tarragona Cathedral; 12th to 13th centuries. The Gothic style in Catalonia is severe and reflects French influence. It tends to be structurally adventurous.

Right Saragossa Cathedral; begun in the 12th century. Fully Gothic in structure, it has the common Spanish feature of the choir to the west side of the crossing.

Below Toledo, Puerta Visagra; 1550, restored 1575. A Spanish blending of strength and charm.

The Renaissance

Renaissance architecture came late to Spain and Portugal. It was already established in Italy when Granada, the last Muslim stronghold, fell in 1492, the same year as Columbus sailed to begin the discovery of America under Spanish royal patronage.

Gothic and Renaissance ideas merged in what is called Plateresque in Spain and Manueline in Portugal. This is perhaps the most characteristic and delightful architecture of these countries. It is highly ornamental but not licentious and may be compared in this respect with Benelux.

Owing to an extraordinary constellation of marriages the throne of Spain was inherited in 1516 by Charles, son of Philip the Fair, ruler of the Low Countries, and Joan of Castile. In 1519 Charles was also elected Holy Roman Emperor and took the style of Charles V. He had been born in Ghent in 1500 and educated in Malines (Mechlen) in Belgium. Thereafter it is possible to discern Spanish influences in Flemish architecture. The other way round is more doubtful but there was a parallel development of extremely decorative architecture in the late fifteenth and sixteenth centuries.

For English-speaking people (and there are parallels in other languages) a long-lasting qualitative judgement was imposed upon history in the early eighteenth century by the Palladians. It may be expressed thus. There is a pure Classical stream of architecture which has been polluted from time to time, especially during the Gothic period. Renaissance architecture in Italy, as practised by a very small group of architects between about 1450 and 1527 represented a return to purity, but Mannerism and Baroque muddied the waters

The Infantado Palace, Guadalajara; 1440–43, by Juan Güas, a Breton trained in Brussels. Outstanding Gothic Plateresque.

of truth. By publishing illustrated books about architecture, Palladio (for England) and Vignola (for France) consolidated Classical doctrine and set standards for the modern age. Architecture would henceforth be, in the words of Inigo Jones, 'proportional according to the rules, masculine and unaffected'. There can be little doubt that this puritanical doctrine took much of the fun and some of the beauty out of architecture.

Even in Italy pure Classical architecture of the Renaissance is rare. Major buildings, like the Certosa in Pavia (p. 185), were extravagantly ornamental within a deeply established Italian tradition and national talent for elaborate craftsmanship.

Above Hospital of Santa Cruz, Toledo, by Enrique de Egas; 1504–14.

Left The west front of the Cathedral of Santiago de Compostela, which is otherwise completely Romanesque in style (see p. 209). Its complex planes and heavy decoration are typical of the so-called Churrigueresque period of late Baroque in Spain. It was built in 1738–49; by Fernando Casas y Novoa.

Left and below Jaén Cathedral, 1546–56, by Andres Vandelvira. It is a hall church (see p. 329) of great beauty, marking the transition from Plateresque to a more pure Italian style. This brief period of High Renaissance design quickly gave way to Spanish influences, and culminated in the full Spanish Baroque style.

Opposite above Hospital Real, Granada, 1511 by Enrique de Egas. The building of hospitals in the early 16th century provided opportunities for developing the renaissance Plateresque style.

Left Belém Tower, Lisbon; 1515–19. Built to command the river Tejus, its Manueline style incorporates Moorish features.

In sixteenth-century Spain and Portugal the 'spirit of the age' inclined, as in France, England and Italy, towards richness.

Charles V started to build a palace adjoining the Alhambra in Granada (p. 140). It was Renaissance in style but far from pure Classicism. The overwhelming taste of the Spanish and Portuguese was for richness, in a society which was becoming progressively wealthier as the Spaniards destroyed the civilisation of Central America for the sake of gold – the biggest planned robbery in history, until the twentieth century.

If we were to look at the moral background of most architecture we might come to the same conclusions as St Bernard: that if suffering has gone the creation of something, that may be all the more reason to preserve it, so that at least something has been achieved. Many people say Plateresque is bad because it is unrestrained and over-exuberant. If we adopt this attitude we may miss beauty.

Early Renaissance architecture in Spain and Portugal is rich and full of delight, of superb craftsmanship and, if you will but care to notice, a powerful sense of design. It is not chaotic, nor is the Baroque architecture of Spain which succeeded it. But there was also a 'High Renaissance' which in some ways anticipated Neo-Classicism, a setback in the natural progress of Spanish architecture imposed by the authority of Philip II (r. 1556–98) and his doctrinaire architect Juan de Herrera. King and architect instituted an artistic dictatorship with a mania for supposed academic purity. Buildings were stripped of their ornaments in the search for the so-called *estilo*

desornamentado (cf. Fascist Italy).

In Philip's brief to Herera for his colossal granite retreat of El Escorial, he wrote *Above all do not forget what I have told you, simplicity of form, severity in the whole, nobility without arrogance, majesty without ostentation.* Yet the main purpose of this vastly costly structure could have been equally well served by a cave in the nearby mountains, if Philip had not also suffered from regal vanity.

After Philip II, and in reaction to Herrera's dictatorship, Baroque flourished and gradually merged with other movements, in parallel with developments in other countries, particularly France.

Around 1900, a group of architects in Catalonia, among whom Antoni Gaudì (1856–1934) is best known, practised in a fantastic style, with a great deal of weird elaboration which has affinities with Plateresque and is contemporary with Art Nouveau, but it lacks the linear co-ordination which is truly characteristic of that style.

Left Dome of the Escorial, built in 1559–84 by Herrera in the *estilo desornamentado*.

Above Detail of the decoration above the doorway of The Hospital of S. Fernando in Madrid, by Pedro de Ribera; 1722.

Left The Palace of the Marqués de dos Aguas, Valencia; 1740–44.

Left The façade of Murcia Cathedral, built in 1737–54 by Jaime Bort y Melía. The doorway is flanked by columns supporting a half-dome.

Above The Puente de Toledo at Madrid, built in 1723–24 by Pedro de Ribera, adding a Baroque flourish to a structure that otherwise recalls Roman engineering.

Above left Detail of the exterior decoration of Murcia Cathedral; 1740–44.

Left Cathedral of La Seo, Saragossa; the façade and tower were built in the 1680s in a restrained Baroque style. For the interior see p. 211.

Right One of the two houses built of the 60 originally planned for the Parc Güell, by Antoni Gaudi; 1900–14. The bright tilework covering the houses and many of the walls in the park reflect Moorish work but the buildings have soft, vegetable forms. Gaudi was leader of a highly individualistic school of Art Nouveau architects in Catalonia.

Left Façade of the Casa Battló, designed by Gaudi; 1905–07.

Folk Architecture of Iberia

Who are the indigenous 'folk' of Spain? Greeks, Phoenicians, Carthaginians, Romans came but long before them the Iberian and Basque languages were giving the names to places which they still have today. The Iberian speakers probably came from Africa and were akin to the Berbers. The Basques were probably an indigenous people, the descendants of those whose accomplished artists painted pictures on the walls of caves at Altamira in about 10,000 BC. They used red ochre and carbon, two basic elements of the present iron and steel industry of Basque provinces which form one of the two industrialised regions of Spain. There is linguistic and ethnic evidence of genetic survival from the Stone Age, and Basque culture extended well outside the present boundaries in Spain and into France, possibly up to the Dordogne.

It is ironical that the only direct descendants of the first Europeans have been overtaken by the Industrial Revolution. They feel separate, as do the Catalans at the other end of the Pyrenees and the Ebro valley. Catalonia had close religious and cultural links with south-west France. Navarre, whence came Henry IV of France, is in both countries. Over in the west, Portugal is actually a separate country and the configuration of Spain (like Italy) makes for regionalism and small communities of differing origins which have emerged from the

Below A harmonious blend of arcane and common architecture at Segovia (see also p. 210).

Above Toledo was already an important town when it was taken by the Romans in 192 BC, and has long been famous for sword blades and silk. Note the defended bridge.

Left A typical rural community set in open country; near Almansa, south-eastern Spain.

ebb and flow of wars and the conflict of Christianity and Islam.

But in spite of all the diversity there is the common factor of aridity, due to low rainfall and great heat in summer. Only the north-west corner of the peninsula has substantial rainfall. Buildings are naturally dry, which means that they can be loosely constructed. Thick walls provide insulation, the cool, cave-like interior being desirable. Generally the Mediterranean style of folk architecture prevails, with modification towards the alpine type in some mountain areas. Single-storey buildings are common, partly because of a law requiring owners of houses of more than one storey to place half of them at the disposal of the monarch.

Generally the wealth that has flowed into Spain has not gone to the builders of folk architecture. It is the architecture, mainly, of relatively poor people. It is simple and sensible. Where decoration does occur, its character may indicate Christian or Muslim origins. Elaborate projecting balconies, roofed and closed with fretted screens are an obvious survival from the Muslim way of life but also suited the relative seclusion of Christian women in Spanish towns.

Left Alhambra, Granada, the Patio de los Arragones. Arcane architecture in a simple traditional setting gains by the contrast of richness and plain walls.

Below Montblanche; the ingredients of many Spanish towns: fortified, on a hill, agricultural environment, suburb developing at the bridge.

Bottom Houses in Burgos with elaborate balconies, possibly derived from the 'roshans' of Islamic architecture.

Above Santa Creus; towns such as this have a deep feeling of history.

Left Fermancabellero: the basic folk architecture of Spain, with low tiled roof, thick walls and small openings.

Below left A modern doctor's surgery near Córdoba, in deliberately traditional style.

Below Williams & Humbert bodega at Jerez. Sherry wineries can be as attractive as their products!

France

Each region of France has its own architectural characteristics but all have been influenced by the architecture of the region round Paris – the Île de France – in or near to which all the major innovations in French architecture since the twelfth century have occurred. The architecture of this region is therefore described first because it is relevant to all other regions.

The Île de France

The Île de France, which covers approximately the geographical area of the Paris Basin, is the heart-land of France. It contains most of the major Gothic cathedrals, the royal palaces and Paris itself. To a greater extent than in any other country the cultural, social and political life of France was and is concentrated upon Paris. This was the deliberate policy of French monarchs and their ministers and is preserved in the Republic. In a sense, provinciality in France is proportionate to distance from Paris, but extreme centralisation has led to the development of strong provincial cultures.

Little Roman and Romanesque architecture survives, partly because of the devastation by Vikings in the ninth century – they sacked Paris in 845 – and partly because of continuous redevelopment in the wealthy towns, villages and countryside. In the Middle Ages the Île de France was a target defended by castles and walled cities. In the cities the walls caused congestion and encouraged high building.

Even cathedrals were restricted in site area. Verticality thus became habitual in urban architecture and this set fashions in proportion which were imitated in rural buildings. The typical French window is tall in proportion to its width (2½ to 3 times the width) and flanked by shutters which are, so to speak, twice as vertical.

Height was also an important component in the effectiveness of town and castle walls. 'High-is-strong' pervaded military architecture and gave social status to verticality. High-pitched roofs were the traditional response to a fairly wet climate and the taste for verticality encouraged an enduring fashion for exaggerating the roofs with spikes and pinnacles. Iron railings along the ridge of a roof are not uncommon as a lacey fringe to the skyline of essentially vertical buildings.

The pre-eminence of Paris begins with the emergence of a strong French monarchy under Philip II (r. 1180–1223). Prior to that its fortunes had fluctuated and the seat of government had been successively at Tournai, Soissons, Metz and Aix-la-Chapelle while Tours, Cluny and Rheims had been more important ecclesiastically. But with the king of France established as the apex of the feudal pyramid in the western part of the former Carolingian Empire, Paris became more and more the political, social and cultural centre of France. From the seventeenth century it was deliberately cultivated as the artistic capital of the western world, with the arts supported by an elaborate educational, patronal and bureaucratic system in reaction against which many of the major French achievements in the arts later took place.

The outstanding achievement of

the region is the great Gothic cathedrals: Nôtre Dame de Paris in the centre; then, clockwise from Amiens to Soissons, Laon, Rheims, Sens, Chartres, Evreux and Rouen.

The main period during which the French Gothic building style was perfected was about 1160–1290. A recommended experience where French Gothic can be seen at its best, and normally without the distraction of crowds is: Laon (the Durham of France, on a splendid acropolis); Soissons, a very elegant and beautiful church in what was, for a time, the capital of France; and then Amiens which is the 'ideal' French cathedral.

There are dozens of superb Gothic churches, some of them cathedrals, among which Noyon may conveniently be visited with Laon and Soissons. The abbey church of St Ouen at Rouen is one of the best in France and should not be missed, but wherever you go in the Île de France there are interesting and beautiful churches. Later Gothic tended towards elaboration and the display of incredible skill in masonry. It is fashionable to call it decadent but it's marvellous!

Little survives of the once-splendid medieval castles and city walls, but the external appearance has been re-created in the nineteenth-century restoration of Pierrefonds by Viollet-le-Duc. The dismantling of city walls, in Paris and elsewhere, created the opportunity to construct the ring roads or boulevards which surround many French towns.

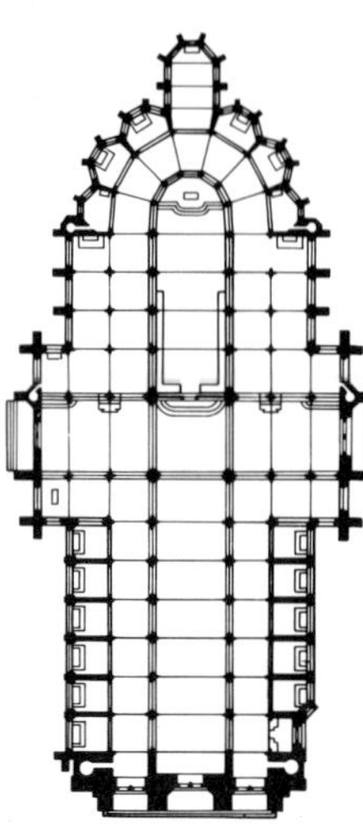

Above, left and plan The cathedral of Amiens; 1220–88. One of the largest and highest Gothic cathedrals in France, its architects achieved a lofty simplicity by extending the pier-shafts uninterrupted. Its plan is typical of the unified French cathedral, with a chevet comprising seven chapels.

Below The façade of Nôtre Dame, Paris; 1163–1250.

Right Soissons Cathedral; 1180–1225 (restored). Less spectacular than Amiens but one of the most beautiful cathedrals.

Below The massive castle of Pierrefonds; 1390–1400. It was restored in the 1860s by Viollet-le-Duc.

Above Chartres Cathedral; 1194–1260. The south doorway (above left), like the west and north, carries in sculpture the history of creation, God's revelation in the Old and New Testaments and the Last Judgement. Instruction is part of the architecture. See also p. 119.

Left The Hôtel de Ville of Compiègne; 1502–10. Still within the Gothic idiom, but the emphasis has shifted from ecclesiastical to civic architecture – the beginning of bureaucracy.

Right The *Cour du Cheval Blanc* at Fontainebleau; 1528–40. This building by Gilles le Breton formed an important prototype in the development of a French Renaissance style.

The Renaissance style was encouraged by Francis I (r. 1515–47), who was a passionate builder. Most of his châteaux are in a mixture of Gothic forms with some Classical details, but at Fontainebleau the architect Gilles le Breton created a synthesis of French traditions with Classical proportions in what may be considered the prototype of the French Renaissance style. When Italian architects, who were already skilled in Classical design, came to France at the invitation of Francis I and his successors, they accepted this compromise; Primaticcio perfected it in the *Aile de la Belle Cheminée* at Fontainebleau. If you enter the forecourt of the Palace of Fontainebleau and look at the range of simple buildings to the left, you are seeing the work of a comparatively unimportant and almost unknown architect (presumably a Breton), but one who not only influenced French monumental architecture until the early twentieth century but sowed the seeds of common architecture throughout France.

The great age of French architecture is commonly said to be the reign of Louis XIV (r. 1643–1715) who came to the throne at the tender age of five; but the really creative period was from about 1525 to 1666, when François Mansart died. Although the French public and guide books identify the name of Mansart with his niece's son, J. H. Mansart (1646–1708), only François of that name can be considered to be one of the greatest architects of all time and it is sad that this is recognised almost everywhere except in France.

Above The *Aile de la Belle Cheminée* at Fontainebleau; 1568. This is a scholarly fulfilment of Le Breton's invention by the Italian Primaticcio.

Right and left Château de Maisons, near Paris, by François Mansart; 1642–48. It was considered a near-perfect example of Classicism, with a unified design and strong use of the Orders.

Above The courtyard façade of the Louvre; the section to the left of the tower is the oldest part of the palace, built 1546–78 by Pierre Lescot. The tower was added in the 1630s.

Left The east front 1667–74, is attributed to Perrault but was really the work of a committee.

It is also ironical that the career of France's greatest Classical architect coincided with the establishment of a system of patronage based upon education in state-controlled schools – the *Écoles des Beaux Arts* – which led to a rather pompous aridity in monumental architecture, while at the same time, the establishment of state-patronised schools and factories for the decoration and furnishing of buildings led to an extreme emphasis upon decoration of the interiors.

This contrast between interior and exterior was common throughout post-Renaissance Europe.

The most obvious effect of academicism in France is the disappearance of the roof and its substitution with the cornice line surmounted by a parapet, behind which there is a concealed, metal-lined gutter (which, sooner or later, leaks). Classical temples had roofs which threw the water clear of the building, and in countries of low rainfall the Classical cornice was a sensible design treatment of the eaves of a low-pitched roof. The French tradition favoured a much more steeply pitched roof to throw off the rain and disposed of it through gargoyles or 'down-comers' – pipes made of lead. After the death of François Mansart, and with the growth of academic studies in architecture, buildings began to look much more Italian (Roman) and balustrades (resembling that on Bramante's Tempietto p. 134), which were originated for quite different purposes, appeared above cornices. Roofs were kept low so as to disappear behind the balustrades. One can see the evolution of this in the Palace of Versailles, from the old *Cour du Marbre* in the centre with mansard roofs, to the great wings designed by J. H. Mansart with no visible roof. But the chapel, also by J. H. Mansart does have a roof.

Under academic influence and growing intellectualism in Paris society, eighteenth-century architecture became more sedate and Neo-Classicism culminated in the Panthéon (p. 145), which set standards for the post-revolutionary period. Under Napoleon the architecture of imperial Rome was favoured but throughout the nineteenth century the taste for elaborate ornamentation flourished, and a type of monumental planning, developed in the *Écoles des Beaux Arts* from Roman planning, produced majestic and controlled interiors not only in great buildings like the Paris Opera House (p. 33) but also in domestic accommodation behind the bland façades of avenues.

Left The Pont Neuf, Paris, built in 1607 as part of Henry IV's planning of Paris. Right, also part of the plan, the Place Royale, now Place des Vosges. It is in the style of Roman Bridges.

Right St Étienne du Mont, Paris; 1492–1625. Slow, perhaps reluctant, change from Gothic to Renaissance architecture is evident in its plan and exterior.

Below The Place Royale, now called the Place des Vosges, 1604; by C. Chastillon in red brick and stone.

Above The Royal Chapel of Versailles; 1692–1710. Built by J. H. Mansart, it is a Baroque re-interpretation of *La Sainte Chapelle*, Paris.

Left The gardens at Versailles by André le Nôtre extend the conception of the palace into the countryside. Best seen on horseback!

Left *Le Hameau* or Hamlet, adjoining the Petit Trianon at Versailles, indicates the revolt of Marie Antoinette against the artificiality of the palace, and the influence of both Rousseau and English romanticism.

Below The Petit Trianon at Versailles, by J. A. Gabriel; 1762–68.

Bottom The Garden Front of the main palace at Versailles, built by Louis Le Vau; 1668–74. It became the model for royal palaces throughout Europe in the 18th century.

Town Planning

Since the seventeenth century France has led the world in civic design. It began with the Château du Louvre and the desire of French kings to keep a way open to the country. So as Paris grew the gardens were extended to the edge of the city and the axis of the Louvre was eventually prolonged to the Arc de Triomphe, and from what is now the Place de l'Étoile the road was, and remains, open to the forest which extended from the Bois de Boulogne to Versailles.

This great axis was a prototype for monumental town planning – from the Mall in Washington D.C. to the Avenue Jules Ferrey in Tunis, and similar 'malls' in many other places.

From the gardens of the Tuileries came Louis XIV's landscape architect, André Le Nôtre, and it was he, more than anyone, who established a kind of garden design which extended the formal planning of buildings into their environment, as in his gardens at Versailles.

The consummation came with the re-planning of Paris by Georges Eugène Haussmann (1809–91). As préfect of the Seine from 1853 he reorganised the

water supply, constructed the sewerage system, devised the boulevards, constructed new bridges, and sited the Opera House. By walking in the gardens of Versailles you can experience the prototype of Haussmann's Paris with trees instead of buildings; and wherever possible trees were planted in the streets of Paris and the many towns and cities in France, its colonies and all over the world, which imitated the delectable civic pattern of Paris. This pattern was devised for people to live and be in, not merely for maximum efficiency of traffic flow.

Above right Le Havre; part of the monumental post-war redevelopment by Auguste Perret, an attempt at modernistic Classicism.

Left The Champs Elysées, Paris, with the old royal palace of the Louvre in the far distance.

Right The Place Henri Bergson, Paris. Urbane common architecture enhanced by formal gardening.

Above La Madeleine, Paris; 1806–42 by Pierre-Alexandre Vignon, based on a Roman temple.

Above The Church of the Sorbonne, Paris; 1635–53. It is the earliest surviving example of a series of domed churches derived from Italy.

Left Portal of the Petit Palais by Charles Girault; 1900. It exploits the French genius for sculpture which culminated in Auguste Rodin.

Below An example of the intricate style of French wrought-iron work which has persisted from the Middle Ages to the present century. From the Hôtel de Cluny, Paris.

Above Diana in the Champs Elysées! Classical mythology was an essential element in French landscape design.

Left The Eiffel Tower, Paris; 1887–89. It is coarse compared with many earlier iron structures but remarkable for its size.

Folk Architecture of the Île de France

In the Île de France folk architecture is a reflection of Renaissance architecture as interpreted by Parisian architects. So, in most villages within 150 kilometres of Paris – and indeed throughout France – one finds not only the *Mairie* and the houses of local dignitaries in French Renaissance style but also the common houses of the streets and the farm buildings in the adjoining countryside. If, on driving through France, you stop at an old garage, above the showroom fascia you will probably see a Renaissance façade and a roof derived, however remotely, from the palace of Fontainebleau or houses and palaces designed by François Mansart for the nobility and the *nouveaux riches*.

But it is not quite so simple as that. The bourgeoisie might have aped the manners of the aristocracy but at Versailles itself Queen Marie Antoinette escaped from boredom with the pompous style of the palace by building *Le Hameau* (Hamlet) in the grounds of the most sophisticated Classical villa in France, *Le Petit Trianon*. The Hamlet was an idealisation of peasant architecture, a curtsy to the fashionable naturalism and a tribute to the English school of landscape gardening.

The Hamlet at Versailles was in the hardwood forest style of folk architecture and long after the Revolution it continued to give authorisation to 'folksy' architecture. Almost the last act of the old French monarchy was to endorse folk architecture as a style fit for queens, and because republicanism is no cure for snobbery, (and the French actually use *snob* as a word of praise) the hardwood forest style as interpreted by the architect of the Hamlet has flourished throughout France (and Belgium), especially in the vicinity of the old royal forests which are one of the glories of northern France. These forests have been conserved and managed since the sixteenth century to a standard which makes the forestry of other countries, especially Britain, look incompetent, (though Luxembourg is even better than France in this regard).

French women are notoriously sensitive to fashion and throughout France they have for centuries been extremely influential without being feminist. This seems to be an unbroken tradition from Romano-Celtic times. To be 'folk' or peasant in the style of your house was embarrassing, so even in remote villages the Parisian style, based upon the early Renaissance style, is dominant. This is the architecture of French people,

from Dieppe to Marseilles.

In the Île de France some pre-Renaissance buildings have survived, more by poverty than inclination in most cases. Rouen, despite wartime bombardment, retains some beautiful timber-framed buildings and this medieval character is now preserved – and even extended.

In many towns there are tall houses with gables fronting the street and one may rightly suspect that these are basically medieval. Houses are organisms and change with the times; even if the owners have decided to give them a bland, Classical façade at some time since the seventeenth century there may still be a timber-framed house behind.

Above The *Mairie* of Berny Rivière, near Soissons and the probable site of the first capital of Merovingian France. Renaissance-influenced common architecture.

Above right Rouen; an interesting relationship between a medieval tower with restored roof and a modern redevelopment in traditional style.

Right Royal, Auvergne; an elegant doctor's house. A mini-Trianon a long way from Paris.

Left Paris, houses on the Île St Louis. The common architecture of France, derived from Le Breton, Primaticcio and François Mansart.

Normandy

Normandy gets its name from the Northmen – the Vikings – who conquered it in the tenth century. Their fleets rowed up the Loire and the Seine, first pillaging and later settling. In 945 they sacked Paris and were paid to go away, but they settled between Brittany and the Île de France, extending their influence both east and south. It is interesting that Gothic architecture developed its finest forms in parts of France which came under Viking influence.

The Normans came from a land of timber buildings, but when they settled and became Christians they quickly learned the Romanesque way of design to which they gave a new simplicity and directness. The style they created flourished in Sicily and southern Italy, which they conquered from about 1060 and in England, where the best Norman architecture is to be found (pp. 262–3).

The conquest of England in 1066 reduced the Duchy of Normandy to the status of an insecurely held province, lost to the French in 1204, and major architecture of Normandy is in the Gothic style of the Île de France.

Two buildings are of outstanding importance: the cathedral of Coutances (p. 51) and Mont St Michel. The interior of Coutances is one of the most beautiful ever created. Mont St Michel is spectacular because of its site and its picturesque quality was enhanced in 1897 by building the belfry and spire, whereas three bays of the nave of the church and the west front were demolished in 1776 so that something of the majestic dignity of the medieval design was lost.

One of the most prestigious guide books states that 'a tour of the Mont on foot is not very interesting', so it needs to be said here that for people who are interested in architecture the succession of enclosed spaces is one of the most moving of architectural experiences and the design – often compared with Chartres cathedral – is among the highest achievements of Gothic art. Unfortunately, as almost everywhere in France, visitors are compelled to go in parties with official guides whose patter makes it difficult to experience this profoundly religious building. If you care about architecture, don't go in the high season.

Norman folk architecture is basically of hardwood forest style but the incursion of Vikings from a softwood region and the skills of the Norse shipwrights, carpenters and smiths are still to be detected in external detail and in the adventurous construction of framed buildings and high-pitched roofs.

High-quality slate from Brittany and superb limestone from such quarries as Caen are also found.

Right The west front and *flèche* of St Maclou, Rouen; 1432–1520. The ultimate richness in flamboyant Gothic design.

Below The high arches of the choir (1456–1521) of Mont St Michel, Brittany.

Right A bistro on the Côte Sauvage, displaying the modern end of Celtic architecture.

Left The *Alignements* of dolmens at Carnac.

Below The Castle of Josselin, built in the early 16th century but showing no sign of Renaissance style. Its steeply-roofed and circular towers are typical of medieval French military architecture.

Below The Palais de Justice, Rennes, built in 1617–25 as a *parlement* building by Salomon de Brosse. The roof surmounted by iron railings exemplifies French nostalgia for Gothic frills.

Brittany

The legend that St Anne, mother of the Virgin Mary, was a Breton, enshrines, like most myths, at least a grain of truth because Brittany, and especially Carnac, was a religious centre at least a thousand years before the first dynasty in Egypt and the architecture there embodied axial planning, formal geometry, parallax, orientation, climax and occlusion long before the pyramids and the temples of Egyptian Karnak. Although its system of religious belief is obscure it seems to have been outward-looking to the firmament while Egypt was introverted towards personal survival and the idea that money spent on building tombs was the best route to reincarnation.

The *Alignements* at Carnac should be approached, like cathedrals, from the entrance, along the axis, towards the climax standing up against the sky. No cathedrals have ever been built on such a scale: defined on the ground and vaulted by the sky. Apart from the mystical immanence of the stones, which can be overwhelming in some weather conditions, these structures pre-figure the highest aims of architects of all ages.

Devotion to and respect for divine power characterise Breton architecture. If you visit Brittany thinking it is quaint to believe in God you had better not go at all. The numerous cathedrals form a religious circuit and the churches are the focal points of village life. Church architecture is derived from Normandy and the Île de France but scaled down to the economy of the country and simplified externally by the hardness of granite. Internally, and on shrines and calvaries, the intricacies of the Celtic tradition are preserved.

The porch of the church at Carnac.

Along the indented and dangerous west coast, folk architecture is predominantly of the basic Celtic type – stone walls, gable ends, thatched or slated roofs – but the interior of Brittany was formerly dense forest. The local granite is hard to work and houses are generally in the hardwood forest style. Apart from the intricacy and smallness of scale, timber-framed houses differ little from those of southern England. Brittany is indeed culturally closer to the Celtic fringe of Britain than to France and it has an unbroken tradition of Catholicism since its conversion by missions from Ireland, Wales and England from the sixth century.

Brittany was not properly conquered by the Romans and remains a country in its own right – possibly the oldest in Europe.

The Loire to the Dordogne

The Loire castles date mainly from the early sixteenth century and are there because of the fine hunting country south of the river. Blois and Amboise are on ancient sites crowning cliffs above the river. The Orleans wing at Blois is François Mansart's finest work, done in the late 1630s and externally the noblest Renaissance building in France. Amboise retains some of its medieval character and was the home of Leonardo da Vinci in his last years. Chenonceaux and Azay-le-Rideau owe much to their watery setting. Chambord is an uncompleted compromise between a medieval castle and a Renaissance palace.

The main interest of the Loire *châteaux* is that they created a style based upon Gothic and executed by Gothic masons, with the Classical trimmings required by fashion at the court of Francis I. Like the English Tudor style this has been much admired.

Orleans cathedral is truly Gothic Revival in conception; it was rebuilt 1601–1827 after its destruction in 1567 by the Huguenots, and is the major French example of the persistence of the Gothic style. Tours cathedral, originally the shrine of St Martin, has a fascinating history. Le Mans contrasts a superb Romanesque nave with an equally fine Gothic chancel. Beaugency preserves the sedate atmosphere of a comfortable medieval town; but all along the Loire there are pleasant villages and country houses, mostly built of stone, quarried locally or brought in barges. Wherever there is water transport it is common to find materials and styles of design which come from a distance.

South into Poitou, Anjou and the Limousin, the country preserves more of the Roman way of living and eating than anywhere else; its most interesting architecture is Romanesque, in which the colour of the interiors of churches, such as N.D. la Grande at Poitiers, is better preserved than anywhere else. At Limoges, a centre of ceramics and enamelling, Gothic architecture can be seen with its colours restored, giving an impression of what Gothic churches were really like.

Right The Château of Chenonceaux, built like Venice on piles over the River Cher; 1515–23. A bridge gallery on the left was added by Philibert de l'Orme in 1556–59, with the upper gallery added in 1576. Chenonceaux is smaller than some of the royal châteaux of the Loire, such as Amboise, but its picturesque use of water, corbelled and circular turrets and Italianate details is typical.

Below Nôtre Dame la Grande, Poitiers; c. 1130–45. The central tower conceals a dome; the interior has some of the best-preserved wall-paintings in France.

Poitiers was the limit of the Muslim invasion from Spain in the eighth century, but from Angoulême to Périgueux and across France to Le Puy and the passes through the Alps, Hellenesque domed architecture came in from the east. The outstanding example is St Front at Périgueux, which in plan and structure is a replica of St Mark's at Venice (p. 180) but stripped of colour and ornament. It appeals to people with austere taste and compared with its Venetian twin it indicates the enormous part decoration plays in architecture. Angoulême cathedral is also domed, but has a typical elongated Romanesque plan. There are over 70 domed churches in the region, and the reason for this incursion of Hellenesque to the Atlantic coast is not clear.

Folk architecture, where not overlaid by Parisian decoration, is hardwood forest in style with bricks quite commonly used, even in castles.

Above Angoulême Cathedral; 1105–28 and later. It has three stone domes over the nave and a double dome over the crossing, on pointed arches though round ones are used elsewhere. The façade is richly sculptured.

Right The Hôtel de Ville at Beaugency, near Orleans; 1526.

The Château of Blois, begun in the 13th century. The east wing (right) was built in 1498–1504 in a late Gothic style. The open staircase was added by Francis I (1515–24), and the Orleans wing (above) is the master-work of Francois Mansart; 1635–38.

Central and South-west France

Approaching Auvergne from the direction of Paris on a clear day, one sees a cluster of volcanoes rising suddenly out of the plain and dominated by the Puy de Dôme. It is the dramatic frontier of a different kind of France, which extends through mainly rugged country, from the upper reaches of the River Loire to the Pyrenees and the Mediterranean. The English visitor, at least, may be interested to know that the region was depopulated by plague in the sixth century and Auvergne was re-peopled by Saxons.

The Romans had a spa at Le Mont Doré but until the building of the railway this valley was all but cut off from the outside world and there are many such places in the Massif Central which have a long history of seclusion. Others, like Clermont-Ferrand dominating the fertile plain of the River Allier, have flourished as regional capitals, or like Rocamadour and Le Puy, as centres of pilgrimage. Though there are some Gothic churches and Gothic and Renaissance additions, all this is fundamentally Romanesque country. The Romanesque church architecture excels even that of Burgundy, in such major examples as St Austremoine at Issoire (pp. 112–3) and St Saturnin in Auvergne, and one of the greatest of all Romanesque churches, St Sernin (Saturnin – he was the fourth-century martyr who evangelised Languedoc) at Toulouse.

For architecture this is one of the richest regions in France and there is the bonus of spectacular scenery. But the buildings do not fall into tidy categories. They were built by small communities of sturdy people and contain many surprises, like the unpretentious door-jamb at Souillac which is a masterpiece of Romanesque sculpture (p. 121). All a guide book can say is 'go and enjoy it. Experience the architecture for what it is' and that, it could be said, is the right way to experience all works of art – with informed spontaneity.

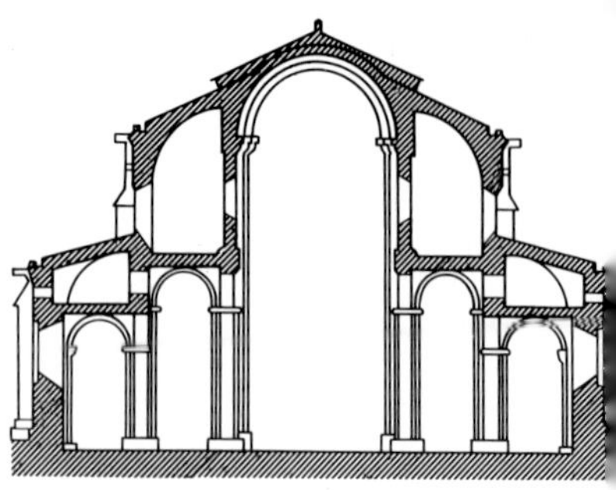

Part of the necessary information is that much of this region was settled in the fifth century by Visigoths, not Franks as in northern France, that they were heretics from the Catholic point of view, that they were persecuted in the middle ages and that later Protestantism flourished in south-west France and through the Pyrenees to the Ebro valley in Spain.

Folk architecture is predominantly Mediterranean but mountain-style at the highest altitudes and not infrequently with a cheeky, small-scale 'baronial' flavour.

Right and far right, St Nectaire and St Saturnin, both typical of the Romanesque churches of the Auvergne, with spare, barrel-vaulted interiors and the characteristic 'shouldered' tower, caused by raising the transept vaults to buttress the towers.

Left and plan right Cross-section of St Sernin, Toulouse; 1077–1119, with the flying buttress concealed below the roof. Right Plan of St Sernin, Toulouse, the largest pilgrimage church on the way to Santiago de Compostela, which it resembles (p. 209).

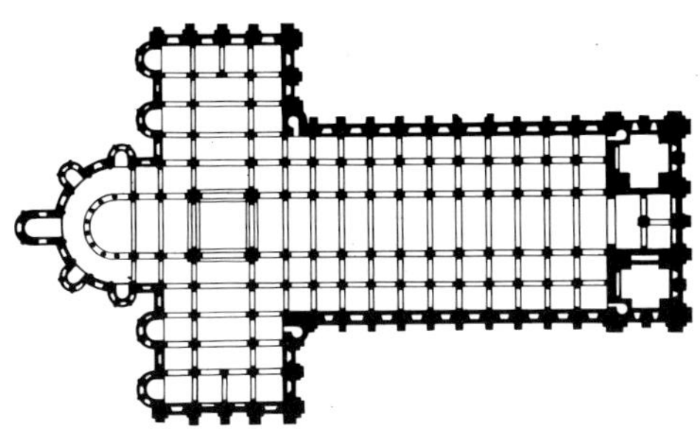

Below The 13th to 15th-century walls of Carcassonne, one of the most complete examples of medieval town fortifications. It was a frontier fortress until Roussillon was annexed to France in 1659. Restored by Viollet-le-Duc from 1844, it is an outstanding example of French conservation policy.

Above The Papal Palace, Avignon, 1349–68. Part palace and part fortress, its layout reflects the monastic background of its builders.

Above right The bridge of Avignon; 1177–85. Bridges were vital communication links and commonly had dedicatory chapels.

Above Aigues Mortes, a new town planned by St Louis as a base for the Seventh Crusade in 1248.

Right The massive towers and barbican of St André fort, Villeneuve-lès-Avignon, built in the mid-14th century.

Provence

This is a predominantly mountain region with substantial Roman remains but it includes the lower Rhône Valley, with Avignon, and the marshlands of the Camargue. Folk architecture here is mainly Mediterranean. The most famous monuments are Roman and the Maison Carrée at Nîmes is the best preserved example of an Augustan temple in existence (p. 31). The Pont du Gard is the most spectacular aqueduct and there are many other Roman remains. Some are incorporated in buildings and one of the best examples is the circular colonnade inside the cathedral of Aix-en-Provence. The Popes lived at Avignon from 1309 to 1377 in a fortified castle. Villeneuve-lès-Avignon, on the opposite side of the Rhone, has a very impressive fortress with all the old inconveniences.

Aigues Mortes was planned as a new town in 1240 with a constable's house in one corner, formidable walls and a harbour leading out to the Mediterranean. Marseilles is famous for one of the seminal buildings of Modernism, the *Unité d'Habitation*, but whether the seed has borne good fruit in European high-rise housing is open to question.

Below The *Unité d'Habitation*; 1946–52, by Le Corbusier. A totalitarian concept paying homage to a proportional system derived from the physique of man but oblivious of human nature. Its influence on the design of 'housing' all over the world has been enormous and disastrous.

Eastern France

'Of all the geographical names' it has been said, 'Burgundy has changed its meaning the greatest number of times'. At the fall of the Roman Empire it was a kingdom which included the Saône and Rhône valleys, much of the western Alps and Provence. Although this kingdom was ruled by a grandson of Clovis I and subsequent history confirmed its adherence to the western branch of the Franks, its barbarian immigrants were Burgundians not Franks. They became established at a crossroads of trade on what was for centuries to be a cultural frontier.

The Burgundian achievement in architecture is comparable with the wine, but it was made in the eleventh and twelfth centuries, mainly through the influence of the Benedictine monastery at Cluny. It extended as far as Santiago de Compostela (p. 209).

Folk architecture of the region is varied, from Alpine in Haute Savoie to mountain and hardwood forest, which is the predominant style. This timber architecture looks towards the east and is at its best in Alsace.

Right Town houses in Colmar, Alsace, showing multi-storey gable-ends, which are typical of this border region.

Left A vintner's courtyard in the small town of Riquewihr.

Right Autun Cathedral; 1120–32. The sculpture over the west door is a very rare example of a medieval artist signing his work, thus: 'Giselbertus fecit'.

Left The St Lazare fountain in Autun, built in 1543 in Renaissance style.

Right The Porte St André at Autun, built by the Romans in about AD 20. Its upper storey of Ionic pilasters may have influenced the design of Autun Cathedral.

Below Auxerre Cathedral, built from 1215 in early Gothic style and including much fine stained glass.

Left St Philibert, Tournus; c. 950–1120. The transverse barrel-vaults of the nave permit full clerestorey lighting. This ingenious idea, like Vézelay, was to be superseded by ribbed vaulting, as at Durham (p. 113).

Right The narthex of St Madeleine, Vézelay; c. 1132. A large multi-purpose vestibule with early pointed cross-vaulting. The nave has transverse arches, a clerestorey and domical groined vaults.

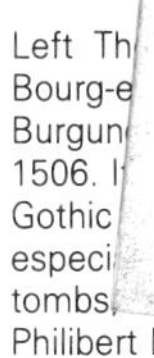

Left Th
Bourg-e
Burgun
1506. I
Gothic
especi
tombs,
Philibert le Beau.

Below The triumphal arch of Nancy, which forms part of the superb mid-18th century planning of that city. A sequence of squares and vistas leads to the palace – smaller but better than Versailles.

Isles

Stonehenge, like the Gothic cathedrals, was built over a long period. It embodies many of the major ideas which have been employed by architectural thinkers up to the present day. In its final form, it is a circular temple related to an axis (an arrow and a target). The axis and the circle are resolved by a horseshoe (like an ambulatory) which forms the setting for an altar. Gothic architects concentrated upon the axis and Renaissance theory upon the circle. Neither achieved the logical clarity of the Stonehenge plan.

The classification of pre-historic 'cultures' by similarities in their fragmentary artefacts is an academic mask for our almost total ignorance of people and a way of life. Megalithic temples were related to the heavens and particularly to the Sun at the mid-summer dawn. They were probably also related to electro-magnetic phenomena in the Earth's surface, possibly to dynamic effects of the Sun's energy. The fact that stones were often brought from a great distance may have been due to their electro-magnetic properties. The existence of altars suggests intercession and propitiation but we should not assume that these ancient people translated their awareness of divine power into human or animal-like deities.

Stonehenge is the most important prehistoric building in the world and one of the most profound examples of arcane architecture from any age. There are stone circles and alignments throughout the western parts of Britain and Ireland. None approach the grandeur of Stonehenge but all exemplify arcane architecture created by relating earthly and celestial geometry. Forget about spurious druids and neurotic imaginings of rites belonging to later ages. Megalithic architecture has an intellectuality seldom equalled in the whole subsequent history of architecture.

Deep intellectual concepts in art affect the emotions profoundly, sometimes awefully. Ideally one should be alone to receive the full impact and this is easier to achieve at the more remote sites. But whatever the time of day or night – and this applies to all religious architecture – the relationship of man to the divine is thoughtful as well as emotional.

Soon after the completion of Stonehenge about 1600 BC ecological changes and movements of peoples throughout Europe led to a dark age in British architecture. Many Bronze and Iron Age sites are known, some with impressive defensive earthworks, but buildings were probably of timber and have perished. They may have been spectacular (as early Norse timber buildings, p. 316).

Roman architecture had its roots in Italy. In Britain it was provincial, lacking the refinements of high Roman fashion even though most of the creature-comforts were provided – baths, theatres in the larger towns, temples for the Roman gods and for mystery cults which offered personal solace and, eventually, on a small scale, for Christianity. But Roman remains in Britain always have to be judged in the context of Continental superiority, fascinating though they are as archaeological source material for British history.

Above Stonehenge, Wiltshire; an open-air cathedral to the source of life.

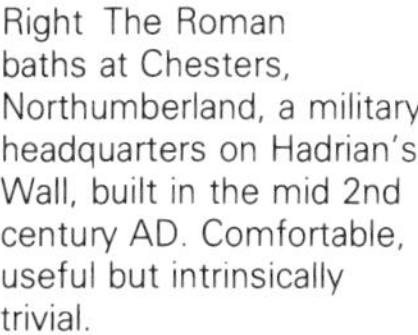

Right The Roman baths at Chesters, Northumberland, a military headquarters on Hadrian's Wall, built in the mid 2nd century AD. Comfortable, useful but intrinsically trivial.

Above The 7th-century monastery of Jarrow. The triangular 'arch' is often described as typical of Anglo-Saxon Romanesque but is in fact rare.

Above right The tower of All Saints, Earls Barton; c. 975. The surface decoration of strips and arches probably derives from Continental sources.

Right The crypt of Hexham Abbey, Northumberland; c. 675–80. The church was on a basilican plan.

Far right The Romanesque church of Sompting, Sussex, c. 1010. The tower, which is unusual for England, resembles the churches of the Rhineland.

The Anglo-Saxons

The Anglo-Saxons were by no means so crude as has commonly been supposed. Their naval and military prowess made Britain untenable by the Romans who withdrew at the beginning of the fifth century. The invaders had beautiful ships of the kind later used by the Vikings. Their arms, costume and jewellery compare with the best that was being produced in the Western Empire at that time.

English settlements were often on new sites, rather than in the Romano-British towns. Buildings were generally of timber and the most significant Anglo-Saxon introduction was the hall where the chieftain held audiences and assemblies. The hall remained a central element in English domestic architecture and became the name for the main house in a locality (eg Haddon Hall).

Although Christianity survived the pagan Anglo-Saxon invasion the missions of St Augustine to Kent in 597 and St Aidan from Iona to Northumbria in 635 accomplished the conversion of kings, and the building of permanent stone churches followed. Those in the south were influenced from France (Gaul) and the Roman apse was favoured. In the north, Celtic influence was dominant. This is reflected in the square east end, which much later became characteristic of English Gothic architecture and gave scope for the development of the great east window, one of the principal glories of English architecture.

Anglo-Saxon church architecture has survived mainly in the settlements that did not develop, as the major buildings of the period were destroyed and superseded by Gothic cathedrals and churches in the more successful places.

The Normans

The Normans saw their conquest of England in 1066 as the beginning of a new era. They brought their architecture with them, just as they took it to Sicily. The informality of Anglo-Saxon monasticism gave way to the discipline of the reformed Benedictine Order and the Continental abbey plan. Castles, which were initially strongholds in subjected territory, were mainly earthworks, quickly built by impressed labour, consisting of a motte (fortified mound) and a bailey (enclosed parade ground, barracks and cattle fold, cf. Tiryns p. 45). Later, stone towers and shell keeps (p. 114) replaced or surmounted the stockaded motte, but living accommodation for the Norman nobility remained austere. They lived rough and so did their wives. A castle bedroom for a king or a duke was about the size of a modern prison cell and less well furnished. Manor houses were possibly more comfortable but were seldom more than substantial two-roomed cottages. Privacy was a rare luxury in buildings (hence the importance in stories of 'bowers' in the woodlands and the elaborate tents and pavilions shown in medieval pictures). It was in churches and abbeys that the major architectural achievements were made (pp. 120–9). Living accommodation in monasteries was well above secular standards and the main building, the church, upon which the monastic way of life focussed, was often magnificent.

The new Norman clergy wanted quick results and had sufficient confidence in the security of the kingdom to use timber roofs instead of vaulting which had become normal on the mainland (but see Durham pp. 112–3). Many of the refinements of Anglo-Saxon building were lost. Walls became thicker again with rubble infilling, suggesting the use of unskilled labour (as for much Roman building). The semi-circular arch was usual. Decoration was simple and repetitive, requiring little skill and a lot of hard work. Forceful and effective with no niggling is a fair description of early Norman architecture.

The chief characteristics of Norman ecclesiastical architecture in England include the aisled nave, transepts, rectangular chancel with apsidal end, low tower over crossing. Round churches, often called St Sepulchre, partly derive from Carolingian and Hellenesque precedents but mainly were inspired by the Church of the Holy Sepulchre in Jerusalem.

Major Norman churches have twin western towers, probably of Frankish origin.

Walls are thick and self-sufficient, but sometimes with slight buttresses.

Arches are round and (later) occasionally horseshoe. Interlacing arches produced a pointed arch, and as in France (p. 111), the pointed arch was occasionally used structurally.

Columns are often simple drums with base and capital echoing Classical columns. The tendency towards sub-division and clustering of columns follows the continental manner but the capital was retained as support for arches and/or vaults. Decoratively arches are multiplied concentrically, each one being supported on its own 'border' or column.

Sculpture is rare and decoration mostly geometrical. Walls and

Above and right Southwell Minster, Notts. Begun in the early 12th century, this is the epitome of Romanesque and Gothic achievement in Britain.

columns were commonly covered with paintings done in earth colours – white (lime), red and yellow ochres, and carbon black. Bright reds, greens, blues and yellows were costly and rarely used.

Vaults are barrel or groined, but the ribbed vault, which made Gothic architecture possible, was probably invented in this period and first exploited on a large scale at Durham.

Domestic and military architecture had plain walls, round arches, newel (spiral) stairs, and square towers.

Ely Cathedral, begun c. 1090, has typical English carving on its south door (left), while the west front, central octagon and western transepts (above) make it highly original.

Left The nave of Norwich Cathedral; 1096–1145. One of the few English cathedrals to retain the round east end (plan, below), in which Gothic grows harmoniously out of Romanesque.

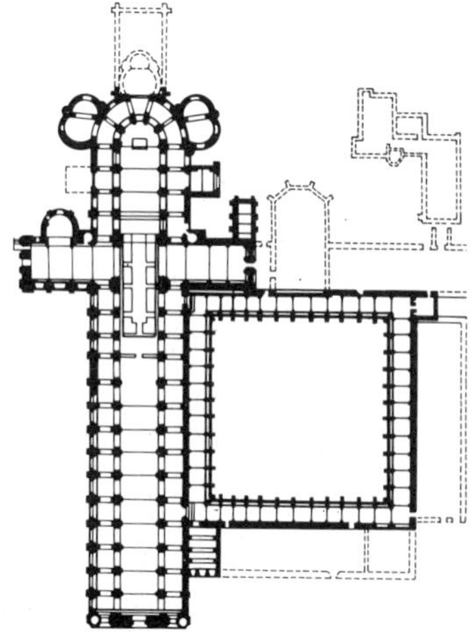

Left The west door of Selby Abbey, begun in the late 11th century. The rings of Norman arches are related to basically Classical Orders of columns.

Below left Bury St Edmunds; the 12th-century abbey gateway tower.

Above The mid-14th century nave of Exeter Cathedral.

Left Winchester Cathedral; 1079–1235 – the intersection of the main axis and transepts.

Gothic

In 1817 Thomas Rickman classified the different kinds of Gothic architecture as though they were Classical Orders. This was part of the movement (see Gothic Revival p. 148) to establish Christian Gothic architecture on an academic basis comparable to that of pagan Classical design. Rickman discerned three styles of Gothic, and called them Early English, Decorated and Perpendicular, assigning dates to each style. It was a brilliant achievement and the dates may be accepted as a very rough guide. The names, though misleading, have come to be accepted but they came only in the nineteenth century and medieval builders had no knowledge of them.

In England the term Gothic is normally applied only to church architecture built in stone. Castles were designed functionally with a few stylistic features borrowed from ecclesiastical architecture. Little domestic architecture of the Gothic period has survived. It was mostly timber-framed (p. 74). Mansions, inns and colleges built of stone followed the style of the domestic quarters in monasteries.

Throughout the Gothic (later medieval) period English kings claimed sovereignty in France and the lilies of France were quartered in the English royal arms, but constant dynastic strife with France did not disrupt ecclesiastical accord and the headquarters of the monastic orders were on the Continent.

Gothic architecture developed from Romanesque architecture and in England some features of Norman design persisted until the beginning of the fourteenth century. After the invention of ribbed vaulting had separated the structure from the enclosing panels, the next stage was to carry the idea of a structural frame into the walls and down to the foundations. The walls, like the vaults, were divided into structure and enclosure. Gothic churches became skeletal and more and more of the enclosure was effected with coloured glass, so that the interior became a space transfused with coloured light. Thus the marvellous atmosphere of Gothic interiors was created. The pointed arch came into general use because of its flexibility (p. 122) though according to Classical theory it was a less satisfactory shape than the semicircle.

Although French and English Gothic developed in parallel and masons travelled between the two countries, there are important differences which seem to reflect social, political and

Left Flying buttresses supporting the nave of Chester Cathedral; 12th century.

Right The ruined nave of Rievaulx reveals the structure of the flying buttress.

Above The quad and 13th-century chapel at the heart of New College, Oxford.

Right The elegant internal structure of Gloucester Cathedral below the 15th-century tower. The consistency of the flying arches, vaulting and tracery may be compared with the work of Modernist architects such as Nervi (p. 35); but here it is much more refined, though executed in stone rather than re-inforced concrete.

temperamental differences between English and French people.

The Norman cruciform plan, with a long processional nave, persisted in England. Emphasis was upon the vista to the altar, upon the horizontal rather than the vertical. English churches covered more ground and had more space around them, either as a church-yard or as a close.

Partly under the influence of the Cistercian Order with its dedication to simplicity, partly because of the Celtic tradition and partly for ease of construction, the apse and chevet gave way to a square east end. What started with acceptance of a tradition and continued as the avoidance of a difficult architectural extravagance became the principal glory of English churches, both great and small, the east window, a wall of illuminated pictures behind and above the main altar and a congregation looking symbolically not into a caged enclosure but into the light.

Early east ends have three lancet windows. If joined under one arch, these became united as *tracery* (see pp. 126–7). Tracery is the decoratively elaborated framework of stone which carries a wall of glass. In the vertical plane this is not so difficult but the pressure of wind must be resisted in the lateral plane without spoiling the beauty of the tracery. This is one of the three-dimensional structural marvels of English Gothic architecture.

So much attention has been given to tracery, since Rickman, as a means of dating Gothic churches that it has distracted attention from more important aspects. Tracery is a means of supporting pictorial glass within a structure which is independent of it, as can be seen in many ruined abbey churches. It is no more structural than curtains are, and is equivalent to what is called in modern architecture a curtain wall.

A good way of understanding Gothic architecture is to start with ruins like the abbeys of Rievaulx or Tintern. The roofs, robbed of their lead, rotted and collapsed upon the vaults, cracking them like eggshells, but the architectural skeleton of the church remains. If you can recognise this in un-ruined churches you will begin to be aware of the essential architectural form into which tracery, ribs, screens and even roofs are fitted.

Ruins are not melancholy: they are a revelation, even though one may regret the loss of so much human endeavour and so much beauty, sacrificed to prejudice, greed, pugnacity and destructiveness.

Right The 12th-century Cistercian Fountains Abbey, sited, like many other such abbeys, beside a river that could provide clear water and fish.

Melton Mowbray, Leicestershire – the splendid parish church of a prosperous Midland market town, internally and externally offering a vivid record of the history of the place and its people. With continuous benefactions the architecture of such churches has been accumulated rather than designed.

This is also true for the East Anglian church of Long Melford (below), which expresses proper pride and due respect under God; the good side of medieval civilisation.

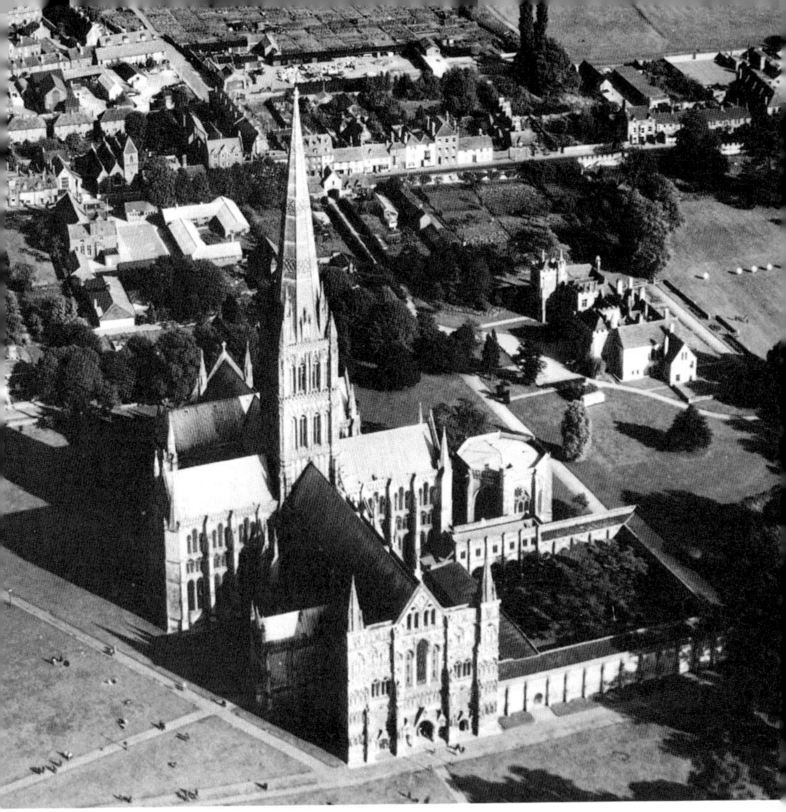

Above Salisbury Cathedral; 1220–58; the 'ideal' English cathedral, commonly contrasted with Amiens (p. 226) as the French 'ideal'. It was built during the reign of Henry III (r. 1216–72), a time notable for the development of English constitutional ideas and a golden age of English architecture.

Right The gateway to the Cathedral Close, Salisbury.

The Periods of English Gothic

In England the transition from Romanesque or Norman to Gothic began at the end of the eleventh century. Up to the end of the thirteenth century a simple and elegant style was based upon the pointed arch and slender columns, often clustered and made of marble, with formal capitals derived from Classical Corinthian. Tracery was formed by intersecting pointed arches, cusping, and circles. The tracery is called geometrical and the style of architecture Early English. Vaulting echoed tracery in providing a web of ribs to reduce the size of the enclosing panels.

About the end of the thirteenth century a new mood is reflected in architecture, a sensitive appreciation of the beauty of nature. This is the great age of English sculpture and its supreme exemplification is to be seen in Beverley Minster. The artists of this period may have reflected the unique contribution to Christianity of St Francis of Assisi (d. 1224) and they did so with tenderness for the physical beauty of the world and a strong sense of humour about humanity's place in it. In Rickman's classification this period is called Decorated.

The joyous period of English Gothic architecture coincides with the development of universities throughout Europe and especially in England at Oxford and Cambridge, the ascendancy of collegiate institutions over the traditional monasteries (see pp. 54–5) and, in Italy, the beginnings of the Renaissance.

Medieval society broke down with the emergence of an economy based upon money rather than service. Though usury (the lending of money at interest) had been condemned by the medieval Church, battles and buildings came to depend upon money to a much greater extent. Inflation, after a long period of stability, brought social troubles and suddenly in 1348 the disaster of the Black Death fell upon England.

The so-called Perpendicular style is a unique and insular phenomenon which strangely anticipates the political isolation of England from Europe and the development of a specifically English culture, which was to have world-wide influence. After the Black Death (but not because of it), church architecture came under secular patronage and flourished most in prosperous regions where merchants and landowners provided the money for building. Strangely, sculpture in stone almost disappeared but a new era of sculpture in timber began and this culminated in the seventeenth century at St Paul's Cathedral in the work of Grinling Gibbons.

Though the Perpendicular style produced some magnificent and intricate vaulting, which is the apogee of mason-craft in Europe, the typical church was capacious, congregational and generally roofed in timber. This was a great age of English carpentry.

Henry VIII consummated the secularisation of architecture by the Dissolution of the Monasteries (1536–40). The adoption of cannon as a weapon of war made castles obsolescent. A new nobility, deriving their revenues from farming, from trade, from speculation and increasingly from colonisation overseas, became the main patrons of architecture and built palatial houses which were centres of regional administration and remained so, in fact if not in theory, until the nineteenth century. England recreated the Roman villa system and, sustaining the principles of Magna Carta, the land-owning classes kept the monarchy in a state of relative poverty. As a result the great royal palace, characteristic of mainland Europe never happened in England.

1 Brinkburn Priory, Northumberland; mid-12th century. Lancets, pointed arcade and a round, arched Norman-style triforium.
2 Geometrical, Early English tracery in Lincoln Cathedral.
3 Cartmel Priory, Cumbria; a typical Perpendicular window.
4 King's College Chapel, Cambridge; 1446–1515. One of the finest examples of late medieval fan-vaulting.

1

2

3

4

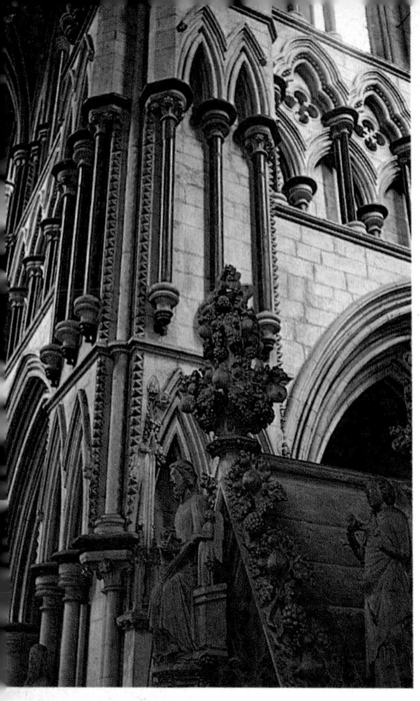

Left, right and detail below Beverley Minster; 1220–19th century, one of the most precious churches in England. The Percy Shrine (left) is the masterpiece of the sculptor who also did the portrait of Queen Margaret (1300), with Edward I and II, perhaps the best medieval royal portraits surviving. Beverley is also notable for the 14th-century nave triforium built in 12th-century style to link the old with the new, refuting the myth that medieval architects always built in the 'modern' style.

Below Gawsworth House, Cheshire; a half-timbered manor-house; 15th-century.

Below The Abbot's Kitchen in the monastery of Glastonbury: a chapter-house design modified for culinary purposes.

Below Montacute House, Somerset; 1580–99. A perfect example of the Elizabethan development of Gothic architecture, for a stately home.

Renaissance Influence

The development of a unique English tradition in architecture comparable with English music and literature of the sixteenth century was suddenly reversed under the patronage of James I's unhappy queen, Anne of Denmark, who in 1616 gave Inigo Jones the opportunity to build an Italian Palladian villa at Greenwich. Inigo Jones (1573–1652), who was primarily a draughtsman and designer of costumes and theatrical scenery, had travelled as a kind of courier with the Catholic Lord Arundel, and had acquired a knowledge of late High Renaissance architecture in Italy.

The commission for the Queen's House was followed in 1619 by the opportunity to rebuild the Banqueting Hall in Whitehall which was the court theatre. Italian Renaissance architecture of the Palladian kind was thus established from the court of James I (r. 1603–25) and confirmed under his son Charles I (r. 1625–49), but it remained exceptional and the English style, derived from Gothic, flourished in the Jacobean period as it had in the sixteenth century, with slight concessions to Classical details

but with great freedom in planning, massing and the handling of materials.

The Revolution, Commonwealth and Protectorate period (1649–60) gave little opportunity for architecture but germinated the idea of a new kind of church which emphasised the sermon rather than the liturgy. The pulpit became more prominent than the altar. Domestic architecture continued in either the Jacobean or the Palladian mode without significant variations.

The restoration of the monarchy in 1660 and the Great Fire of London in 1666 gave Christopher Wren (1632–1723) an opportunity, the fulfilment of which is only comparable with the achievements of Sinan the Great in Istanbul (p. 104).

Wren was a scientist (professor of astronomy at Oxford) and a founder member of the Royal Society under the patronage of Charles II (r. 1660–85), who himself played a decisive role in the design of St Paul's Cathedral by overriding the committee men and giving Wren latitude to vary his hastily prepared Royal Warrant design.

Wren's first major building was the Sheldonian Theatre in Oxford, the model for which was exhibited at the Royal Society in 1663 and aroused great interest because of its structural ingenuity in creating a Classical theatre with a flat ceiling. In style it is a highly original amplification of the English tradition. In 1665 (the year before François Mansart's death) Wren visited Paris. In 1669 he was appointed Surveyor of the Royal Works and until his death in 1723, and indeed afterwards, he had an enormous influence on English architecture by the example of his work, by the nobility of his character and through the hundreds of craftsmen who learned to work in the Classical manner on his buildings.

Wren designed in the Classical and Gothic styles and he was probably the first architect to use that word 'style' which was to become so important. His approach to design was intellectual and theoretical but not dogmatic, indeed he had much the same investigative and open approach to the problems of architecture as his friend Isaac Newton had in physics. He thought perspective was extremely important and in this respect, at least, he was in line with contemporary Baroque architects on the Continent, but his closest affinity seems to be with François Mansart and the culmination of the French version of High Renaissance design (pp. 229–31).

Left Hardwick Hall by Robert Smithson (1590–97); notable for its internal spatial planning.

Right The Queen's House, Greenwich by Inigo Jones (1618–35), which introduced the Palladian version of the Classical style to England.

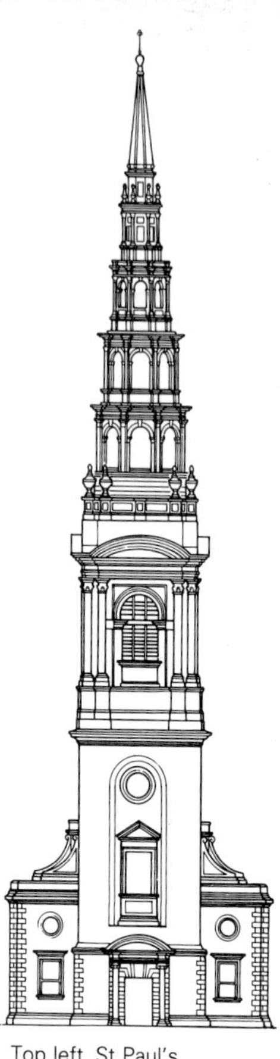

Top left St Paul's Cathedral, London, by Sir Christopher Wren; 1675–1710. The dome is arguably the finest built during the Renaissance.

Centre left The east wing of Hampton Court Palace, Middlesex; built by Wren in 1689–1701.

Left The Sheldonian Theatre, Oxford; 1664–69. A brilliant early work by Wren based on a Roman theatre, but with a roof.

Blenheim Palace by Sir John Vanbrugh; 1704–20. Magnificently scenic and often called 'Baroque' in line with Continental architecture but really quite different: despite its Classical Orders it has romantic affinities with Romanesque. The interiors (left) are pompous but ordinary, but the exterior (below) maximises the effect of a not particularly large country house.

Left St Bride's, Fleet St, (1671–78), one of 52 churches Wren built in London after the Fire.

Below Capheaton Hall, Northumberland; by Robert Trollop; 1668. Its decoration is in a rustic Baroque style based on well-meaning ignorance of Classical detail.

The Eighteenth Century

Wren had gone beyond the derivative Palladianism of Inigo Jones and followers. For him architecture was a living and growing art. But by the end of the seventeenth century there were ambitious men who thought he had reigned too long and a new kind of patron, represented by and indeed to a large extent created by Lord Burlington (1694–1753), turned away from creative architecture to impose a long-out-of-date Palladianism upon England.

The result was that English architecture became governed by text books. These began with theories of Alberti (p. 132) which had been based upon science as understood in the fifteenth century. Wren had brought architecture and seventeenth-century science together in his work but he had been far too busy to write books. Alberti was really too abstruse for the eighteenth-century aristocracy and his follower, Palladio, whose ideas had already been introduced by Inigo Jones, now provided the standards by which English architecture was to be designed.

This was an extraordinary phenomenon. The eighteenth-century gentry, led by Lord Burlington, cut completely away from European developments and went back to the High Renaissance as interpreted by Palladio who was, it must be said, already out of date in Italy when he published his famous *Four Books of Architecture* in 1570. It was an English renaissance of the Renaissance and its leaders felt very virtuous about it. The snag was that it took the life and creativity out of architecture and substituted books, enabling the client who could afford them, to instruct the architect who often could not.

The results in actual building were not disastrous. In the resultant Georgian style, built by craftsmen who had learned their trade under Wren, England had an orderly, well-proportioned and dignified style of design and a few architects rode on the band-waggon of Palladianism and aristocratic patronage to produce buildings of great originality and beauty.

There was Nicholas Hawksmoor (1661–1736), Wren's former assistant, who carried on in his master's manner but with some interesting idiosyncrasies of style and without Wren's flair for unity in his compositions. All Souls College, Oxford, was designed in the Gothic style by Hawksmoor in 1715.

James Gibbs (1683–1774), architect of the Radcliffe Camera at Oxford and the famous church of St Martin-in-the-Fields, London, greatly enriched the English tradition and produced books of designs which he was unable to build, for lack of patronage; but they became copy-books for many English architects and were even more influential in America.

But the most un-Palladian architect of the age was the Restoration playwright, Sir John Vanbrugh (1664–1726). His approach to design was grand and theatrical, the very opposite of Palladianism, but he prospered and built the nation's tribute to the victorious general John Churchill, Blenheim Palace.

The most important effect of Palladianism was upon common architecture. The orderly Palladian formula was adopted by estate developers who built town houses for the gentry and, in Bath especially, places for them to stay on holiday. (The custom of going to 'watering places' for annual holidays began in this period and had a great influence upon architecture). The façades of Georgian squares and terraces are not skin-deep architecture. Behind them there are well-proportioned rooms, elegant staircases and Classical detailing, though one has only to look at contemporary paintings of interiors (especially by Hogarth) to realise that some of these rooms are now more beautiful than they were in the eighteenth century.

The reaction to Lord Burlington's Palladianism came in a Rococo interpretation of Gothic design led by Horace Walpole, Earl of Orford (1717–97). The supreme example is his own house at Strawberry Hill, Twickenham, but the prevalence of charming and licentious Rococo design on the Continent did not escape the notice of English aristocrats who had quickly tired of Classical correctness. The Duke of Northumberland imported Italian stucco workers who enriched many houses in northern England with Rococo plasterwork. Lord Chesterfield created a French Rococo interior for his London home (it is now in the Bowes Museum at Barnard Castle). Robert Adam sensed the desire for something different, which he found in late Roman design.

The Radcliffe Camera, Oxford, built by James Gibbs; 1737–49. The culmination of the ideal circular plan, but for a library rather than a church.

Above Detail of a corner pavilion in the Royal Crescent, with Giant Orders unifying two storeys of a simple domestic building.

Top The Royal Crescent Bath, by John Wood Junior; 1767–75. This continued the admirable scheme of civic design in Bath begun by Wood's father in 1728.

Above The Neo-Classical church of Redland, near Bristol; 1740–46.

Right Chiswick House, near London, built by Lord Burlington and William Kent from 1725. This house is polite and Palladian through and through, built for a formal style of living.

Above The stable block of (right) Belsay Hall, Northumberland, designed by Sir Charles Monck, an enthusiastic amateur of things Greek; 1810. His original drawings are dimensioned *in decimals* to 0.001 of an inch.

Below Strawberry Hill Twickenham, 1747–63; the Long Gallery by Horace Walpole, Earl of Orford (see also p. 148).

The Nineteenth Century

By the late eighteenth century Eclecticism was being born, with a philosophy which was opposed to the Renaissance idea that beauty was the result of conformity to natural law. David Hume's *Essay on the Standard of Taste* (1757) epitomised a growing conviction that beauty was not an objective quality of things. The Romantic idea of 'the sublime and beautiful' remained, but beauty became a matter of taste and cultivated judgement. But whose judgement? Whatever the philosophical truth of the matter, the effect was disorderly. Hitherto, in both the Classical and the Gothic styles, there had been a consistent discipline in theory and established practice. Styles in many lands were also seen to have established consistent and orderly ways of design. 'Purity of style' became a cult, but one could choose whatever style one liked. An alternative was to make a synthesis of two or more styles; but whichever course of Eclecticism was adopted, architecture became backward-looking and historicist. The study of architectural history boomed in a series of erudite books which tended to emphasise decorative details rather than structural or design principles. Although these principles were not entirely ignored by the authors, architects tended to use history books as quarries for design. Even a Gothic Revival purist, A. W. N. Pugin, (1812–52), chose to use Flemish rather than English Gothic precedents for the Houses of Parliament.

The late eighteenth and the early years of the nineteenth century are commonly known as the Regency period, though the actual regency lasted only from 1811 to 1820. Taste remained conditioned by the Palladian version of Classicism and this was

Below Grey St, Newcastle upon Tyne, built mostly in the 1830s by Richard Grainger under Greek Revival influence.

reinforced by the Classical Revival in France (pp. 144–5), as well as the belated growth of academic studies architecture in England. This happened to coincide with the rediscovery of Greek architecture of the fifth century BC, and then with the potent influence of Lord Byron and his involvement in the liberation of Greece from Turkey, which engaged the sympathy of the British people. Awareness of the qualities of Greek architecture had its effect even upon design in exotic styles, as we can see in Brighton Pavilion (p. 13) by John Nash (1752–1835) who also designed the Doric colonnades of Carlton House Terrace. His more academic contemporary Sir John Soane (1753–1837) established the study of architecture at the Royal Academy and built the new Bank of England. But Soane also designed in various styles.

The Great Exhibition of 1851 revealed an amazing richness of ornament in arts and manufactures and, to some people, an astonishing lack of taste. This seemed to result from the use of industrial processes for making articles which had formerly been made by craftsmen. In fact the workmen in factories and foundries were marvellously skilful, but design was passing more and more on to the drawing boards of people, including architects, who had no part in the actual making of what they designed. Despite the efforts of William Morris, the Art Workers Guild, and the Europe-wide Arts and Crafts Movement which they inspired, this is still true, although the bleakness of Modernist architecture has helped to create a market for hand-made works of art and craftsmanship.

By the end of the nineteenth century England was achieving high academic standards of Eclectic design and the quality of workmanship and building construction was as high as it had ever been anywhere, except possibly in fifth-century Athens.

A normal architect's specification, not only for public buildings but for houses, required simply 'best quality'. In what is now called the 'public sector', Office of Works specifications set perfection as the standard for government buildings. In any district of England which was developed, even by speculative builders, in the period 1890–1914 you may see window frames and sashes made of red deal with oak sills and they are as sound today as they were when they were made. We do still have very high standards of craftsmanship, at a high price, as is right in the modern context, but the materials which are today being destroyed by developers are irreplaceable – unless the human population of Earth drops to about a million and stays there for a thousand years.

Despite World War I the first three decades of the twentieth century were a golden age in English architecture, reflecting the culmination of the British Empire. There was a return to the disciplines of Classicism combined with awareness of traditional English values, implemented by a building trade based upon extremely high standards of craftsmanship and led by architects who proudly saw themselves as masters in the greatest of the arts. Judged by the standards we use when considering ancient Greece and Rome or Renaissance Italy, this was a great age.

Above The Houses of Parliament by Charles Barry and A. W. N. Pugin; 1840–65.

Right The Natural History Museum, London. Alfred Waterhouse; 1868–80.

Above The porch of Babbacombe Church, Devon; 1868–74 by William Butterfield, a leader of mid-Victorian Gothic.

Above Detail of Dame Allen's School, Newcastle-upon-Tyne; 1883, by R. J. Johnson.

Left Scarborough, Yorkshire; typical 19th-century holiday architecture in a tradition based on Bath (p. 282).

Left A timber-framed, or half-timbered, urban house in Canterbury, Kent, in the hard-wood forest mode.

Below A cottage in Rockingham, Northants, built of local stone and thatched with local straw, the usual roofing material for humble dwellings in much of England before the 19th century.

Above A timber-clad, or clapboard, house in Robertsbridge, Sussex, a style common in southeast England.

Right Sturdy stone houses in the fishing village of Portloe, Cornwall.

Folk Architecture in England

England is one of the richest countries in Europe in the variety and quality of its folk architecture which, for the tourist industry, is one of its greatest assets. It is noteworthy that the Anglo-Saxons settled off the Roman main roads; that the Norman Conquest led to insular integrity for England, Wales and Scotland over nine centuries; that apart from dynastic squabbles, border skirmishes and the sixteenth-century revolution, England has enjoyed internal peace and relative prosperity for 900 years.

In this period political and social institutions have evolved in England which, in one way or another, have affected many other countries. Most importantly for folk architecture, the long experience of parliamentary democracy, however imperfectly conducted, has fostered the idea, not merely of the responsibility of government to the people, but the responsible participation of an ever-growing sector of the people in the corporate life of the nation. An ever-growing number of substantial people have been able to make their homes an expression of their responsible individuality and, in longer term, the family continuity of that role. Pride may be a deadly sin but it is very good for architecture, so long as it doesn't corrupt the architects.

The social stratification of English society linked arcane architecture with the aristocracy and the Church, and common architecture with the gentry (from the sixteenth century). But the economic and political conditions favoured the building of folk architecture by unpretentious yet fairly prosperous people.

Another important fact is that England is a natural garden and what nature provides man has improved to such an extent that the English concept of a garden has had a world-wide influence.

The modern demand for by-passes is consistent with the Anglo-Saxon belief that you should not build a town on a main road. English towns and villages developed their own magnetism within the locality, rather than relying on external influences for their growth.

English folk architecture was based upon prosperity and individuality, upon a combination of respect and self-confidence.

To understand the distribution of the styles of English folk architecture we must consider the effects of surface geology, botany, ethnic history, water transport and cultural influences.

Botanically the whole country was once predominantly deciduous forest. Ethnically the Celts survived in Cornwall, Wales and possibly Northumberland. The Anglo-Saxons penetrated to the edge of the Celtic territories but were displaced in the east and Midlands in the ninth century by Scandinavians.

The transport of exotic materials certainly goes back as far as Stonehenge before 2000 BC and until the building of railways this was almost always done by water. Putting stones on rafts is the easiest way of moving them.

Opposite top The Old Grammar School, Burnsall, founded in 1602, and typical of the Yorkshire Dales.

Centre Handsome cottages in West Auckland, County Durham, with a continuous pan-tiled roof.

Right The Pantiles, Tunbridge Wells, Kent: a sophisticated 18th-19th-century precinct in a fashionable spa.

Scotland

Like Ireland and the west of England, prehistoric Scotland and its islands were occupied by people who built with great stones (megaliths). They built circles, avenues, and graves as in other countries, one of the most spectacular being at Callanish, Isle of Lewis (p. 94).

Peculiar to Scotland are the round stone castles called *brochs*, dating mainly from about 100 BC to AD 100. The Broch of Mousa, Shetland was about 55ft (17 metres) high with six storeys of galleries, a single entrance and an unpierced external wall. The ideal of a high tower persists in Scottish military architecture.

The monastery of Iona, which is now restored, was a nucleus of Celtic Christianity in the seventh century, its influence reaching into Northumbria.

After the Norman Conquest of England there was a peaceful immigration into Scotland of Anglo-Normans who introduced the Norman version of Romanesque architecture. Benedictine, Cistercian and other monastic houses gradually replaced the Celtic monasteries.

Under David I (r. 1124–53), brother-in-law of Henry I of England, feudalism became established, but relations with England were soured by a dispute over the right of Scottish kings to rule in Northumbria. In 1136 David I took Carlisle and Newcastle, and Newcastle was ceded to Scotland for a time though recovered by Henry II for England. A century of peace and prosperity ensued until the death of Alexander III (1286), last of the Celtic Royal line.

Under Edward I (r. 1272–1307) of England a period of war began that lasted for two and a half centuries. This had a profound effect upon Scottish architecture: at the time when Gothic was becoming firmly established it encouraged the fostering of foreign influences other than from

Left The ruins of Jedburgh Abbey, Roxburgh; a late 12th-century Benedictine monastery.
Above Abbotsford House, Roxburgh, built by Blore and Atkinson for Sir Walter Scott; 1816–23.
Right Dalkeith Palace, Lothian; c. 1705 by J. Smith.

England, and especially from France, with which Scotland had intermittent relationships. Scottish architecture, as well as confectionery, shows marked French influence: the prime source of the characteristic turrets and trimmings of the Scottish Baronial style is to be found in northern France.

The Reformation reached Scotland in 1560 and the secularisation of church property promoted the building of residential castles, and the French version of early Renaissance architecture, as seen in the Loire *châteaux,* gave a 'baronial' character to Renaissance architecture in Scotland. Netherlands influence, mainly introduced through pattern books, is also evident in some great houses.

The restoration of the Stuart monarchy in 1660 inaugurated a period of English influence and the development of Classicism. Some Scottish architects practised in England with distinction, notably James Gibbs (1683–1774) and Robert Adam. The New Town at Edinburgh is one of the major Classical urban developments.

The Greek Revival flourished in Scotland but the Baronial style had more romantic and patriotic appeal. In Eclectic architecture traditional Scottish features were naturally chosen. Stone is the characteristic material for major buildings. Sandstone and, even more, granite gives a certain hardness to much Scottish architecture. Harling (rough-casting) was frequently used to pleasant effect in folk architecture and in some major buildings. The basis of folk architecture is Celtic, modified, as in Ireland, by Georgian windows and other details. Corbie-stepped gables are a national feature (possibly of Netherlands origin) and the custom of painting the outsides of houses, sometimes with very bold pseudo-masonry patterns, may also have come from there.

Right Glasgow Art School, built by C. R. Mackintosh; 1897–1909. One of Europe's major Art Nouveau buildings, and one in which its principles permeate the whole design, not simply the decorative detail.

Below Charlotte Square Edinburgh by Robert Adam; 1791. It is part of the New Town initiated by James Craig in 1767, one of Europe's most important Classical urban developments.

Above St Giles Cathedral, Edinburgh; 1385–1495.

Ireland

At New Grange, near Drogheda, there is the astonishing architectural phenomenon of a chamber tomb, roofed with a corbelled vault and approached by a passage, all underneath a man-made tumulus. It is contained within a megalithic circle and the walls of the passage and chamber begin with a plinth of vertical megaliths. The date is probably 2000 BC or earlier.

The Treasury of Atreus at Mycenae (p. 103) has the same elements (a passage, *dromos,* a domed chamber, *tholos,* and a single *exedra,* rather than three as at New Grange). We tend to think of the beehive tombs of Mycenae as prototypes of the great corbel domes from Hagia Sophia (p. 105) to St Paul's London. The Mycenae dome is dated about 1325 BC and is a fully developed masonry interpretation of the original idea.

Irish megalithic architecture is thought to have been developed by people who migrated from Brittany and Spain into Britain and Ireland. They are generally thought of as post-and-lintel architects (cf Stonehenge p. 34), if indeed they ever got beyond marking out infinite space on the ground with standing stones; but in chambered tombs of this kind they actually put roofs on stone circles and their imagination far outran the limitations of contemporary technology. Such tombs are very mysterious.

Christianity came to Ireland, we are told, by St Patrick's mission about 432 and monasteries were then founded. They were not of the kind which was later to be established by the Benedictine Order. Instead, Irish monasteries may be understood as collections of hermits worshipping in small shrines, not one central church. It is instructive, in this context, to compare with some of the Aegean islands such as Mykonos where God is served in many small, domed chapels, not a great church. This practice reflects an intimacy with God which perhaps gives people a sense of social independence.

But the Irish monasteries were not undisciplined and the idea of working for the glory of God rather than any selfish aggrandisement did produce such masterpieces as *The Book of Kells* and, for the simple purpose of fastening a plaid at the shoulder, the Tara Brooch.

People lived in very simple buildings constructed sensibly in what we call the Celtic fringe style. From about 3000 BC if not earlier, Ireland seems to have been part of a culture which looked towards the Atlantic, extending from North Africa to the Shetland Isles and with an unknown but not menacing hinterland to the east.

In the sixth century the Irish took Christianity to Scotland, through Iona and Lismore and thence to Northumbria.

Ireland was harried and to some extent colonised by Vikings but the major assault upon this predominantly Celtic (and earlier) island came from the descendants of the Normans who had conquered England in 1066 and from Scotland in the sixteenth century, under the plantation policy of Oliver Cromwell.

From the point of view of the Irish Celtic nobility and peasants alike, England has taken much and given little in exchange, but in the eighteenth century Dublin did become one of the most civilised capital cities in Europe and from Edward Gibbon,

Above A Regency doorway in Rathkeale, Limerick, typical of refined Irish taste of the early 19th century.

Left Killarney Cathedral, County Kerry; designed in 1842 by A. G. W. Pugin.

Below A substantial cottage on Sherkin Island, County Cork, in Celtic fringe style.

Right The Four Courts, Dublin, built of granite in 1776–1802 by Thomas Cooley and James Gandon: the lantern and dome cover a large central concourse.

Below A Georgian street in Limerick.

Jonathan Swift and George Berkeley, through Bernard Shaw and James Joyce, to name only a few, the Anglo-Irish contribution to literature has been, to say the least, impressive, and Handel's *Messiah* was given its first performance in Dublin in 1742.

In architecture Dublin developed a form of Palladianism which produced both there and in other places such as Limerick some of the most beautiful Classical streets in the world. Georgian architecture in Ireland is beautiful in town and country houses and public buildings. Some of the best Victorian Eclectic architecture under the influence of John Ruskin is to be found in Dublin.

Belfast has one of the grandest of Neo-Classical city halls, complementing the Dock Board building in Liverpool, and modern Irish architecture has shown considerable sensitivity in interpreting and adjusting Modernism to Irish needs.

Great estates were imposed upon the Irish way of life by the English, and some, like Powerscourt, now a major tourist attraction, have survived the danger of arson during the 'troubles'. These tensions may be seen as the fundamental conflict between a Celtic society which values the family and divides the inheritance, against a predatory society which sends the younger sons out into the world.

The tiny fields and cabins of the west of Ireland, following in the Celtic Fringe style, tell their own story of the effects of these Celtic values and in these areas the Irish were racked by poverty.

Benelux

Belgium, The Netherlands (Holland) and the Grand Duchy of Luxembourg comprise Benelux. The three countries are here considered together.

There is a tendency for historians, who are occupationally concerned with kings, cardinals, dukes, and victorious generals to identify themselves with these exalted people and look down upon the industrious, ingenious and enterprising citizens whose skill, acumen and not a little courage have created the wealth which has made palaces and cathedrals, castles, and civic buildings possible.

From another angle Marxist historians decry the bourgeoisie, so from both sides prejudice operates against appreciation of the corporate achievements of the citizens who made the architecture of The Netherlands, Belgium and Luxembourg. So don't hate the middle class if you want to enjoy the architecture of Benelux!

In the late Roman period the whole region was a transit area for barbarians who established counties and duchies which later allied themselves with France or the Empire from time to time, but exercised little influence upon the enterprising townsmen whom they exploited as much as they could without killing the geese that provided the golden eggs.

It happened that the Emperor Charles V (r. 1519–56) was born at Ghent. As Archduke he inherited and ruled the Low Countries (modern Belgium and The Netherlands combined) but in March 1516 he also became King of Spain. When the Emperor Maximilian I died in 1519 Charles' family connection enabled him to beat his rival, the Valois king Francis I of France. He was elected Emperor and crowned at Aachen in 1520. Immediately he faced the most serious internal crisis Germany had ever known, the Lutheran Reformation. The Diet of Worms in 1521 brought a confrontation of Martin Luther with Charles V and divided the Empire and Germany. It was also to split the Low Countries – with Holland adhering to Protestantism and Belgium, disastrously, to Spain. In the continuing struggle between the Empire and France, Flanders became a Spanish-occupied territory and suffered appalling persecution remembered as the 'Spanish Fury'. Despite the hatred of the Flemings for the Spanish, Flemish art was influenced by the harrowing neurotic element in Spanish art. It is still palpable in many Belgian churches, though not in the mainstream of Belgian architecture, which was civic and commercial.

Churches in predominantly Protestant Holland were large and austere, with the most beautiful Baroque organs in the world, both visually and musically. But the main differences between Belgian and Dutch architecture are due to geology, not religion. Except around Maastricht, Holland is short of building stone; Belgium is rich in limestones and marble. But the general character of architecture is consistent with the cities of the Baltic coast which, until they were absorbed into the Soviet empire had close cultural and trade links with the North Sea ports.

Romanesque in Benelux looks more to Germany than to France, for the obvious reason that the main centres of Romanesque

Left and below Tournai Cathedral, Belgium; 1066–1340. It has Romanesque apsidal transepts and the cluster of towers that was envisaged elsewhere (such as at Chartres) but seldom built. The chancel is a typically French Gothic chevet. Much of the city centre was destroyed in World War II but has been rebuilt in facsimile. Left, the transept with round and pointed arches. Below, note the pantile roofs and zinc flashings of typical Belgian common architecture.

development in France lay to the south and west. Tournai, first Frankish capital and still venerated as a cradle of French civilisation, has one of the great cathedral churches of Europe and because of its associations with the French monarchy has an amazing treasury going back to Carolingian times (a must for the tourist, as is the Tournai Folk Museum). The Germanic Romanesque nave with transepts lead to a splendid French Gothic choir (c. 1242).

Echternach in Luxembourg has a Germanic Romanesque abbey church which has a special interest for British visitors as the shrine of St Willibrord (658–739), the Northumbrian monk who brought Christianity to this region and is the patron saint of Holland.

From Tournai through the Ardennes to Luxembourg, folk architecture changes with the geology to mountain style modified by the abundance of fine timber, both hard and soft, and excellent quality slates. These were used with a precision usually expected in metal roofs for the churches.

Below left The Benedictine abbey church of Echternach, Luxembourg. It is the shrine of St Willibrord, a Northumbrian monk of the 8th century who proselytised the region. He is buried in the crypt.

Centre The tower of Malines Cathedral, Belgium; 1452–1546. Although unfinished, it is 97 m (318 ft) high, and was described by the 17th-century French military architect Vauban as the 'eighth wonder of the world'. The rest of the cathedral is 13th–14th century.

Below The west tower of Utrecht Cathedral, the Netherlands, built in 1321–82, and typical of the Dutch later medieval belfry. Though originally attached to the rest of the cathedral, it was isolated when the nave collapsed in 1674. The cathedral shows a strong French influence.

Left The Cloth Hall and belfry at Bruges; 1282–1487. Such halls served as expressions of civic pride in the mercantile centres of the Low Countries as in Italy (compare the Palazzo Pubblico, Siena, p. 184).

Below The 12th-century Castle of the Counts, Ghent.

Below The Cloth Hall, Ypres, Belgium; 1202–1304 (and rebuilt in 1934). It is the largest, grandest, and most simple in design, of the medieval halls.

An interesting feature of rural architecture in the Grand Duchy is the large farm houses, sometimes grouped, looking like enormous multistorey chalets, all under one low-pitched roof. Luxembourg sets an example in landscape conservation and forest management. The picturesque town of Vianden looking across the river to Germany is a spectacular mixture of styles of folk and common architecture from the surrounding countries.

Gothic architecture flourished luxuriantly in Belgium, not only in churches but in public buildings. Extreme richness of decoration, emphasis of vertical lines and high towers are characteristic. England owes its Houses of Parliament building mainly to Flemish precedents.

So strong was the Gothic decorative tradition in Belgium that the main effect of the Renaissance was to add Classical details to the decorative repertoire. Where attempts were made, mainly in mansions, to build with Classical discipline, French precedents were usually dominant.

In Holland there are notable affinities with the development of Renaissance architecture in England, especially Elizabethan and Restoration (pp. 276–81).

Below The castle of Beersel, Belgium; 14th century. It comprises three massive circular high-roofed gabled towers, linked by walls. Somewhat unusually for a castle, it is brick-built.

Below Middelburg Town Hall, Holland; 1412–1599. It was built by the Kelderman family, who also built the tower of Malines.

Above The 17th-century house in Tournai, now the celebrated Folk Museum. The stepped gable-end facing the street epitomises the urban common architecture of the Low Countries.

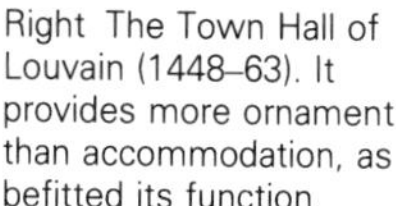

Right The Town Hall of Louvain (1448–63). It provides more ornament than accommodation, as befitted its function.

The European tendency towards elaboration and Eclecticism could hardly enrich Belgian architecture and generally it remained very much within local tradition in Holland and Luxembourg, but two developments are noteworthy. The Arts and Crafts Movement (p. 150) was accepted in Holland, produced a major work in the Amsterdam Exchange by H. P. Berlage (1898) (p. 63) and led on to a Dutch version of restrained Modernism which was influential in many countries.

In Belgium, the monstrous Palais de Justice in Brussels (1866) by J. Poelaert is an impressive example of the grandiosity in public architecture which emanated from the *École des Beaux Arts* in Paris. In the context of European architectural values, built up through the centuries, it can be called a very good example of really bad architecture.

Art Nouveau (p. 151) also flourished in Belgium, mainly as an opportunity to extend the Flemish genius for decoration into the realm of fantasy.

Right Typical canal-side houses on narrow sites in Malines. Such houses generally have coarsely ornamented fronts, and whatever the period, style and building materials used, the character persists.

Below Antwerp Town Hall; 1565. It shows a blend of traditional and Renaissance features, and is ornamental but practical. The style influenced the architecture of Elizabethan England (compare Wollaton Hall, p. 141).

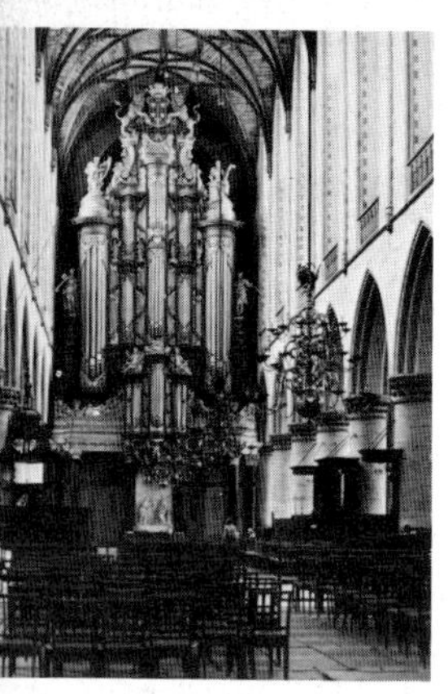

Above The Baroque organ (1738) of St Bavo, Haarlem; 1400–1550. It is perhaps the most famous organ-case in the world. The pure tin pipes in the side towers are 12 m (40ft) high.

Top Canal-side houses in Amsterdam. Note the elaboration of the traditional gables which are needed to light the very deep rooms.

Above St Aubain, Namur, Belgium, in restrained Baroque style; 1750–72.

Right A pavilion in the park adjoining the abbey of Echternach, a cheeky example of true Mannerism.

Above The elaborate guild houses, mostly dating from the late 17th century, surrounding the Grand Place, Brussels.

Right The Town Hall of Leiden, Holland; 1594. Its fusion of local and Classical style is typical and resembles early French Renaissance architecture. This robust style has also been miscalled 'Mannerist'.

Right The Dining Room of the Maison Horta, Brussels; designed by Victor Horta in 1895. This is an early example of Art Nouveau as it developed in Belgium, one of its main centres.

Below The Town Hall, Hilversum, Holland; 1929. Its architect W. M. Dudok relied on simple brick surfaces to effect a Cubist reversal of Dutch tradition.

Right A tall and compact Dutch farmhouse, economical in its use of land. Interesting to compare with the elegant Palladian brick houses of Georgian England.

Right A simple Belgian farmhouse in the Ardennes region, strongly contrasting with the elaborate houses of the urban merchants.

Below The Stocklet House, 1905–11, by Josef Hoffmann; a geometrically controlled version of Art Nouveau.

Part Four

Central, North and East Europe

This vast region was either on or beyond the frontiers of the Roman Empire. The Rhineland, it is true, was a flourishing and integrated part of the Empire but it will be convenient, in the light of later history, to consider modern Germany, Switzerland, and Austria together with Scandinavia, Russia and its dependencies from the Baltic to the Black Sea. Snowy winters and the prevalence of timber (mainly pine) as a building material affected architecture. Indigenous styles were mainly based on timber construction; imported styles were modified. In Alpine regions (pp. 78–9) low-pitched roofs were used to exploit the insulating properties of snow but elsewhere the steep roof was more usual and everywhere churches and public buildings were designed to shed the snow and have striking profiles against mountains and sky. Furthermore, timber constructions sheathed with shingles, boards or metal are more durable, when treated decoratively, than stone exposed to severe frost, icicles and slipping snow.

Peoples have moved into Europe from East to West. Trade routes have brought silks and spices from the East and Mongolian hoards have penetrated far into central Europe; but it is a mistake to think that the elaborate spires and onion domes of central Europe are of oriental origin. They are, in fact an indigenous architectural form and, with dormer windows, high pitched roofs, bonnet hips and helmet towers are the major contribution of this region to the architectural repertoire. One should not assume a single origin for this architectural style, but one major influence did come through the Orthodox Church as it extended into Russia.

Right The town hall of Alsfeld, near Frankfurt, West Germany; 1512.

Below The 13th-century church of Densis, Romania.

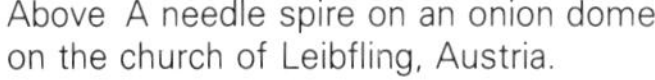

Above A needle spire on an onion dome on the church of Leibfling, Austria.

Below The church of Nereditsa, near Novgorod, first built in 1198, rebuilt in 1904 and destroyed in the 1940s. It adds the onion dome to a structure of Byzantine origin.

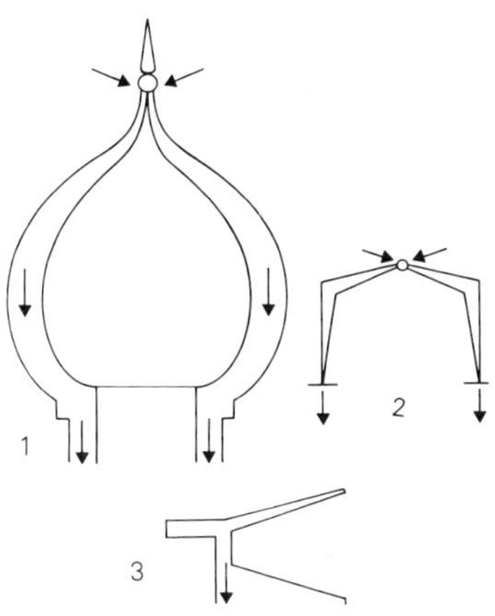

The logic of the onion dome is that the weight of the bulge balances the structure to exert a vertical load (an alternative to buttressing). Conveniently, the bulge also serves to throw snow clear of the walls. The onion dome may be constructed in timber or in reinforced concrete, and with a limited overhang in brick, stone or concrete. It may be compared (1) with modern stadium construction (2) or pin-jointed balanced structures (3).

Below Onion domes on a timber-framed house at Gottlieben, Untersee, Switzerland.

Russia

The trade route from the Black Sea to the Baltic was developed in pre-Christian times and was significant in the transmission of Celtic and Greek art to north-west Europe. The spread of Orthodox Christianity brought Hellenesque architecture along the trade route to Kiov which Norsemen had conquered in 878 (p. 315). Trade with Constantinople (furs, wax, amber, honey and slaves in exchange for the rich merchandise of the greatest city in the western world) facilitated the spread of Christianity. The eleventh-century cathedral of Hagia Sophia at Kiev observed the Byzantine traditional plan but did not attempt a dome spanning more than 9 metres (30 feet). The church had 13 domes in all and set a precedent for multiple small domes. These were unsatisfactory in that they tended to collect the snow and obscure the form of the church besides possibly over-stressing a rather vulnerable structural form.

Further north, at Novgorod, we find the elevation of the dome and the beginning of an onion form. This was not fantastic: it was conventionally practical (see diagram p. 309) whether it was constructed in stone, brick, or timber. As timber was abundant it was commonly used and so the Hellenesque dome (p. 104–5) was translated into timber.

Throughout modern Europe there is a marvellous tradition of decorative folk art, especially in costume, but the patterns which are appropriate for embroidery may equally decorate the gable of a house in Bohemia and persist in Russian ballet and circus.

Romanesque architecture penetrated from Germany, particulary in Cistercian Catholic monasteries; but wherever the Orthodox faith prevailed Hellenesque traditions persisted.

Modern Russia emerged with the expansion of Muscovy in the fifteenth century, as the princes of Moscow, which had been a staging post on the caravan route from the East to the Baltic, established their rule over a territory which was to become the Russia of the Czars. A profound change took place in Russian architecture in 1697 when Czar Peter the Great returned from a visit to western Europe; thereafter Russia looked to the West and became Baroque. This developed to Neoclassicism and indeed Russian culture was dominated by the West. In less than a century the Russian upper classes changed from terror that they might be mistaken for foreigners to the fear that they might not be.

The two main aspects of Russian architecture are exemplified in the Hellenesque cathedral of St Basil in Moscow (p. 51) and the Baroque Smolny cathedral in Leningrad (p. 313).

The 1917 Revolution established a social-political system of western origin and a return to isolationism, to the suspicion of foreigners which had prevailed before Peter the Great. In architecture there was a brief flirtation with Modernism but the International Style was unsuitable for the Russian climate, as it produced thick layers of ice by condensation on the insides of Modernist windows. Regimes established by revolution, though often initially supported by progressive artists, tend to clothe themselves in the decor of the regime they replace, discourage innovation and eliminate the avant-garde who had helped to create the conditions for change.

Left The Church of the Transfiguration, Kizhi; 1714. The climax of the formal development of the Russian timber style, it has extreme simplicity in plan and walls, surmounted by an elaborate but rigidly formal roof structure.

Below left S. Sophia, Kiev, founded in 1018 and probably the first masonry church in the region. Its 13 domes symbolise Christ and the Apostles. The present structure dates from the Baroque restoration under Polish, Austrian and Italian influences.

Below S. Sophia Cathedral, Novgorod; begun in 1052. The tall drums on which the domes are placed served as a prototype for St Basil's Cathedral, Moscow (p. 51).

Above The Cathedral of the Annunication, Moscow; 1484–89. Its complex gables derive from the style of timber churches.

Below left The Grand Palace, Pavlovsk; begun in Classical style by Charles Cameron; 1782.

Below The archway of the Admiralty, Leningrad, 1806–15; by A. D. Zakharov and fusing many diverse architectural elements.

Above The Smolny Cathedral, Leningrad, by Bartolomeo Rastrelli; 1748–55. Almost unbelievably the chapel of a convent school for poor girls.

Below The Winter Palace, Leningrad, also by Rastrelli; 1754–64.

Scandinavia

For architectural history (as for literature) Scandinavia comprises the modern countries of Norway, Sweden, Denmark and Finland as well as the Baltic states, now absorbed by Russia. Indeed Russia itself gets its name from the Swedish Rus (or Varangian) merchant-adventurers who established themselves in Kiev and Novgorod, and traded with Constantinople, attacking it in 907 and 944, each expedition being followed by a commercial treaty! This was in the great age of Viking expansion, which has commonly been represented as the descent of pitiless savages upon civilised communities, especially in the British Isles and northern France, though northern Germany and central Europe suffered as least as much. In fact this expansion built on the commercial intercourse between Scandinavia and the Bosphorus and the Black Sea coast that began at least as early as the fourth century BC. Possibly the original basis for this trade had been amber from the Baltic and gold and bronze from the Greeks.

These early Scandinavians built in timber and their architecture has not survived, but it is clear that there must have been flourishing and relatively civilised communities long before the Viking expansion of the eighth to tenth centuries. The basis for this expansion may have been threefold: the decline of Constantinople after the rise of Islam in the seventh century; the invention, probably in Sweden, of better ways of working iron to make weapons and tools; and, in contrast to the Franks and Celts, the practice of inheritance by primogeniture, instead of dividing land equally among the sons. This made for a strong agricultural economy at home and presented a challenge to younger sons to go out into the world. The long-established mercantile techniques would provide the equipment, while those who stayed at home as craftsmen were unsurpassed in making ships and weapons.

There can be little doubt that the main influence upon Scandinavian architecture was Hellenesque, but the style had to be translated into timber construction. Surviving stave churches in Norway reflect this. If you wanted to make a Byzantine basilica in wood this is how you would do it. Domes were not logical in timber, but they were stylistically desirable features; so throughout eastern Europe they were displayed on towers with considerable pride and ingenuity. Some influences may have come from further east, and the minaret may have suggesed the spires which became common in Hellenesque and in Gothic architecture at a later date.

These Hellenesque influences persisted in Scandinavia until the present century and are evident in Stockholm Town Hall (1911–23), as well as in the flavour of much architecture in Russia and elsewhere round the Baltic.

The consummation of this Scandinavian tradition is in Denmark, especially in Copenhagen. It is a mistake to see these masterpieces of Scandinavian architecture as aberrations from the Renaissance. They have different roots, going back to pre-Christian Scythian/Celtic/Greek origins and this should be kept in mind when looking at all non-Classical architecture around the Baltic and

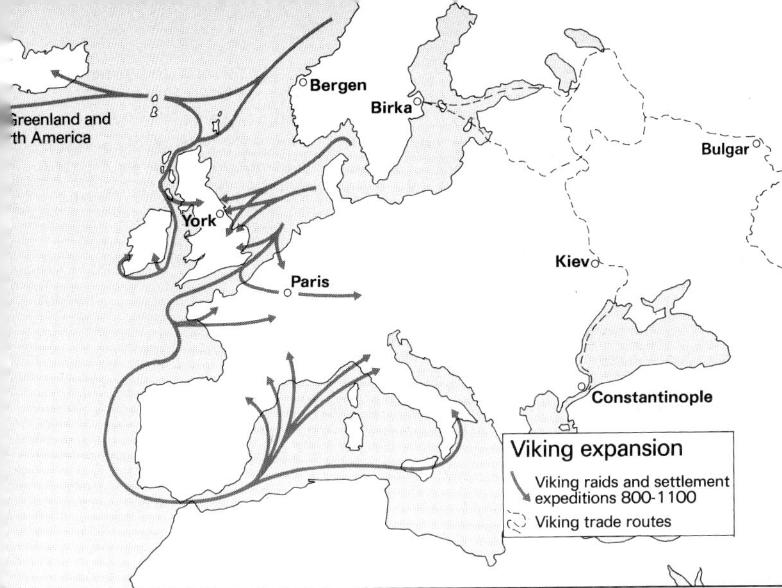

down the North Sea coast as far as Dunkirk.

The Viking expansion was both destructive and dynamic. There can be no doubt that it was followed by a period of rapid and exciting innovation in architecture wherever the Vikings had been but, whether this was through their creative efforts or in reaction to them, or a combination of clearing up the mess with the co-operation of a new people and new craft skills, can hardly be more than a matter of opinion, nine hundred years later.

In the later Middle Ages and since, the Scandinavians have looked to the west, involved themselves with west European politics and since the Reformation mainly with Protestantism. They have built well, maintained high traditional standards in folk and common architecture and generally followed west European fashions.

In the present century the Arts and Crafts Movement took firm hold in Scandinavia and the inherited sensitivity to design values, going back into the remote past, together with cultivated skills in craftsmanship and industry, produced superb design and workmanship in architecture which embodied many crafts. More recently a zealous concern for the maintenance of standards by bureaucratic control seems to have stifled creativity, but because of the preservation and cultivation of craft standards Modernist architecture in Scandinavia has qualities which are difficult to find elsewhere.

The descendants of the stay-at-home Vikings have good taste. Many modern architects admire Alvar Aalto (1898–1976) of Finland as the supreme genius of the movement and Arne Jacobsen of Denmark as its most elegant practitioner, but generally Modernism in Scandinavia has been subservient to strong traditional values.

Above Old farm buildings now at the Oslo folk museum. Round-faced timbers and planks were often made by riving or splitting with wedges, which was easier than sawing.

Right The stave church at Hoprekstad, Sögn, Norway; c. 1150. One of the earliest such churches, it explored the potential of its timber construction in developing the steeply-pitched roof. The doorways are intricately carved with mythological scenes.

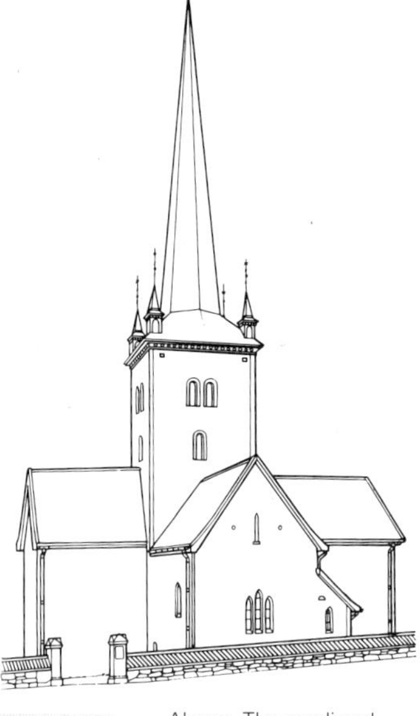

Above The medieval church of Rinsaker, near Lillehammer, with a broach spire (rising octagonally from a square tower) and corner turrets. This type of spire was often used in Early English parish churches.

Above left Tynset church, Hedmark, Norway, with Renaissance influences in its plan, doors and windows, but retaining a slightly eastern European flavour in the shape of the cupola.

Left Heidal church, near Sjoa, Norway; a development of the ancient tradition, but with sawn timbers.

Left Kalmar Castle, eastern Sweden. An important stronghold built in the 14th century, its accommodation was enhanced by the addition of Renaissance elements in the 16th century.

Right Östelar church, Bornholm, Denmark; 12th century. Its circular plan reflects King Sigard's pilgrimage to Jerusalem (1107–11) and the church of the Holy Sepulchre.

Above Trondheim Cathedral, Norway; 1130–1290. Counterpart to the Viking invasions, Christianity was established in Norway from Britain.

Right Lund Cathedral, Sweden; from 1103. Its plan (below) derives from German models, but the style of decoration, including the aracading, is Italian in origin.

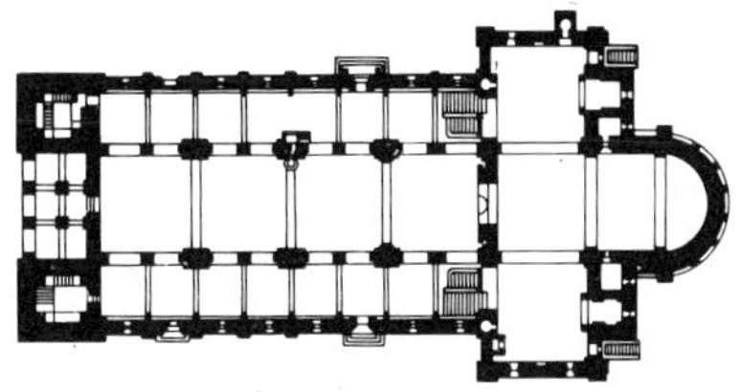

Left Frederiksborg Castle, near Copenhagen, built in 1602 by van Steenwinckel, of brick with stone dressings and elaborate copper roofs, reflecting the Dutch style in their gables.

Right The Amalienborg Palace, Copenhagen, by N. Eigtved; 1754. This ambitious and extravagant palace was built under German influence.

Below right The Old Church, Helsinki, built in 1826 by C. L. Engel in Neo-Classical style but using timber.

Below The University Library, Helsinki; 1836. Its Neo-Classical style was introduced to Finland from Russia.

Above Helsinki Cathedral, by Engel; 1830. It forms the climax to Engel's rebuilding of the centre of the city. The design is a curious travesty of the Villa Capra, Vicenza (p. 37)

Left Kina Slott, or the Chinese Pavilion, of the Castle of Drottningholm, near Stockholm, Sweden; c. 1760. Rococo *chinoiserie* was a fashionable manifestation of Eclecticism.

Left Stockholm City Hall, by Ragnar Ostberg; 1911–23. Perhaps the crowning achievement of Eclecticism under the influence of the Arts and Crafts movement.

Below Grundtvig Church, Copenhagen; 1913–26, by P. V. Jensen Klint. A modernist reinterpretation of the Gothic ideal, which also reflects the stepped gables of Baltic common architecture.

Central Europe

Germany

Germany became a nation-state in 1871 but the distinct character of German architecture was not a product of political unity; indeed the preceding disunity was a more powerful factor, making for individuality and strong local traditions. There was no German capital comparable with Paris to set the standards. Vienna, the cosmopolitan capital of the Austro-Hungarian Empire, was a meeting place of cultural traditions, and apart possibly from its adoption of the Italian Baroque style in the seventeenth century Vienna had little influence upon German architecture.

The unifying influence was the German language. Despite the great differences between various parts of Germany a common language facilitated a common culture, manners, customs, the interchange of ideas, awareness of a mythology and the sharing, somewhat unevenly, of a droll sense of humour. When printing was invented the adoption of the black letter typeface was characteristic of Germany and completely different from the Classical type-faces which were quickly developed in Italy.

The German language and mythology originated with the so-called barbarian peoples who invaded the Roman Empire from the fourth century AD. The western part of what is now Germany had been conquered by the Romans, who adopted the line of the Rhine, north of Mainz, and of the Danube as their main eastern frontier. In the fourth century Trier, on the Mosel, was the administrative capital of the Western Empire. Trier has some of the most impressive Roman remains in Europe as well as a superb museum. Its cathedral has a Roman plan and the Basilica (now a Protestant church) is one of the largest Roman buildings still roofed and in use. The Roman Black Gate is the most significant link with Romanesque architecture.

When the Salian Franks invaded the empire in the fifth century their first capital was at Tournai (now in Belgium), and they pushed on to settle in France. Other Franks moved into the Rhineland and established themselves in the rich Roman territories. These have been called Ripuarian Franks (from *ripes* – river banks). The Franks, like the Celts, divided a man's property among his sons when he died and kingdoms were treated in this way, as personal property. Partly as a result of the unworkable division of territory at the death of Lothar I in 561, two kingdoms eventually emerged. These were Austrasia with its capital at Metz, and Neustria with its capital at Soissons and then Paris. The Neustrian monarchs seem to have become interested in the arts and religion, thereby earning the title of *rois fainéants.* They were eventually displaced by Austrasian usurpers whose military prowess threw back the Muslim invaders coming in from Spain in the eighth century. From the Austrasian usurpers sprang Charlemagne who was crowned Holy Roman Emperor by the Pope on Christmas Day 800.

Top left The Partition of Verdun (843), by which Charlemagne's Empire was divided into the regions that would develop into modern France and Germany.

Above left The Austrian Empire as it was constituted in 1815 after the Congress of Vienna.

Above The unification of Germany, from the disparate Holy Roman Empire of 1648 to the German Empire, led by Prussia, of 1871.

Left The abbey gateway of Lorsch, near Mannheim, built in c. 800, the year in which Charlemagne was crowned Emperor. Its style it derives from the propylaeum of Old St Peter's, Rome, and its stonework from French craftsmanship.

Above The sturdy parish church of Reichenau, Lake Constance, West Germany. German churches commonly have the weight towards the west as here. This is known as *westwerk*.

Left The Rathaus, Paderborn, North Rhine Westphalia, built in the 13th century and its façade remodelled in 1612–16. A delightful formal design raising the folk style to an arcane level.

Left Maria Laach Abbey, near Koblenz; 1093–1156. The west end is apsidal and towered, and approached through an atrium. Churches with an apse at each end were characteristic of German Romanesque.

Below The Church of the Apostles, Cologne; 1190 and later. The trefoil choir consists of three apses. The west helm tower is typically Rhenish (a style that spread to England – see p. 261), but the attached columns and arches echo Roman architecture.

The Holy Roman Empire

The reconstituted Roman Empire was to have a profound influence as an idea throughout German history. It extended from the Pyrenees to the Elbe and the middle Danube. When Charlemagne's son, Louis the Pious, died in 840, the Empire was partitioned among his three surviving sons by the Treaty of Verdun (843). Lothar received a central strip from Frisia to Italy, including the Rhine and Rhône valley. Charles the Bald had the west which was to become France, and Louis the German had the east.

In the east the Carolingian line died out and the Franconian duke, Conrad, was elected king in 911 but devastation by Vikings and Hungarians was not halted until, on Conrad's death, Henry the Fowler, Duke of the Saxons was elected king. Henry and his son, Otto the Great (r. 936–73), halted the Hungarian invasions. Such strength and unity as were achieved under Otto and his successors relied upon close alliance with the Church, but this disintegrated in conflict with the reforming Pope Gregory VII (r. 1073–85) over investiture, principally of abbots and bishops. Out of this dispute came a long era of conflict between the Empire and the Papacy.

Meanwhile Catholic monasticism had been developing and pushing east. In the infinitely complex secular power struggles, abbots and bishops acquired great influence and wealth leading to a princely life-style and, eventually, to the building of palatial Baroque monasteries and churches in those parts of Germany which did not become Protestant.

In architecture the alignment of central Germany (Lothar's portion) with Italy and the constant intercourse between Germany and Rome favoured the influence of Italy rather than France upon German Romanesque architecture.

Throughout German history, when unity looked possible new divisions arose and in the prolonged tension between Empire and Papacy churchmen in Germany became, in some cases, more princely than the princes. The existence of an irresponsible feudal and ecclesiastical aristocracy led to a stratification of German society in which townsmen, sometimes under ducal or episcopal leadership, but more often autonomously, created corporations and an urban way of life which derived its architecture mainly from local folk traditions.

While Gothic architecture was developing in France and England, Germany was in a state of disorder and decline which did not favour architecture. Moreover the version of Romanesque which had developed from Carolingian times was congenial to the Germans. Gothic was French and was naturally resisted, so the Romanesque style persisted into the Gothic period and seems to have a permanent place in the German idea of architecture. Splendid though some German Gothic buildings are, marvellous in workmanship, enormous in height and ingenuity of construction, they are mainly French in inspiration and do not reflect the Germanness of German art.

But if Germany did not produce a Gothic style in church architecture it made up for it in the development of timber-framed folk architecture into a delightful common architecture and even, in town halls and other public buildings, to an arcane level. Likewise in large areas of north-eastern Germany where there is no good building stone but plenty of clay and vast reserves of timber, design in brick created a style which is shared with Scandinavia and the Low Countries.

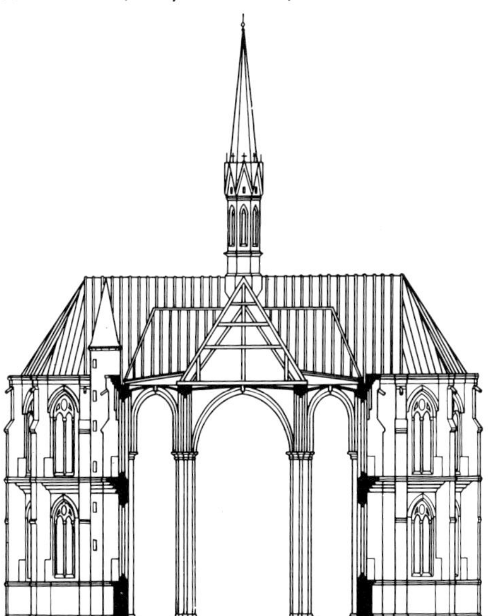

Left and plan below St Elizabeth, Marburg; 1257–83. The nave and the nave aisles are the same height, eliminating the triforium and creating the 'hall' type of church, typical of the Gothic period in northern Germany. The usual German *westwerk* is here replaced by western towers with spires in the French style.

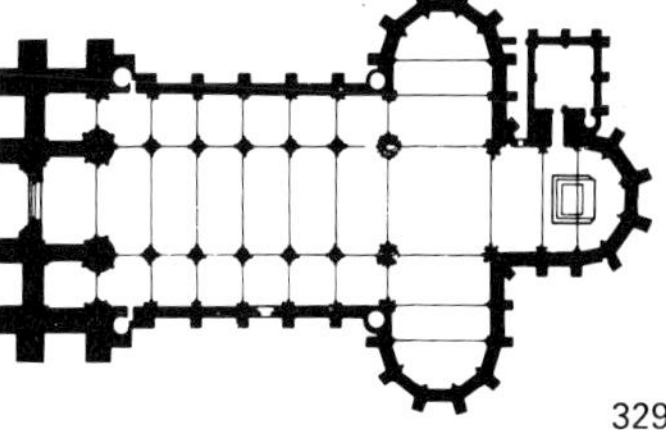

Left The Palatine Chapel, Aachen; 792. It was modelled on S. Vitale in Ravenna (p. 181), and though a palace chapel it had cathedral status from the first.

Above Dinkelsbühl, Bavaria; a well-preserved, mainly medieval walled city which withstood ten sieges during the Thirty Years War (1618–48). The church of St George, late medieval with a Romanesque tower, is a fine example of a hall church.

Left Heidelberg, one of the grandest castles in Germany; 13th century and later. On the right is the Ott-Heinrichsbau (1556–59), typical of early Renaissance in Germany.

Above The castle courtyard of Langenberg, near Heilbronn. How beautiful common architecture based on a folk tradition can be! The stylish cupola evidently crowns a previously machicolated tower – nice idea to leave the corbels.

Left Munich Marienplatz and New Rathaus; a magnificent example of 19th-century German Gothic revival (completed 1905).

Left Castle of Chillon, near Montreux, Switzerland; 13th century. It is built on a naturally defensible site guarding a trade route and occupied since the Bronze Age.

Right Burg Karlstein, now in Czechoslovakia; an extended medieval tower house with curtain walls on a rocky site.

Below High-density common architecture in Nuremburg, clustered round the castle.

Above The Rathaus, Heilbronn; 1535–96. There is a covered market on the ground floor.

Left The Golden House, Innsbruck, Austria; c. 1500. The copper-roofed balcony, or oriel, was added to dignify a rather plain house. This act of family pride created a national monument.

Left The Würzburg Residenz Chapel; from 1722, built for the Prince Bishop of Würzburg by Balthasar Neumann. A fusion of Austrian Baroque with French Rococo style.

Below A house in the Austrian Tyrol with typical wall paintings.

Right A traditional Austrian house in Walchsee am Wilden Kaiser; basically an Alpine chalet but made-up with paint to look like a little palace.

Below The Brandenburg Gate, Berlin; 1789–93 by C. G. Langhans. It is a Neo-Classical cross between the Athenian Propylaea (p. 158) and a Roman triumphal arch.

Above Wilten bei Innsbruck, Austria; mid-18th-century Rococo at its best in a parish church. The stucco-work is by Feichtmeyer of Wessobrunn.

Left Birnau church; 1746–58 by Peter Thumb. Rococo; traditional but inventive.

Baroque and After in Central Europe

From 1618 to 1648 the Thirty Years War, essentially between Catholic and Protestant interests but also involving dynastic, economic, political and personal ambitions (and the Catholic French siding with the Protestants to weaken the Hapsburgs), turned much of Germany into a battlefield and a graveyard. When economic recovery came, Italian Baroque found its most lavish fulfilment in Germany.

The development of Baroque and Rococo depended to a large extent upon the participation, in design and decoration, of German skilled craftsmen. This collaboration remained characteristic of German architecture until the Bauhaus movement of the 1920s, which was theoretically dedicated to the involvement of craftsmen in design but effectively led to their virtual elimination from Modernist architecture.

With Hanoverians as the English royal family, from the early eighteenth century, and a common interest in defeating Napoleonic France in the early nineteenth, there were some affinities between English and German architecture, most importantly a common interest in the revival of Greek architecture. A growing movement for German national unity in the nineteenth century was reflected in an inward-looking Eclecticism, not uninfluenced at a later stage by Wagner's operas. Concurrently folk arts were cultivated, partly with an eye to tourism.

Germany after World War I was one of the originators of Modernism but with the rise of Hitler a brutal version of Neo-Classicism was imposed. After World War II international Modernism prevailed but with a growing concern for conservation of resources, nature and the architectural heritage which seems to open the way for yet

The music room of the Palace of Sanssouci, Potsdam; built in the 1740s for Frederick the Great. Rococo in the fashionable French style.

Melk Abbey; 1702–14, on the Austrian Danube, by Jacob Prandtauer. A splendid example of Baroque, relying mainly on geometry and dramatic massing, with sparing use of decoration.

another new architecture.

The great divide in European architecture is neither racial nor linguistic. With Germany we must group Poland, Bohemia (Czechoslovakia) and Yugoslavia with Slavonic languages, Hungary with a Uralian language and Austria which is Germanic. Throughout this vast area the dividing line is between Orthodox and Catholic Christianity (reformed or otherwise). Politically the influence of the Hapsburg emperors is important in this division, but the dividing line is confused by the fact that from the 17th century onwards Russia, despite the Orthodox Church, looked to the West for architectural inspiration. It is generally true, however, that from Gdansk to Dubrovnik common architecture and folk architecture prevailed within an admirable tradition, whereas arcane architecture followed the inspiration of Italian Baroque in the seventeenth century and of French Classicism and Rococo in the eighteenth, and western Neo-Classicism and Romanticism therafter in public buildings. Throughout, there was a strong under-current in favour of folk architecture, which is now developing into environmentalism.

Perhaps the clearest evidence of the divide is between the music of the West, with its infinite fertility, and the solemnity of the Eastern Church which persisted even into Russian operas in the Western style. Among the greatest gifts of the Catholic Church is music and the architecture in which it was created. Plain-song belonged to the echoing Gothic cathedrals and counterpoint to the precise auditoria of the hall churches decorated in the Baroque style.

Austria and Switzerland

Looking back upon the infinite convolutions of war, diplomacy and inheritance which have involved and surrounded the modern countries of Austria and Switzerland, we need not be surprised that neither country has a national style of architecture. Yet both countries have notable public and religious buildings, castles, palaces and local traditions of common architecture which are sometimes very beautiful. These derive partly from outside, from Italy and France and even from England (in Swiss Victorian hotels), from Germany and from the Middle East. But there is a delicious irony in the fact that, despite all the pretensions and achievements of the Austrian-based Hapsburg Empire, the most distinctive and admired architecture is in the Alpine folk tradition.

Less well-known is the beauty of village churches, partly Romanesque and partly Hellenesque in style, and often with Baroque additions. From the west, Burgundian influence was strong in the great period of French Romanesque. From the east came Hellenesque ideas of design. From the south, when the Hapsburgs controlled much of Italy, came the Renaissance of Classical architecture in its Baroque form. In the nineteenth century the glamour of Viennese society was a magnet, the attractiveness of which was enhanced by the building of the railways. In the 1880s skiing, an ancient Norse way of moving over snow, was introduced from Norway by British sportsmen. The modern development of alpine folk architecture as a common style for mountain resorts is mainly a result of this sporting initiative promoted by the British pioneer of skiing and tourism, Sir Arnold Lunn. The chalet has proved to be an admirable prototype for Alpine holiday architecture and it has spread to many other places.

Vienna is on the Danube, which provides a waterway (with a short portage) from the Black Sea into the heart of Germany. Hellenesque architecture seems to have come this way as well as through the Alps, to meet Burgundian Romanesque in the great days of the monastery of Cluny. The other route through Austria was from Ravenna and Venice through Turin, Aosta and the Mont Cenis pass.

But the Hapsburg Empire and the city of Vienna were, from the sixteenth century, on the edge of the Ottoman Empire. Their interests were defensive to the east and political to the west. Their language was German. Their architecture was rooted in the Germanic ethos and tradition. The Renaissance came late in the form of Baroque from Italy and its music, a vital part of Austrian culture, was also linked with Italy – from Rossini to Mozart and on to Johann Strauss.

The Rococo court of France was assassinated in the 1790s by the French Revolution. Vienna's survived to remain the European capital of dignified frivolity, elegance and beauty, until in the early twentieth century the Hohenzollern dynasty pledged Germany to re-enact the old feud between the Austrasians and the Neustrians a thousand years on.

Left The monastery of Einsiedeln, Switzerland; 1704–20; one of the great pilgrimage centres of Europe.

Below The Karlskirche, Vienna; 1716–37 by J. B. Fischer von Erlach. It combines a thoroughly Baroque dome with a more formal Classical portico and is fronted by two columns based on Roman models.

Left St Nicholas, Prague; 1703–52, by C. Dientzenhofer and others. An outstanding example of curvaceous Baroque and superbly controlled spatial design internally. The design is an essentially simple one, of a dome carried on pendentives.

Right Vienna; an interior of the Upper Belvedere; 1721–24. A summer palace by Lukas Von Hildebrandt, with splendid gardens.

Left The castle of Linderhof, Bavaria; 1870–86, for Ludwig II of Bavaria. A pretty Rococo minuet in architecture, genteel and remote from the problems of 'ordinary people'.

Below left Entrance hall of the I. G. Farben dyeworks at Höchst, Germany; 1920–24 by Peter Behrens. Behrens' geometrical and utilitarian style influenced much modern German architecture.

Below Tower of Birsfelden church, Switzerland; 1958 by Hermann Baur.

Author's Acknowledgment
This book could not have been the work of one person. My name is on the title page but I want to thank all those members of the team who have made it possible. Peter Furtado as begetter and editor and Ian Muggeridge in charge of design and artwork have been wonderful to work with and have made many visits to my home in Northumberland; without the back-up I have had from my publishers and their staff, and the totally frictionless collaboration I have enjoyed throughout, this book could not have been produced in anything like its present form. I am also indebted to photographers and agencies in many countries and in particular to Ursula and Peter Chatfield. Though I have travelled widely in Europe and studied architecture for more than half a century, and much of what is here derives from my own experience, the writer of a synoptic book must acknowledge an enormous debt to scholars and travellers, past and present. Individual references cannot be made but I am only the presenter at the end of a long line of people who have made, recorded and interpreted the history of architecture. Without the creative artists and enlightened patrons there would have been nothing to write about.

All line illustrations by Hayward Art Group. Monochrome illustrations by Ivan Lapper appear on the following pages: 5, 40, 43, 64, 67, 69, 72, 73, 75, 77, 78, 80, 82, 83, 84, 101, 111 top, 129, 145 bottom, 157, 158, 162, 172, 173, 193, 228, 245, 251, 287.

Left A shrine, cultivated land, village and church at Igls, Austria: architecture of a coherent way of life in which all architecture – whatever the religion – was rooted until the modern age. It is a question whether architecture as previously understood is possible in the modern age. If not, it is a great loss.

Photographic Acknowledgements

Colour Bruce Allsopp 162 top, 162 bottom, 163 top, 166 centre, 166 bottom, 167 top, 167 bottom, 170 top, 170 centre, 170 bottom, 171 top, 171 centre, 171 bottom right, 174 top, 174 bottom, 175 top left, 175 top right, 177 top, 177 bottom right, 180 top, 180 bottom, 181, 185 top left, 188 top left, 188 top right, 188 bottom right, 189 centre, 189 bottom, 192 top, 192 bottom left, 192 bottom right, 210 bottom left, 214 top, 218 top left, 219 top, 226 bottom left, 227 top, 230 top, 230 bottom, 234 top, 235 top, 235 centre, 235 bottom, 238 top right, 238 bottom, 239 top right, 239 bottom, 274 top, 275 top, 275 bottom right, 278 top, 278 centre, 279 top, 279 bottom, 282 top, 282 centre left, 283 top, 283 centre, 283 bottom, 286 centre left, 286 bottom, 287 centre 287 bottom left, 335 centre right; British Tourist Authority, London 286 top right; Ursula Clark 219 bottom, 222 top, 222 centre, 222 bottom, 223 top, 223 centre, 223 bottom left, 223 bottom right; C. Daniels 189 top; Department of the Environment, London, Crown copyright 282 bottom; Hamlyn Group Picture Library 226 top, 234 bottom; Angelo Hornak 334 top; A. F. Kersting 330 bottom, 331 bottom; Oriel Press Ltd, Newcastle upon Tyne 175 bottom, 177 bottom left, 274 bottom; Portuguese National Tourist Office, London 214 bottom; Scala, Florence 184 top, 185 centre, 185 bottom; Spanish Tourist Office London, Arnaiz 210 top; Stockholm Information Service 322 bottom, 323 top; Zefa, London 326 top, 327 top, 327 bottom, 330 top, 334 bottom, 335 top, 335 centre left.

Black and white ACL, Brussels 297 bottom; Aerofilms, Boreham Wood 259 top, 271 top; Fratelli Alinari, Florence 10, 27, 34, 47, 121 bottom left, 121 bottom right, 130–1, 135, 137, 159 bottom right, 168 bottom, 176 top, 178 top, 182; Bruce Allsopp 116 top, 117, 124, 154, 155 top, 155 bottom, 156 top, 157, 159 bottom left, 160, 166 top, 168 top, 169 top, 169 bottom, 171 bottom left, 176 centre, 179, 183 top right, 185 top right, 187 top left, 187 top right, 187 bottom, 188 bottom left, 191 bottom, 193 centre, 193 bottom, 195, 196 top, 196 bottom right, 197, 204 bottom, 211 bottom, 216, 221 top, 228 bottom, 229, 232, 233 bottom, 237 top, 237 bottom, 239 top left, 240, 241 top left, 241 top right, 241 bottom, 242, 243, 244 top, 244 centre right, 247, 248 top, 248 bottom, 249 bottom, 251 bottom right, 252 centre, 252 bottom, 253 top, 254 top, 254 centre, 254 bottom, 255 centre, 255 bottom, 256 top, 256 bottom, 257 top, 257 bottom, 259 bottom, 260 top right, 263 top, 264 top left, 265 top, 265 centre left, 265 centre right, 266, 267, 268 bottom, 270 top, 270 bottom, 271 bottom, 273 top left, 273 top right, 273 bottom left, 275 bottom left, 276, 282 centre right, 286 top left, 286 centre right, 289 centre, 289 bottom, 290 left, 290 right, 291, 292 bottom left, 292 bottom right, 294 top left, 294 top right, 294 centre, 294 bottom, 298, 299 bottom, 302 left, 342;

Archaeological Museums of Istanbul 161 bottom; Architects' Journal, London 59 centre; Archives Photographiques, Paris 212, 226 bottom right, 249 top, 297 top; Austrian National Tourist Office, London/Frischauf Bild 333 bottom; Hermann Baur/R. Spreng, Basel 341 bottom right; Belgian National Tourist Office, London/Cliché C.G.T. 307 centre, Cliché C.G.T.-Photo Desutter 305 top, Cliché C.G.T.-Photo L. Philippe 301 left; Boudot-Lamotte, Paris 306 top, 313 top, 339 top; Donovan E. H. Box 287 bottom right, British Library, London; 29 top; British Tourist Authority, London 23, 29 bottom, 61 bottom, 141, 260 bottom, 268 top, 278 bottom; J. Allan Cash, London 319; P. J. Chatfield 316 top, 316 bottom, 317 top, 317 bottom, 319 centre; Ursula Clark 208 bottom, 213 top, 221 bottom; Country Life, London 139, 143, 148, 273 bottom right; Danish Tourist Board, London/Inga Aistrup 319 top; Deutsche Fotothek, Dresden 340 top; Documentation Française, Paris 253 bottom; Department of the Environment, London, Crown copyright 116 bottom, 269; Farbwerke Hoechst 341 bottom left; F.E., London Crown copyright 116 bottom, 269; Studio Bmöller 322 top; Herbert Felton 120; Finnish Embassy, London/Martti Peltonen 320 bottom; Finnish Tourist Board, London 321 bottom; Foto-Arnold, Füssen 9 top; Foto Fisa, Barcelona 140. Fototeca Unione, Rome 33 top; French Government Tourist Office, London 246; Photo-Edition G.-d'O., Olliergues 113 bottom; Gabinetto Fotografico Nazionale, Rome 132, 138; Gemeente Bestuur van Mechelen 303 top; German Embassy, London 333 top; Giraudon, Paris 109, 125 top, 244 centre left; Greater London Council 41; Haarlem Tourist Board 304 bottom left; Hamlyn Group Picture Library 17, 151, 183 bottom, 186 left, 186 right, 196 bottom left, 228 top left, 261, 295, 300 bottom, 302 right, 309, 311 top, 323 bottom, Keith Gibson 292 top, Hermann Hessler 335 bottom; Michael Holford 58, 123; A. Martin 233 top; Michel Hetier 159 top; Franz Höch, Coburg 142; Institut Belge d'Information et de Documentation, Brussels 300 top; Istituto Italiano di Cultura, London 178 bottom; A. F. Kersting 9 bottom, 51 bottom left, 150, 218 top right, 281; King's College, Newcastle 51 bottom right; Lichtbildwerkstatte 'Alpenland', Vienna 339 bottom; Mann Brothers, London 57; Mansell Collection, London 176 bottom, 184 bottom, 318, Alinari 194 top, Anderson 187 centre, 194 bottom; Bildarchiv Foto Marburg 8 centre, 8 bottom, 11 top, 11 bottom, 35, 49 centre, 125 bottom, 133, 161 top left, 183 top left, 190 top, 190 bottom, 191 top, 201 top, 203 top, 209, 210 bottom right, 210 bottom, 231 top, 244 bottom, 251 top, 255 top, 263 bottom, 264 top right, 264 bottom, 299 top, 303 bottom, 304 top, 304 bottom right, 307 bottom, 311 bottom left, 325, 238, 331 top, 332 centre, 332 bottom, 336, 340 bottom; A. Martin, Paris 147 bottom, 238 top left; MAS, Barcelona 49 bottom, 200 top, 200 bottom, 201 bottom, 202 top, 202 centre, 203 bottom, 204 top, 205 bottom, 207 bottom left, 208 top, 211 top, 215 top, 217 top left, 217 top right, 217 bottom, 218 bottom, 220; Museum of Architecture, Moscow 311 bottom right; National Buildings Record, London 13, 149; National Monuments Record, London, Crown copyright 113 top, 279 centre; Karla Neulerta 312 top; Nordisk Pressefoto/Sven Thoby, Copenhagen 320 top; Novosti Press Agency, Moscow 312 bottom right, 313 bottom, B. Manushin 312 bottom left; Oriel Studios, Newcastle upon Tyne 284; Rapho, Paris/Serge de Sazo 54; Rex Features, London 307 top; Roger-Viollet, Paris 8 top, 31 top, 49 top, 61 centre, 156 bottom, 161 top right, 227 bottom, 252 top, 337; Jean Roubier, Paris 31 bottom, 111, 121 top, 205 top, 341 top; Royal Danish Ministry of Foreign Affairs, Copenhagen 321 top; Walter Scott, Bradford 289 top; Spanish National Tourist Office, London 46, 201 centre, 207 top, 207 bottom right; Strüwing 59 bottom; Studio-Matignon, Paris 231 bottom; Swiss National Tourist Office, London 332 top; Tass News Agency, London 51 top; Dean and Chapter of Winchester Cathedral/Murray Davison 265 bottom.

Index

Places, buildings, architects, technical terms and stylistic terms will be found in this index. Buildings are listed by the city or town in which they are located, but when mentioned more than once in the text they are also listed by name.

Historical and regional approaches can be made through the table of contents. Captions to the illustrations are shown in *italic type*.